A WORLD BANK COUNTRY STUDY

Strengthening Bolivian Competitiveness

Export Diversification and Inclusive Growth

THE WORLD BANK
Washington, D.C.

Manufactured in the United States of America
First Printing: June 2009

Printed on recycled paper

1 2 3 4 5 12 11 10 09

World Bank Country Studies are among the many reports originally prepared for internal use as part of the continuing analysis by the Bank of the economic and related conditions of its developing member countries and to facilitate its dialogs with the governments. Some of the reports are published in this series with the least possible delay for the use of governments, and the academic, business, financial, and development communities. The manuscript of this paper therefore has not been prepared in accordance with the procedures appropriate to formally-edited texts. Some sources cited in this paper may be informal documents that are not readily available.

The findings, interpretations, and conclusions expressed herein are those of the author(s) and do not necessarily reflect the views of the International Bank for Reconstruction and Development/The World Bank and its affiliated organizations, or those of the Executive Directors of The World Bank or the governments they represent.

The World Bank does not guarantee the accuracy of the data included in this work. The boundaries, colors, denominations, and other information shown on any map in this work do not imply any judgment on the part of The World Bank of the legal status of any territory or the endorsement or acceptance of such boundaries.

ISBN-13: 978-0-8213-8021-5
eISBN: 978-0-8213-8022-2
ISSN: 0253-2123 DOI: 10.1596/978-0-8213-8021-5

Library of Congress Cataloging-in-Publication Data has been requested.

Contents

Tables

Figures

Boxes

Preface

Bolivia's trade liberalization, launched in the mid-1980s, has resulted in a relatively open trade regime; but the results have been mixed. Bolivia's export-to-GDP ratio and export entrepreneurship index rating are among the highest in the Latin American and Caribbean (LAC) region and the country has achieved great success in making soya the major export crop in less than 10 years. At the same time, the country's share in world trade has stagnated and exports are increasingly dominated by gas and minerals.

Reinvigorating the nontraditional export sector is important for the government of Bolivia as it implements its National Development Plan. As a resource-rich country, the Bolivian government's emphasis on export diversification is well-placed but the optimal nontraditional export strategy should build on successes in the traditional sector.

This study investigates (1) the role trade should play in Bolivia's development strategy considering the country's natural resource endowment; (2) the lessons of Bolivia's integration to the world economy; (3) the linkages between Bolivia's past trade and economy and a forward-looking analysis of the impact of different scenarios on growth, employment, trade flows, and poverty; (4) constraints to higher export competitiveness and weaknesses related to transport and logistics; and (5) the characteristics of exporting firms and the constraints affecting them.

The main findings of the analysis are that preferential access to world markets is necessary but not sufficient for success in nontraditional exports; rather, success depends largely on increasing the competitiveness of exporting firms. Second, a neutral incentive regime is essential to the growth of nontraditional exports. Third, efficient backbone services are vital for reducing exporters' costs. Finally, the government should be proactive in addressing institutional impediments to cross-border trade.

The study presents prioritized policy implications of the analysis related to (1) trade policy and preferential access to markets; (2) the incentives regime; (3) backbone services; (4) increasing the effectiveness of institutions to promote cross-border trade; and (5) setting the foundations for exports diversification

Vice President:	Pamela Cox
Country Director:	Carlos Felipe Jaramillo
Sector Director:	Marcelo Giugale
Sector Manager:	Rodrigo Chaves
Sector Leader:	Carlos Silva Jauregui
Task Team Leader:	Seynabou Sakho

Acknowledgments

This report was prepared by Seynabou Sakho (Country Economist LCSPE) and Oscar Calvo-Gonzalez (Young Professional LCSPE) under the guidance and supervision of Rodrigo Chaves (Sector Manager LCSPE) and Carlos Silva Jauregui (Lead Economist and PREM Sector Leader LCSPR). Carlos Felipe Jaramillo (Country Director LCC6A) linked the team to the Bank's overall strategy and steered them in that direction. Mauricio Carrizosa (Adviser IEGCR), Vicente Fretes Cibils (IDB), and Rossana Polastri (Senior Country Economist LCSPE) provided initial guidance to the study.

The team also included contributions from Soamiely Andriamananjara (Senior Economist WBIPR), Peter Walkenhorst (Senior Economist PRMTR), Julio Loayza (LCCBO), Julio Velasco (LCCBO), Olivier Cadot (Professor Université de Lausanne), Ernesto Valenzuela (University of Adelaide), Jean Francois Arvis (Senior Economist PRMTR), Martha Denisse Pierola (Consultant), Ethel Fonseca (Rutgers University), Graham Smith (Consultant), Ana Cristina Molina (Université de Lausanne, UNCTAD), Laure Dutoit (Université de Lausanne), and Hector Revuelta Santa Cruz (Consultant). The peer reviewers for this report are Pablo Fajnzylber (Senior Economist LCRCE), Daniel Lederman (Senior Economist DECRG), and Jose Lopez Calix (Lead Country Economist MNSED).

The report benefited from excellent production support from Michael Geller (Senior Program Assistant LCSPE), Monica Torrelio (LCCBO), and Patricia Holt (Language Program Assistant LCSPE). Chris Humphrey (Consultant) provided editorial support. Santiago Flores (Consultant) and Jan Erik Von Uexkull (PREMTR) provided data analysis. The team gratefully acknowledges financial support provided by DFID to finance background papers on the impact of trade scenarios on employment growth and poverty.

This report was enhanced by substantive comments from a variety of people during various stages of this project. Comments were received from Viviana Caro (Executive Director UDAPE, Bolivia), Dr. Valda (Former Vice Minister of Commerce, Bolivia), Pablo Rabczuk (Former Vice Minister of Commerce, Bolivia), Gabriel Loza Telleria (Former Minister of Planning, Bolivia), Enrique Fanta Ivanovic (Senior Public Sector Specialist LCSPS), Antonio Furtado (Division Chief IMF), Ian Walker (Lead Social Protection Specialist LCSHS), Carlos Mollinedo (Strategy Officer IFC Bolivia), Jean Pierre Chauffour (Advisor, PREMTR), Lily Chu (Sector Manager LCSPF), Mike Goldberg (Senior Private Sector Specialist LCSPF), and Jose Guillerme Reis (Lead Private Sector Specialist LCSPF).

The report was prepared based on two missions in Bolivia that took place in August 2007 and December 2007. The team would like to thank the Bolivian authorities, including Ministry of Planning through VIPFE, UDAPE, the Vice Ministry of Commerce, The Bolivian Customs Agency, and the Ministry of Production and Enterprises for their cooperation in delineating the scope of the study and facilitating access to all the information necessary for the study.

The team gratefully acknowledges all the support received.

Abbreviations and Acronyms

ABC	*Acuerdos Bolivianos de Competitividad* (Bolivian Competitiveness Agreements)
ANB	*Aduana Nacional de Bolivia* (Bolivian Customs Administration)
ATPDEA	*Ley de Promoción Comercial Andina y de Erradicación de Drogas* (Andean Trade Promotion and Drug Eradication Act)
BCB	*Banco Central de Bolivia* (Central Bank)
BTBC	Bolivian Trade and Business Competitiveness
CAF	*Corporación Andina de Fomento* (Andean Development Corporation)
CAFTA	Central American Free Trade Agreement
CAN	*Comunidad Andina de Naciones* (Andean Community)
CEDEIM	*Certificado de Devolución Impositiva* (Duty Drawback Program)
CEM	Country Economic Memorandum
COA	*Control Operativo Aduanero* (Customs Operations Control)
COMIBOL	*Corporación Minera de Bolivia* (Bolivian Mining Corp.)
CONEX	*Consejo Nacional de Exportaciones* (National Council on Exports)
CONACAL	*Consejo Nacional de Calidad* (National Council for Quality Control)
DFID	Department for international Development (UK)
ENDE	*Empresa Nacional de Electricidad* (National Electricity Company)
FDI	Foreign direct investment
FERE	*Fondo Especial de Reactivación Económica* (Special Fund for Economic Reactivation)
FTA	Free trade agreement
FTT	*Impuesto a las Transacciones Financieras* (Financial Transaction Tax)
GDP	Gross domestic product
HIPC	Highly indebted poor countries
ICE	*Impuesto al Consumo Especifico* (Excise Consumption Tax)
IFC	International Finance Corporation
IMF	International Monetary Fund
INE	*Instituto Nacional de Estadística* (National Institute of Statistics)
INPEX	*Instituto de Promoción para las Exportaciones* (National Exports Promotion Institute)
IT	*Impuesto a las Transacciones* (Transactions Tax)
IUE	*Impuesto a las Utilidades de las Empresas* (Corporate Income Tax)
LAB	*Lloyd Aéreo Boliviano* (Bolivian Airline)
LAC	Latin American and Caribbean
LGA	*Ley General de Aduanas* (Customs Law)
MDGs	Millennium Development Goals *(Metas del Milenio)*
MERCOSUR	*Mercado Común del Sur*
MFIs	*Instituciones microfinancieras* (Microfinance institutions)
MECE	Ministry of Exports and Economic Competitiveness
NGO	Nongovernmental organization
NTM	Non-tariff measures
OECD	Organization for Economic Co-operation and Development
OMO	Open market operations

PROFOP	*Programa de Fortalecimiento Patrimonial* (Capital Strengthening Program)
RER	Real exchange rate
RITEX	*Régimen de Internación Temporal para el Perfeccionamiento de Activos* (Temporal Regime for Asset Improvements)
TFT	Total factor productivity
SENASAG	*Servicio Nacional de Sanidad Agropecuaria E. Inocuidad Alimentaría* (National Sanitary Service for Agricultural and Food)
SIN	*Servicio de Impuestos Nacionales* (Internal Revenue Service)
SIVEX	One-stop shop for export procedures
SNMAC	*Sistema Boliviano de Normalización, Metrología, Acreditación y Certificación* (National System for Normalization, Metrology, Certification, Accreditation and the Management of Quality)
UNCTAD	United Nations Conference on Trade and Development
UDAPE	*Unidad de Análisis de Políticas Económicas* (Economic Policy Analysis Unit)
UNDP	United Nations Development Program
UPC	*Unidad de Productividad y Competitividad* (Unit for Productivity and Competitiveness)
UPF	*Unidad de Programación Fiscal* (Fiscal Program Agency)
USAID	United States Agency for International Development
VAT	Value added tax *(Impuesto al valor agregado)*
WEF	World Economic Forum
WDI	World Development Indicators
WTO	World Trade Organization

Republic of Bolivia Fiscal Year
January 1 to December 31

Currency Equivalents
(as of as of June 30, 2008)
Currency Unit = Bolivianos
1 U.S. Dollar = Bs. 7.22

Weights and Measures
Metric System

Executive Summary

Bolivia's trade liberalization effort, launched in the mid-1980s, has resulted in a relatively open trade regime. But the results have been mixed. On the one hand, Bolivia's export-to-GDP ratio and export entrepreneurship index rating are among the highest in the LAC region and the country has achieved great success in making soya the major export crop in less than 10 years. At the same time, however, the country's share in world trade has stagnated and exports are increasingly dominated by gas and minerals. Our analysis shows, however, that Bolivia's reliance on a small number of traditional exports—mainly minerals and natural gas—is not necessarily a curse as it can be leveraged to boost nontraditional exports and economic growth. We also identify the reasons for the modest performance of nontraditional exports. These include the business environment, which limits inflows of foreign direct investment (FDI) and constrains the productivity of exporting firms, and weak trade institutions and deficiencies in transport logistics for trade that are so crucial for a landlocked country. In this report, we offer policy options aimed at strengthening the trade sector's ability to stimulate the economy.

Reinvigorating the nontraditional export sector is important for the government of Bolivia as it implements its National Development Plan. The plan's goal is to shift to greater value-added exports, coupled with more balanced trade relations and diversified export markets and products. In addition, the government currently faces several policy challenges regarding the nonrenewal of preferential access to the U.S. market through the Andean Trade Promotion and Drug Eradication Act (ATPDEA), changes in its tariff policy toward the common external tariff of the Andean Community (CAN), free trade agreements (FTAs) between the United States and important regional partners (Peru and, possibly, Colombia), and worsening global economic conditions.

As a resource-rich country, the Bolivian government's emphasis on export diversification is well-placed but the optimal nontraditional export strategy should build on successes in the traditional sector. Diversification matters because a heavy reliance on a few products implies excessive vulnerability to price downturns. Bolivia's nontraditional sector is already exporting a wide range of diversified products but the limited productive capacity implies short (rather than sustained) export episodes and a high attrition rate for new exporters. Leveraging the benefits of the natural resources boom would require investing in human capital and knowledge technology to maintain the country's export edge in natural resources while strategically planning to achieve positive spillover effects in such key areas as infrastructure and transport.

Main Findings

Preferential access to world markets is necessary but not sufficient for success in nontraditional exports; rather, success depends largely on increasing the competitiveness of exporting firms. Preferential agreements alone cannot provide the levels of growth and trade that facilitate long-term economic development. The nonrenewal of APTDEA preferences may be the most costly development that Bolivia now faces. Our analysis indicates that nonrenewal of the ATPDEA with the United States may reduce growth the most, by 0.6 percent. The ratification of the U.S.-Peru and U.S.-Colombia FTAs would reduce growth by 0.4 percent. Deeper integration with MERCOSUR would dampen growth by 0.09 and realignment of Bolivia's tariff scheme to the CAN common external tariff would lower it by 0.01.

Preferential agreements remain critical for trade policy. The small estimated impact of preferential agreements does not reflect these agreements' full effect as second-round effects are not captured in the modeling. The scenarios we analyze are based on products currently traded and current market conditions and do not consider products not yet traded. As a result, the scenarios downplay the impact of increased trade of new products that could take advantage of preferential market access. For example, the incipient trade in the service sector may well yield significant gains through preferential agreements, not only directly through the services sector but also indirectly by lowering the cost of services inputs into goods production and exports. Therefore, there are risks related to a loss of preferential access to the U.S. market and failing to pursue greater trade integration within the region. Bolivia could also be left out from the dynamics of trading blocks, which may reduce its potential to diversify its trade in new products and markets.

Our analysis suggests that policy should focus on increasing exporting firms' productivity and competitiveness to fully exploit preferential agreements. We find that Bolivian exporting firms are no more productive than their nonexporting counterparts, which contrasts with evidence from most countries. This finding, together with the fact that preferential access alone has a limited impact, suggests that increasing exporting firms' productivity is key to improving their performance. Long-standing investment and business environment factors—such as contract enforcement, regulatory uncertainty, and political instability—have undermined productivity and export performance. As a result, the manufacturing sector has only attracted limited FDI. In addition, exporting firms' productivity is further affected by competitiveness issues related to the neutrality of the incentives regime for exporters, the efficiency of backbone services such as transport and logistics, and the effectiveness of institutions for cross-border trade.

A neutral incentive regime is essential to the growth of nontraditional exports

Payment delays under the duty-drawback system are a problem for exporters. Duty drawbacks (called CEDEIMs) allow exporters to claim back duties paid on inputs for exported products, thus partly offsetting the cost of tariffs for exporting firms. Reimbursement requests under the CEDEIMs are accumulating, as the budgeted allocation for CEDEIMs is not keeping pace with export levels. In addition, the program that automatically suspends taxes on imported inputs for exporters (called RITEX) has a very low take-up rate. In the absence of a smoothly operating duty relief mechanism, export manufacturers have to produce at a higher cost than if they had full and easy access to production inputs at world prices. This obviously handicaps their export performance.

The recent rise in import tariffs adds to the cost of imported inputs and worsens the anti-export bias. Our analysis indicates that the increase in import tariffs is expected to reduce exports more than imports: exports by $35 million a year and imports by $24 million a year.[1] Output and welfare are also expected to fall. These results stem from the fact that higher import duties are also taxes for exports. First, they mean higher costs of imported inputs, and higher costs of living may generate higher wage costs. Second, this strategy creates an anti-export bias and reduces incentives to export.

Rapidly rising inflation poses a threat to the competitiveness of Bolivian exporters. Inflation climbed to 12 percent at end-2007, up from 5 percent in 2006, increasing the price of Bolivian exports. The higher inflation is the result of such variables as the global rise in food prices, a slow supply response attributable to low private investment, increased aggregate demand fueled by remittances and commodities revenues, and the destructive effect of the La Niña weather pattern. In response to the rise in inflation, the government issued export restrictions on staple food prices, shifting incentives to producing for the domestic, rather than the international, market. The government also increased its open market operations and brought about a modest appreciation of the boliviano in real terms. Bolivia's currency, however, appreciated less than its neighbors, further eroding competitiveness in the nontraditional sector. In particular, the bilateral dollar-boliviano appreciation eroded the competitiveness of nontraditional exports destined mainly for the U.S. market.

Efficient backbone services are vital for reducing exporters' costs

For a landlocked country like Bolivia, efficient trade services are critical for export competitiveness. Telecom infrastructure is not well-developed, undermining the country's connectivity to international markets and the ability to take advantage of opportunities in dynamic services export sectors, such as call centers and outsourcing. The phytosanitary standards agency SENASAG does not function properly owing to a lack of capacity and resources; exports are delayed for months in some parts of the country because of slow certification procedures. The use of air freight remains limited because of a lack of air transport capacity. This hurts the capacity to develop exports using airfreight in some parts of the country, such as Cochabamba.

Trucking costs appear to be competitive by international standards but the predictability of trip time remains a challenge. The quality of transport logistics in Bolivia is slightly below the level to be expected for its income level. Transport costs of 5–8 U.S. cents per kilometer are competitive, but the great distances to ports make the overall costs high and places Bolivia at a competitive disadvantage. In addition, the predictability of truck trip time is important as most container ships operate out of Arica in Chile (Bolivia's main international port) once a week, hence seasonal damage or road blocks can be costly for exporters.

Institutional reforms implemented in Bolivia's Customs Administration (ANB) have improved trade control and trade facilitation, but smuggling and delays at border crossings persist. Import and export controls have improved and trade facilitation has been enhanced through comprehensive institutional reforms in the ANB. But control of smuggling remains weak. Indeed, smuggling possibly affects a third of total imports, undermining the income of formal-sector importers and producers. Similarly, econometric estimates suggest that Bolivian exporters are hurt by the costs associated with shipment delays at customs. The current administration plans to build on past reforms by upgrading information systems and adapting procedures and regulations.

The government should be proactive in addressing impediments to cross-border trade

Export entrepreneurship is high, even though Bolivia tends to under-export relative to other countries. Accounting for its status as a landlocked country, Bolivia imports more than econometric models predict (by 3 percent) and exports less than predicted (by 11 percent). Not accounting for its being landlocked, Bolivia exports 43 percent less than predicted. But export entrepreneurship—as measured by the number of new products exported—is higher than one would expect given Bolivia's level of income. Bolivia has been able to export a diverse range of products, although only intermittently, in small quantities, and by only a few firms. These results suggest an unrealized potential for diversification through volume rather than new products.

Increasing the effectiveness of trade-related institutions would enhance export competitiveness. The performance of the institutional framework for trade is mixed. While Bolivia has implemented a successful customs reform, key export agencies remain plagued by institutional weakness and lack of resources. As a result, the export promotion agency CEPROBOL cannot fulfill its mandate. In some cases, the private sector has stepped in to provide export promotion services. The large number of products that are exported for only a short duration suggests that sustained government support through effective trade promotion institutions could reap substantial benefits.

Policy Implications

The productivity and competitiveness of Bolivian firms should be the paramount focus for boosting export growth and increasing the impact of the export sector on job creation and poverty reduction. New trade developments have the potential to affect the preferential access of Bolivian exports to several markets. But preferential agreements and regional integration alone have limited implications for employment, poverty, and growth. In addition, preferential access can only be exploited once the goods are produced and ready to be exported. Hence, increasing the productivity and competitiveness of Bolivian firms are crucial first steps.

Trade policy and preferential access to markets

In the short term, the government may seek to reverse the increase in Bolivian import duties as a first best; as a second best, it may consider limiting the economic distortions implied by the tariff increase. Indeed, the tariff increase toward the common external tariff of the Andean Community creates an anti-export bias for domestic producers. The government may consider exploring instruments that minimize those distortions.

Over the medium term, the government may consider alternatives to the use of export bans for staple foods in order to contain price increases. Bans jeopardize the long-term supply of food products to domestic markets, as producers have more incentives to shift their production to other products and the effectiveness of export bans is thus limited over time. Bans also encourage smuggling.

Incentives regime

In the short term, a high-impact and relatively easy-to-implement policy is to pay duty drawbacks in a timely fashion, as delays burden firm finances and, hence, their production capability and competitiveness. Delays defeat the purpose of neutralizing the effects of tax policy for exporting firms. Customs control should be made more efficient to ensure that duty-drawback relief is legitimate and correctly executed.

Also in the short term, the authorities should continue to maintain a stable macroeconomic framework. Solid fiscal accounts, stable monetary policy, and controlled inflation are critical to maintaining economic confidence and making long-term plans needed to develop value-added exports.

A major priority over the medium term, with potentially substantial impact on FDI flows and exports, is to step up efforts to enhance the business environment. This would promote firm productivity and competitiveness and encourage investment in nontraditional exports, which would raise the volume of such exports. Political stability, anticorruption efforts, and reducing informality are key areas for further improvement.

Backbone services

A priority for policy makers in the short term is to evaluate and revamp SENASAG—the agency in charge of issuing phytosanitary certificates—to ensure that it fulfills its mandate in a sustainable manner. This mandate includes providing a sufficient budget to ensure adequate geographical reach and information systems consistent between destination market requirements and SENASAG services, appointing and training qualified personnel, and clearly defining the regulatory framework and delimiting the relationship and responsibilities of the SENASAG relative to other government agencies.

In the medium term, the government could pursue further reforms in customs and border control management, continuing the focus on decreasing corruption and smuggling. Areas for further improvement include: setting up a risk-based selectivity process for inspections, relying on computerized databases; upgrading core software from ASYCUDA++ to the next level, or transition to other software; upgrading IT hardware and other equipment for border stations and expanding joint integrated border facilities with neighboring countries; setting up a system of border-crossing performance indicators; and improving coordination between customs and other agencies, especially SENASAG.

Another medium-term priority is to encourage the consolidation of air freight consignments and give truck trailers their own license plates. Air freight consolidation will facilitate export growth in producing regions without airports. Cochabamba in particular was identified as having the potential to channel exports by air freight via Santa Cruz to North American and European markets. The current law considers tractor and trailer as a single unit for purposes of registration. Allowing tractor units to have separate registration from trailers would enable them to keep moving—and earning revenue—while trailers wait to unload and reload. This change would greatly enhance the efficient use of the truck fleet, allowing transport charges to be lowered by 10 percent or more. An alternative solution would be to allow a single plate to be retained for both units, but permitting the trailer plate to be switched from one trailer to the next.

Increasing the effectiveness of institutions to promote cross-border trade

In the short term, a key policy priority offering high potential returns is to revamp the trade promotion office CEPROBOL by expanding its resources, stabilizing its institutional environment, and increasing the role of the private sector in CEPROBOL's operational support to exporters.

Setting the foundations for exports diversification

Over the medium term, the government can boost export diversification by helping current and prospective exporters export higher volumes and for much longer periods using the revamped export promotion agency. Over the longer term, the authorities should develop a diversification strategy that leverages the country's natural resource endowment. Elements of the strategy may include investing in activities related to hydrocarbons or minerals such as in services, machinery, engineering products, or transport equipment; developing a trade regime that favors the emergence of new export activities; and promoting technological change in manufacture and services.

Notes

[1] All dollar amounts are U.S. unless otherwise indicated.

CHAPTER 1

The Role of Trade in Bolivia's Development Strategy

What role should trade play in Bolivia's development strategy and how does the country's natural resource endowment affect such a role? These are relevant questions for Bolivian policy makers and are a core concern of Bolivia's National Development Plan. The plan seeks to shift Bolivia's exports toward products of greater value added, coupled with more balanced trade relations and diversified export markets and products. In this chapter, we discuss the context for the drive toward export diversification. We describe Bolivia's economy and structure, focusing on value added, trade, and employment by sector. We then briefly survey Bolivia's trade, macroeconomic, and foreign direct investment policies pursued since the introduction of economic reforms in 1985—which included trade liberalization—and the resulting evolution in the terms of trade.

The Structure of the Economy: Value Added, Trade, and Employment

Bolivia's economy has seen limited structural change over the last decade. The share in value added accounted by the three broad sectors of activity changed little from 1996 to 2006. The share of agriculture in value added declined slightly from 16 percent to 14 percent, while industry increased from 32 percent to 34 percent (Table 1.1). The limited structural change in the last decade has been particularly evident in the services sector, which has remained largely unchanged as a share of value added at close to 52 percent—well below the 62 percent of value added accounted for by services in Latin America and the Caribbean. For the region as a whole, however, the share of services in value added has actually decreased slightly. Bolivia's economy also remains more

Table 1.1. Share of Value Added by Sector (Percent)

		1984	1996	2006
Bolivia	Agriculture	22.8	16.4	14.0
	Industry	33.3	32.3	34.2
	Services	43.9	51.3	51.9
LAC average	Agriculture	10.7	7.0	6.2
	Industry	40.2	29.4	31.3
	Services	49.1	63.7	62.4

Source: World Bank WDI.
Note: 1984 is shown to reflect the Bolivian economic structure prior to the reforms launched in 1985.

reliant on agriculture (14 percent) than is the case for the region as a whole. Among Latin American countries, the share of agriculture in value added is higher than in Bolivia only in Guatemala (22 percent), Paraguay (21 percent), and Nicaragua (20 percent).

The mining and hydrocarbon sector—the source of so-called "traditional" Bolivian exports—has increased its share of value added in recent years, owing largely to the rise in commodities prices. While services is by far the largest sector of the Bolivian economy, a more disaggregated analysis shows the most dynamic sectors to be hydrocarbons and mining (Figure 1.1). The increasing weight of these sectors in the Bolivian economy is all the more relevant from a foreign trade perspective since hydrocarbons and mining have traditionally accounted for the bulk of Bolivia's exports ("traditional exports" in this report refers to exports of hydrocarbons and mining products).

Figure 1.1. Sectoral Breakdown of GDP

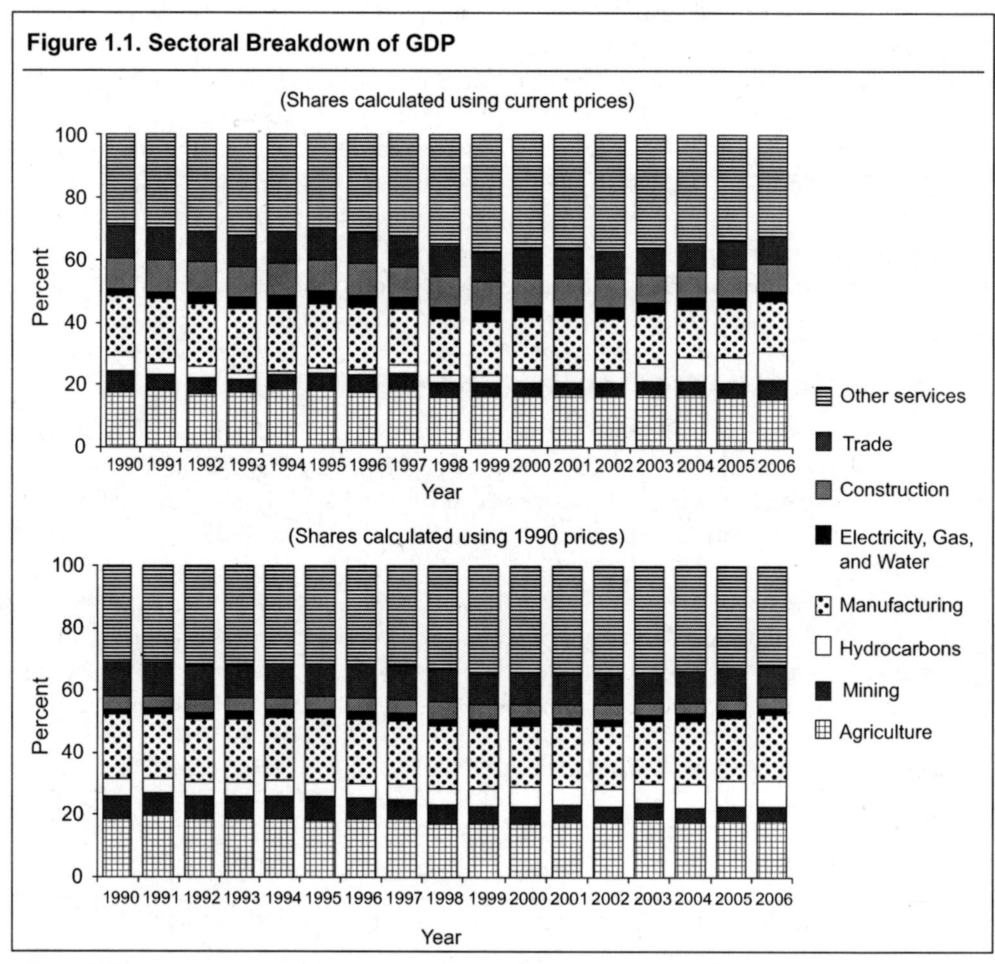

Source: INE.

Note: Other services include finance, personal and social services, restaurants and hotels, and imputed banking services.

But mining and hydrocarbons contribute to employment only in a limited way. The labor share of traditional export sectors such as mining and hydrocarbons is relatively low relative to the labor share of some of the agricultural products or manufacturing activities (Table 1.2). For example, the labor share in natural gas accounts for only 14.2 percent, while in textiles it accounts for 22.4 percent.

Table 1.2. Value Added and Labor Share in Selected Economic Sectors (Percent)

Sector	Value added share	Labor share	Sector	Value added share	Labor share
Primary agricultures			**Processed food**		
Paddy rice	79.2	36.7	Meat: cattle, sheep	29.4	4.2
Wheat	35.8	16.8	Meat: pig, chicken	18.2	4.1
Cereal grains nec	66.9	31.1	Vegetable oils	2.2	1.2
Vegetables, fruit	74.1	34.5	Dairy products	43.8	17.8
Oil seeds	68.7	31.5	Processed rice	19.2	1.1
Sugar primary	33.6	15.5	Sugar	32.1	15.5
Plant-based fibers	56.4	26.3	Food products nec	21.0	13.9
Crops nec	80.1	37.3			
Cattle, sheep, goats	70.4	32.7	**Manufacturing**		
Pig and Poultry	63.6	29.6	Beverages and tobacco	39.3	12.1
Raw milk	61.3	28.3	Textiles	36.8	22.4
Wool	44.5	20.6	Wearing apparel	36.8	22.4
Forestry	67.1	16.1	Leather products	36.8	22.4
			Wood products	25.5	14.9
Other primary resources			Paper products, publishing	32.8	15.5
Coal	42.9	15.2	Petroleum, coal products	21.1	0.8
Oil	64.2	6.8	Chemical, rubber, plastic prod.	25.8	11.7
Gas	66.0	14.2	Ferrous metals	4.0	1.7
Minerals nec	79.5	21.6	Metal products	9.7	1.9
Mineral products nec	52.2	28.2	Motor vehicles and parts	8.0	1.4
			Transport equipment nec	12.4	2.8
			Electronic equipment	6.8	0.9
			Machinery and equipment	11.4	2.2
			Manufactures nec	39.9	28.4
			Utility and construction	41.9	19.9
			Transport and communications	63.2	31.7
			Other Services	77.4	55.4

Source: Andriamananjara and Valenzuela (2008) based on GTAP database.

Traditional exports (hydrocarbons and minerals) accounted for 77 percent of Bolivian exports in 2006—up from 52 percent in 2002. Bolivia's export structure has become less diversified in recent years (Figure 1.2). The share of traditional exports has continued to rise, largely because of rising prices for minerals and gas. In 2006, Bolivian exports were valued at about $2 billion, and imports at about $2.4 billion. Minerals (zinc, silver, tin, and gold), oil seeds, and vegetable oils were the largest source of export earnings, followed by natural gas. Services related to transportation and communication represented 13 percent of all goods and services exports. Imports included mainly capital goods, with machinery and equipment accounting for some 20 percent. Services including transportation and communication accounted for one-quarter of total import of goods and services.

Over the past 25 years, many developing countries have improved the well-being of their population by tapping international markets. Some have benefited from the discovery, exploitation, and (recent) price surge for fuel and commodities, while others have gained strongly from transitioning from centrally planned to market-based economies. Yet, even among the non-fuel exporting, nontransition countries, a large number of economies have achieved sustained long-term growth. Indeed, 16 of these countries managed to more than triple their GDP between 1980 and 2005, which corresponds to an average annual growth rate of more than 4.5 percent.[1]

Figure 1.2. Bolivian Export Product Structure

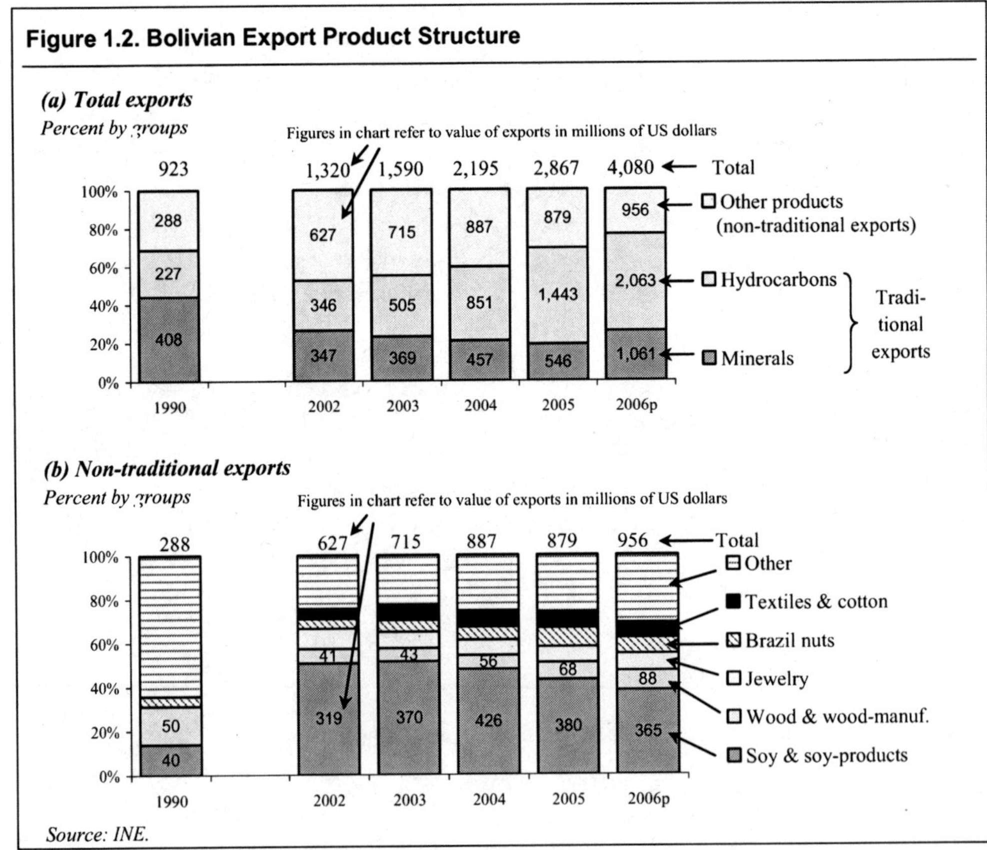

Source: INE.

The success of the high performers has been based on an export-oriented strategy. Such an outward-looking paradigm seems appropriate for most developing countries, given the generally limited size of their domestic markets, which do not allow for economies of scale and competition-driven productivity gains. Jones and Olken (2007) find that growth take-offs are strongly associated with a large and steady expansion of international trade. In fact, since 1980, the 16 high performers pursued a strategy of export-led growth and increased their share of world non-fuel merchandise exports and world services exports each by a factor of three (Figure 1.3).

Figure 1.3. Bolivia's Share of World Exports

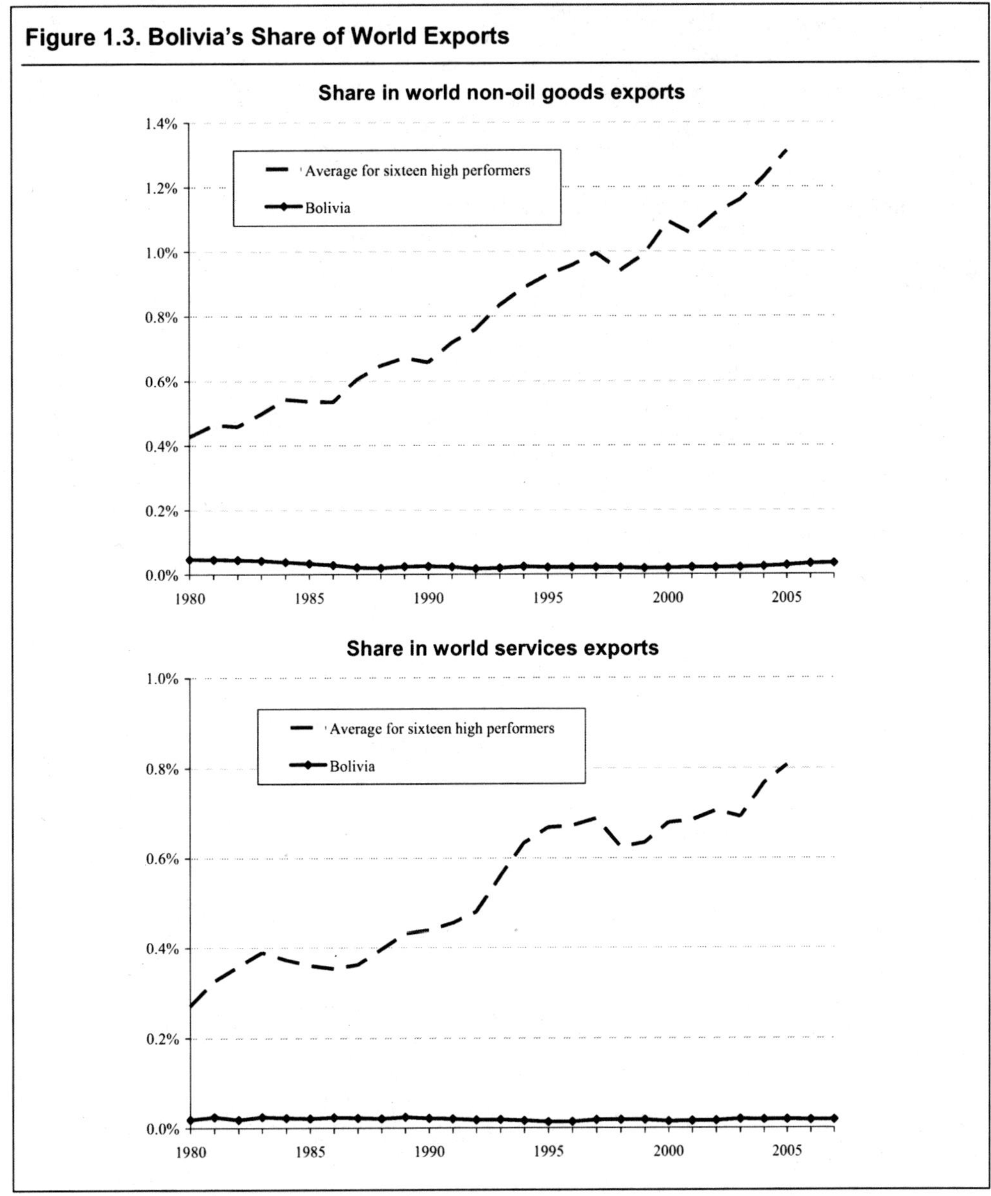

Source: World Bank staff based on UN Comtrade database and IMF Balance of Payment database.

In contrast, Bolivia's share in world markets has remained largely unchanged since 1980. Moreover, Bolivian exports are increasingly concentrated in only a few products and reach only a few markets. An index of export market penetration[2] indicates that Bolivia exploits only a relatively small fraction of the potential markets for its exports (Figure 1.3), falling well short of similar countries in Latin America and East Asia.

The International Trade Center of Geneva (ITC) confirms the view that Bolivia has not realized its full export potential. The ITC, using its TRADESIM model, estimates that Bolivian exports to the United States (the largest market for Bolivia's non-gas exports)[3] are more than 40 percent below their potential. Bolivia's apparent increase in openness, relative to the small size of its economy, and the rapid rise in global trade, suggest that trade liberalization has paid only modest dividends. In fact, such measures as the increase in exports per capita show that Bolivia has underperformed most of its neighbors between 1985 and 2005 (Figure 1.4).

Figure 1.4. Foreign Trade, Selected Indicators for 1985 and 2005

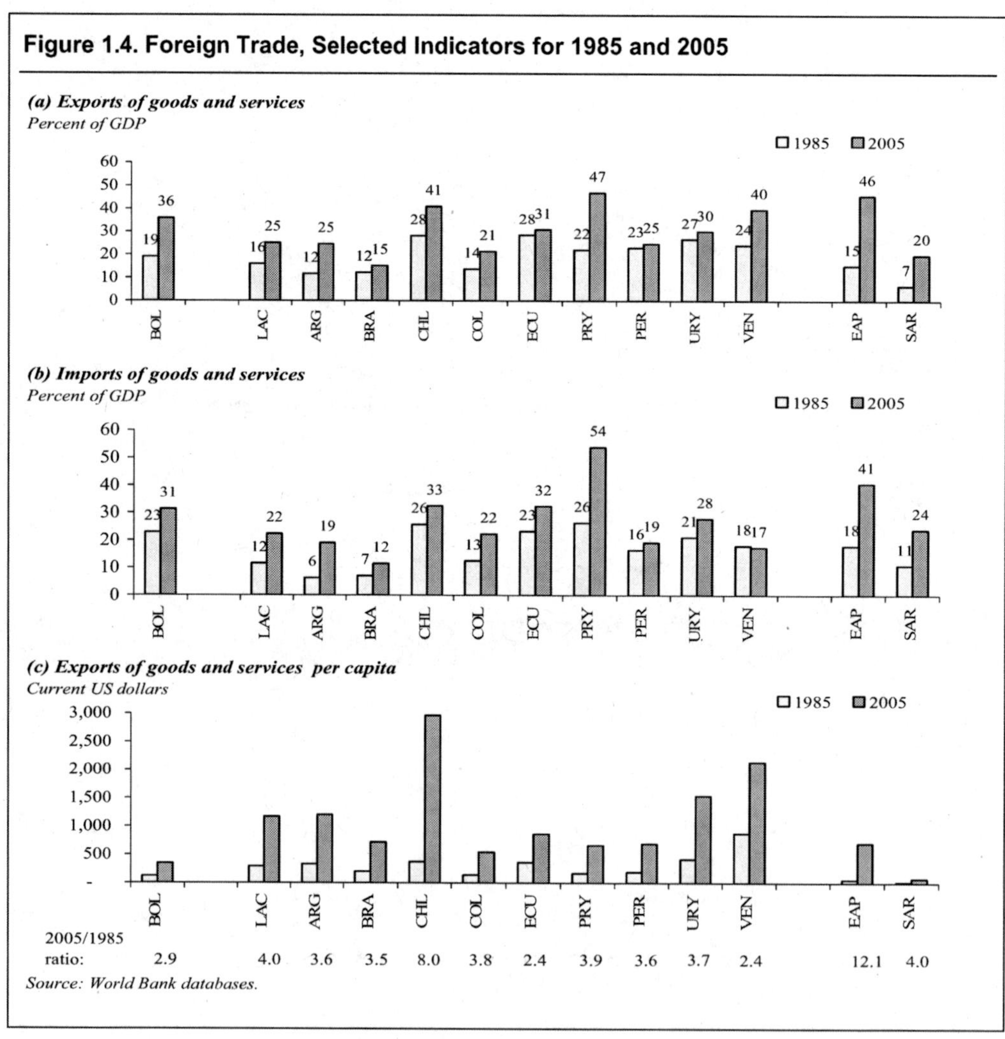

Source: World Bank databases.

Bolivia has, however, achieved some successes: exports as a percent of GDP or exports per capita have improved since the liberalization. Select foreign trade indicators suggest that Bolivia's increase in exports' share of GDP grew faster, from 1985 to 2005, than any LAC country—except Paraguay—and even more than the South Asian average. Of course, GDP growth in Bolivia around that period was modest and biased measurement of GDP due to the large size of the informal sector may have affected the export indicators. In contrast, the evolution of Bolivia's share of exports per capita from 1985 to 2005 highlights a moderate export growth relative to the population growth, with the ratio increasing less than most countries in the region, except for República Bolivariana de Venezuela and Ecuador. See Figure 1.4.

Trade, Macroeconomic, and FDI Policies since the 1985 Liberalization

We now review the evolution of trade policy since the 1985 liberalization, emphasizing trade agreements and their preference utilization rates. We also discuss recent macroeconomic developments inasmuch as they affect trade flows through the exchange rate and inflation. And we look at FDI policies and the evolution of FDI flows at the sectoral level.

Trade Policy

Bolivia's trade liberalization since the mid-1980s has resulted in greater openness. Starting in 1985, as part of a broad-ranging economic stabilization program, Bolivia embarked on a major liberalization of its foreign trade regime. This resulted in a substantial lowering of tariffs—down to an average of 8.2 percent in 2005 for the most favored nation (MFN) tariff rate.[4] Bolivia also stopped using import quotas, surveillance mechanisms, monopolies, export subsidies, and other nontariff measures.[5] Overall tariffs at 10 percent are relatively low. Tariffs of capital equipment and printed material are at 5 and 2 percent respectively. Bolivia rarely uses contingent protection (such as anti-dumping), nor does it resort to quantitative restrictions or licensing (except on public-health grounds) so that the ad-valorem equivalent of nontariff barriers is, at 6 percent, one of the lowest on the continent.[6] The country's uncomplicated tariff regime yields many benefits in terms of predictability and transparency, and in promoting efficient resource allocation.[7]

Preferential agreements with the region and the rest of the world are the key instrument of Bolivia's integration (See Table 1.3). Bolivia is a member of the Andean Community of Nations (CAN), together with Colombia, Ecuador, Peru, and República Bolivariana de Venezuela. These countries are Bolivia's main export destinations, accounting for about one-quarter of total export values. Bolivia maintains an association agreement with MERCOSUR, and the member countries (Brazil, Argentina, Uruguay, and Paraguay, and Chile as associate member) are the second-largest markets for Bolivian exports, with a share of 18 percent. Bolivia has a free trade accord with Mexico, a preferential agreement with Chile and (until 2008) the United States, and a preferential agreement with the European Union. The preferential agreement with the United States was part of the Andean Trade Pact and Drug Eradication Act (ATPDEA); it provided duty-free treatment for a wide range of Andean exports in return for cooperation in the struggle against narcotics production and trafficking in the Andean region.

Table 1.3. Key Policy Mechanisms of Bolivian Integration

Instrument	Since	Until	Notes
Participation in regional integration initiatives			
Andean Community (Ecuador, Colombia, Peru, Bolivia)	1969	Indefinite	Member of free trade area, common external tariff
MERCOSUR (Argentina, Brazil, Paraguay, Uruguay)	1997	Indefinite	Associate member
Venezuela, R. B. de, Cuba (ALBA-TCP)	2006	Indefinite	
Trade agreements			
Chile	1993	Indefinite	Zero tariff on around 200 products
Mexico	1995	Indefinite	Free trade agreement. By 2009 all tariffs will be eliminated
Unilateral preferences granted to Bolivia unilaterally by other countries			
US–ATPDEA	Dec. 2001	Dec. 2008	See Box 1.1
US–SGP	Jan. 1976	Dec. 2008	
EU–SGP Plus	Jul. 2005	Dec. 2015	
Other SGP: Japan, Switzerland, Canada			

Source: World Bank staff compilations.

Nontraditional exporters have benefited from several trade preference schemes. All exports to the Andean Community and most exports to MERCOSUR and Mexico benefit from tariff preferences. Moreover, the Generalized System of Preferences (GSP) favors exports to most developed economies: since 1990, the Andean GSP grants preferential treatment in accessing European countries for all industrial products and many agricultural products. The ATPDEA, which in 2002 replaced the 1991 Andean Trade Preference Act (ATPA), provided substantial preferences to nontraditional exports to the United States. Between the GSP and ATPDEA, about half of nontraditional exports (textiles, leather, wood products, and jewelry) enjoy preferential access to the U.S. market. Soya exports have been benefiting from Andean Community preferences.

Bolivia has taken good advantage of preferential access to EU and U.S. export markets. According to the World Bank's World Trade Indicators (WTI) database, Bolivia claimed, in 2006, 70 percent of the preferences available for its exports to the European Union (Table 1.4).[8] The corresponding number for its exports to the United States was 98 percent. The values of the utilized preferences (estimated at 3.4 percent of Bolivia's total exports to the United States and 3.1 percent for exports to the European Union) were low but were about the same as the average for low-income economies. But those utilized preferences were concentrated in a few product lines, suggesting that Bolivia could increase its preferential access for many other products (Table 1.5).

Table 1.4. Value and Utilization of EU and U.S. Preferences for Selected Exporters

	Preferences (EU) actual value (% of exports)	Preferences (EU) utilization rate (%, actual/potential value)	Preferences (U.S.) actual value (% of exports)	Preferences (U.S.) utilization rate (%, actual/potential value)
Bolivia	3.37	70.05	3.11	98.38
Colombia	1.41	89.45	1.61	97.94
Ecuador	7.16	95.43	0.550	95.49
Peru	1.96	93.96	3.71	99.51
Andean Group Average	3.48	87.22	2.25	97.83
LAC average	8.30	81.17	2.77	83.21

Source: World Trade Indicators (WTI) 2008, available at www.worldbank.org/wti2008.

Table 1.5. Utilization Rate, ATPA/ATPDEA, 1997–2005

ISIC 3 code	ISIC category	1997	1998	1999	2000	2001	2002	2003	2004	2005
311	Food products	0	0	0	0	0	0	0	0	0
312	Food products	0	0	0	0	0	0	0	0	0
313	Beverages	0	0	0	0	0	0	0	0	0
314	Tobacco	0	0	0	0	0	0	0	0	0
321	Textiles	0	0	0	10.32	3.90	0	0	4.73	0
322	Wearing apparel except footwear	99.63	72.49	96.50	19.71	55.65	5.25	10.99	14.51	4.22
323	Leather products	95.99	81.94	75.48	77.77	86.14	18.90	78.38	85.35	78.14
324	Footwear except rubber or plastic	0	0	0	0	0	0	0	0	0
331	Wood products except furniture	0	0	0	0	0	0	0	0	0
332	Furniture except metal	0	0	0	0	0	0	0	0	0
341	Paper and products	0	0	0	0	0	0	0	0	0
342	Printing and publishing	0	0	0	0	0	0	0	0	0
351	Industrial chemicals	0	0	0	0	0	0	0	0	0
352	Other chemicals	0	0	0	0	0	0	0	0	0
353	Petroleum refineries	0	0	0	0	0	0	0	0	0
354	Manufacture of miscellaneous product	0	0	0	0	0	0	0	0	0
355	Rubber products	0	0	0	0	0	0	0	0	0
356	Plastic products	0	0	0	0	0	0	0	0	0
361	Pottery china earthenware	0	0	0	0	0	0	0	0	0
362	Glass and products	0	0	0	0	0	0	0	0	0
369	Other non-metallic mineral products	0	0	0	0	0	0	0	0	0
371	Iron and steel	0	0	0	0	0	0	0	0	0
372	Non-ferrous metals	0	0	0	0	0	0	0	0	0
381	Fabricated metal products	0	0	0	0	0	0	0	0	0
382	Machinery except electrical	0	0	0	0	0	0	0	0	0
383	Machinery electric	0	0	0	0	0	0	0	0	0
384	Transport equipment	0	0	0	0	0	0	0	0	0
385	Professional and scientific equipment	0	0	0	0	0	0	0	0	0
390	Other manufactured products	0	0	0	0	0	0	0	0	0

Source: Cadot and Dutoit (2008) from U.S. ITC.

The uncertainty surrounding the renewal of the ATPDEA raised the risk of preference erosion. Since the original ATPDEA ended (in December 2006), it was extended four times through the end of 2008, but for progressively shorter terms. Despite several extensions, many short-term renewals were already generating uncertainty concerning the sustained application of the agreement. The government has sent signals that it is less interested in signing long-term free trade agreements both with the United States and (through its participation in the CAN) with the European Union. Instead, other long term agreements—like the ALBA (*Alternativa Bolivariana para las Américas*) initiative or with the Republic of Iran—have already been signed, with little or no effect on trade.

While Bolivia is a member of the Andean Community, it did not apply the common external tariff (CET) agreed upon in 1995 for many years. Instead, Bolivia pursued a less restrictive import regime with lower tariffs than the CET for most products, subject to Andean Community administration. Peru does not participate in the CET mechanism at all, while Colombia, Ecuador, and República Bolivariana de Venezuela apply the common tariffs.

Bolivia has moved toward higher import tariffs for more than 2,000 products since April 2008, closing the gap with the CET. Some observers view higher import taxes as partly a means of protecting domestic industry from foreign competition and thus fostering productive development. Yet such an infant industry and import-substitution strategy could easily backfire, undermining international competitiveness and reducing exports. Domestic market protection comes at a cost, notably to consumers and firms that source their inputs domestically. Also, tariff protection introduces an anti-export bias. If firms produce for the export market, they do not receive the same market price support enjoyed by producers for the domestic market. Hence, producers' decisions will be biased against selling abroad.

An analysis of the restrictiveness of the trade regimes in Andean Community countries illustrates what is at stake. An Overall Trade Restrictiveness Index (OTRI)[9] indicates that Bolivia has both the lowest tariff restrictiveness and overall restrictiveness in the Andean Community (Figure 1.5). If the restrictiveness of the Bolivian import regime were to be increased to the average of the CET-countries (Colombia, Ecuador, and República Bolivariana de Venezuela), Bolivia's import restrictiveness would rise by 3.5 percentage points, which would imply an increase in the anti-export bias of the trade regime of almost 50 percent.

Recent macroeconomic policies

Inflation in Bolivia accelerated in 2007 to near 12 percent owing to supply shocks and rising aggregated demand, particularly in private consumption and public expenditures. After several years of relative price stability—average inflation was less than 5 percent between 2000 and 2006—inflation in 2007 approached 12 percent (Figure 1.6). Most of the price increases were related to food and beverages, a heavily weighted factor in the price index (near 50 percent, though recently reduced to 39 percent), making inflation highly regressive. The main factors behind this upsurge were the El Niño Southern Oscillation at the beginning of 2007; imported inflation; the slow supply response, linked to low private investment; and increased aggregated demand, both from the public sector (related to increased gas revenues) and from households (because of increased remittances and state transfers).

Figure 1.5. Trade Restrictiveness in the Andean Community (Uniform Tariff Equivalent)

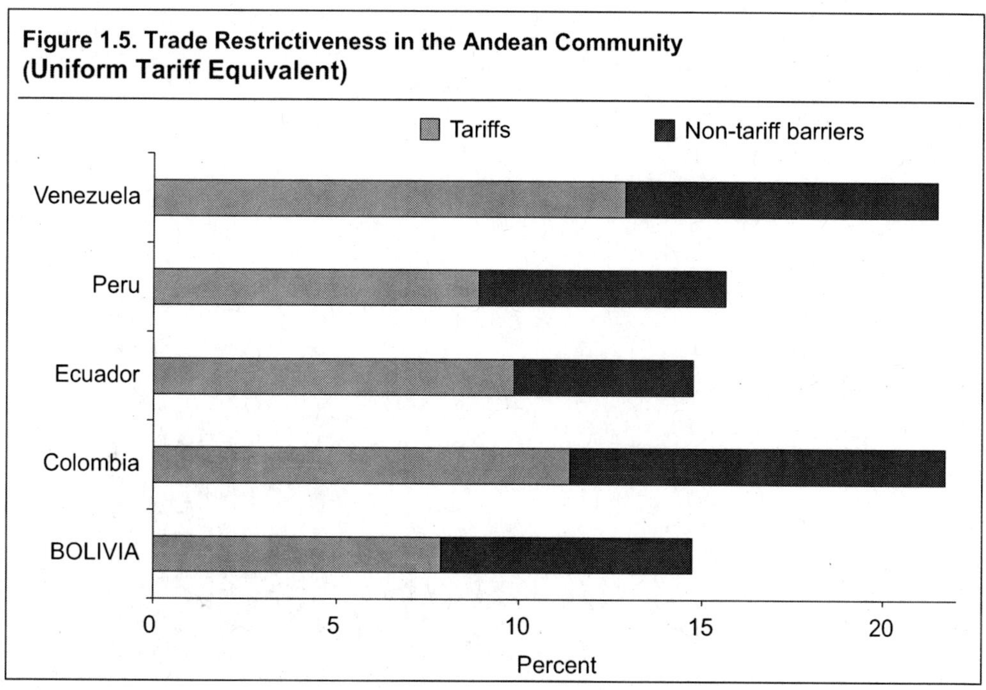

Source: World Bank staff calculations based on Kee *et al*. (2005).

Figure 1.6. Twelve-Month Inflation and Depreciation

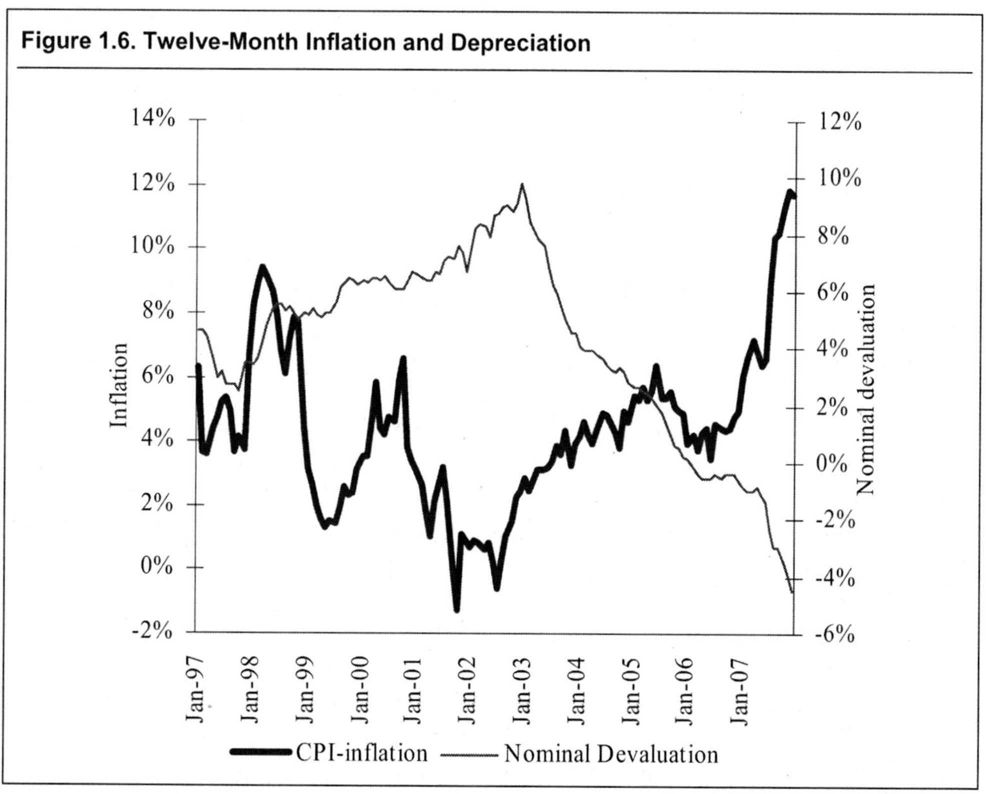

Source: INE.

Figure 1.7. Central Bank Domestic Debt

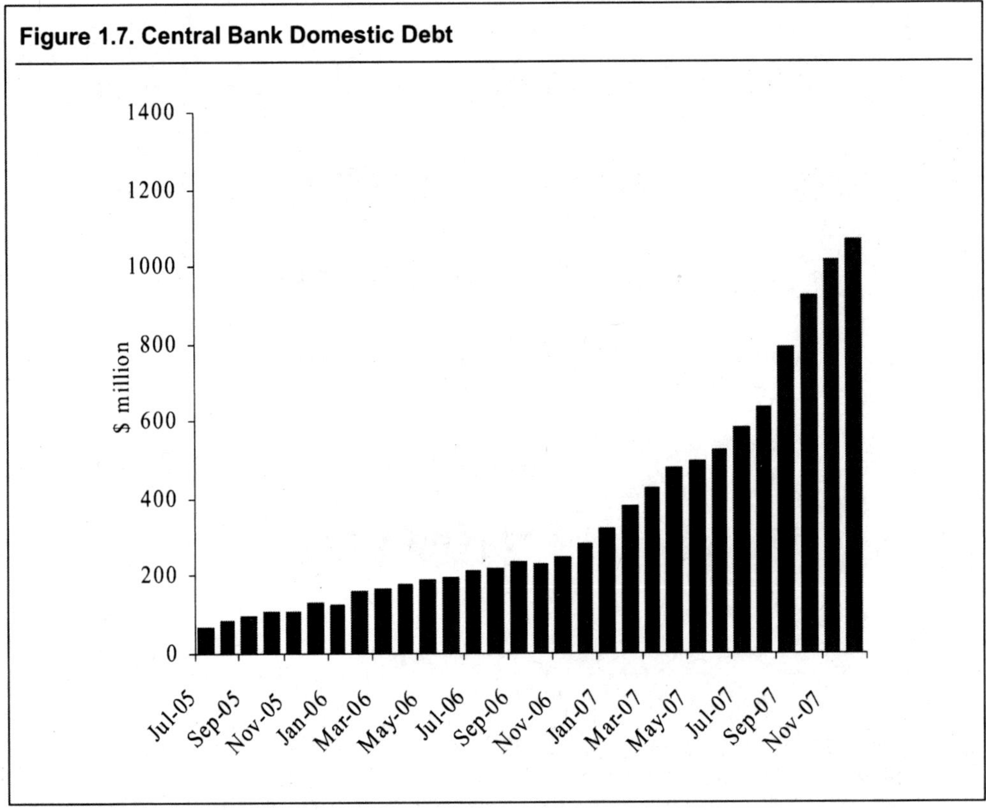

Source: BCB.

Monetary policy focused on contractive open market operations (OMOs) in 2007, while the nominal exchange rate appreciated modestly. The central bank's domestic debt increased considerably last year, underscoring the effort to reduce liquidity through OMOs (Figure 1.7). On the other hand, the nominal exchange rate appreciated by 4.5 percent, in an effort to reduce imported inflation, although without significant effects on the real exchange rate. If the exchange rate was freely floating, the appreciation should have been higher (Central Bank of Bolivia 2008), owing to hydrocarbon export revenues and remittances growth. But the central bank expects that OMOs will affect inflation and inflation expectations more notably in 2008 because of the lagged effects on prices of monetary policy (Orellana and Requena 1999). Additionally, the effect of appreciation may be weak because the pass-through effect is asymmetric—inflation reacts faster to depreciations than to appreciations—and has decreased over the past 20 years, in parallel with falling inflation (Escobar and Mendieta 2004). The central bank expects 8 percent inflation in 2008, although this seems optimistic; the IMF projects 16 percent inflation in 2008 (IMF 2008) and La Niña again imposed a large supply shock affecting inflation in the first quarter of 2008.

Increased inflation and nominal appreciation are hurting competitiveness, at least for some nontraditional products. Despite accelerating nominal appreciation and rising inflation, the multilateral real exchange rate has changed only modestly in the last two years (Figure 1.8) because other trading partner currencies' also appreciated. The effect of nominal appreciation by export type is also similar: nontraditional real exchange rates have also remained mostly stable in the last years. This outcome is more relevant for nontraditional exports, which are more elastic to real exchange rate variations than traditional exports, at least in the short term (Loza, 2000). For example, gas export prices and volumes in Bolivia are defined by contractual rules. But the stability of the real exchange rate of nontraditional exports hides the competitive loss faced by several products owing to *bilateral* real appreciations. This is the case for the United States, the most important buyer of Bolivian nontraditional products. Bolivia has also lost competitiveness relative to Ecuador, Japan, Mexico, Panama, and Peru. Important nontraditional products (such as wood, jewelry, Brazilian nuts, and coffee) are thus facing significant losses of competitiveness because they are largely exported to United States or Peru (Figure 1.8). This effect is partially counterbalanced by the real depreciation with respect to such other countries as Colombia (Figure 1.9). Bolivia has also gained competitiveness relative to República Bolivariana de Venezuela. As three-quarters of soya exports are directed to República Bolivariana de Venezuela and Colombia, this product is gaining competitiveness.

Figure 1.8. Multilateral Real Exchange Rate of Total Trade, and Traditional and Nontraditional Exports

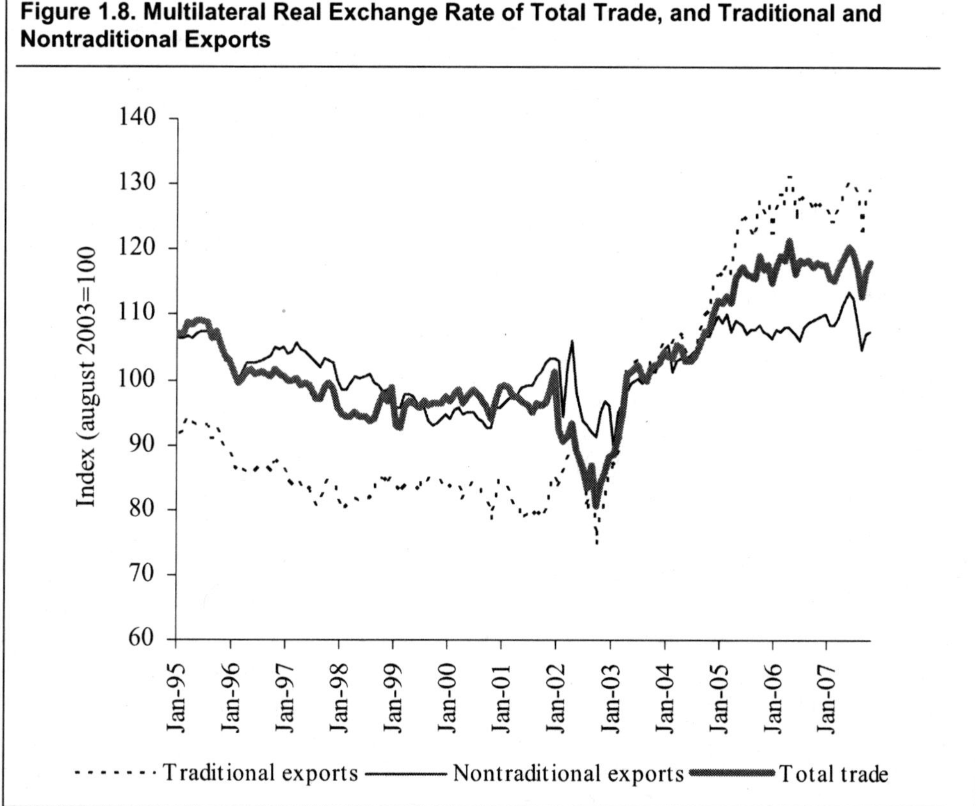

Source: INE and BCB.

Note: Multilateral real exchange rates were estimated considering the 8 main partners in each category.

Figure 1.9. Multilateral Real Exchange Rate of Nontraditional Exports and Selected Bilateral Real Exchange Rates

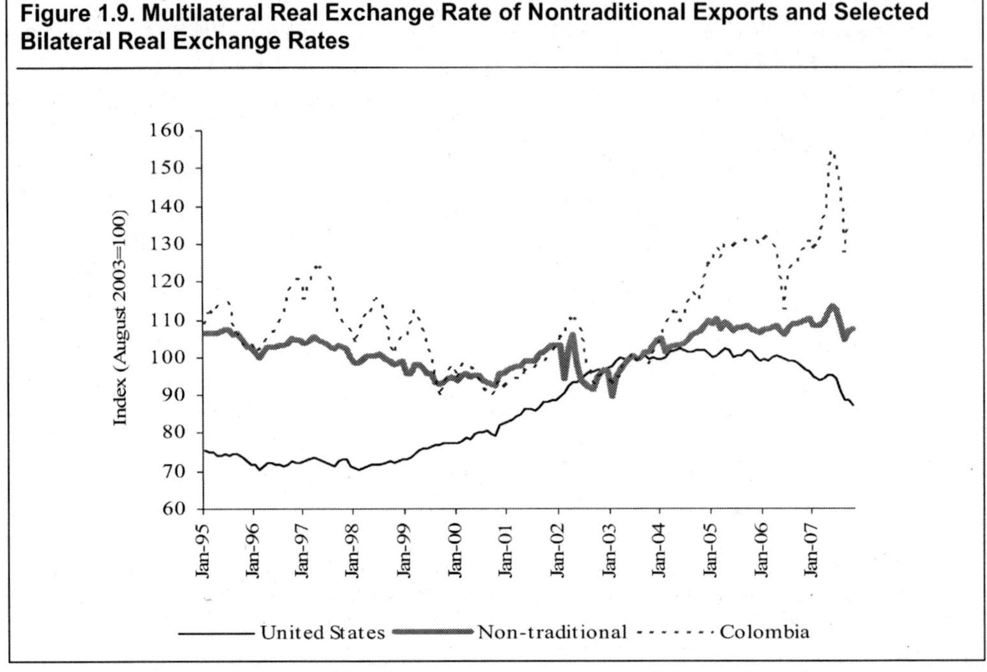

Source: INE and BCB.
Note: Multilateral real exchange rate of non traditional exports was estimated considering the 8 main importers of Bolivia's nontraditional goods.

Several other factors could counterbalance the pressure on competitiveness by the appreciating real exchange rate. Further nominal and real appreciation seems inevitable owing to the large foreign inflows expected over the medium term, and aggregated demand growth would persist (IMF 2007). In other words, some symptoms of Dutch disease[10] could become evident in the coming years. As noted above, this appreciation could have more intense negative effects on nontraditional exports, which are the most labor-intensive.

Fiscal policy has been increasingly restrictive, with the government's overall fiscal position reaching near balance. Strong revenue growth has driven the improving fiscal balance. In fact total government revenues doubled from Bs. 14.9 billion in 2003 to about Bs. 30.1 billion in 2006. This increase in revenues was due largely to hydrocarbon-related revenues, which rose from Bs. 2.8 billion in 2003 to Bs. 10.6 billion in 2006. Mining royalties also fueled the higher revenues, as they surged from Bs. 50 million in 2003 to Bs. 408 million in 2006. The importance of hydrocarbons and mining for government finances helps explain the close correlation between the evolution of the trade and fiscal balances (Figure 1.10). In contrast, government expenses have grown at a much more modest pace. Current spending increased from Bs. 12 billion in 2003 to just Bs. 14.3 billion in 2006, while capital expenditure climbed at a faster rate, rising from Bs. 4.9 billion in 2003 to Bs. 9.3 billion in 2006. The pace of expenditures appears to have accelerated since 2006.

Figure 1.10. Bolivia's Trade and Fiscal Balance (Percent of GDP)

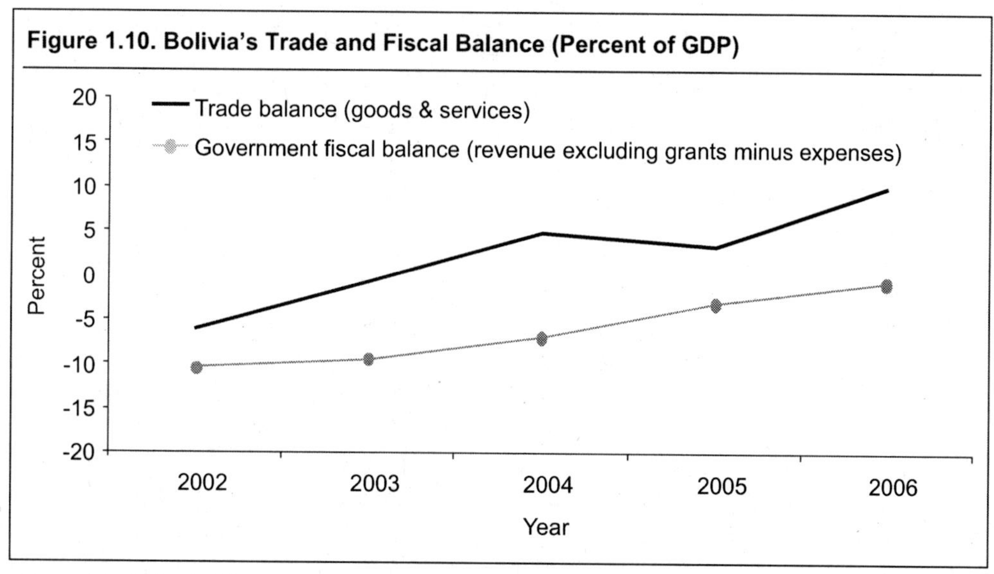

Source: World Bank WDI.

Earnings from customs tariffs have not been a particularly important source of fiscal revenue. In 2006, tariff revenue accounted for some Bs. 907 million, or about 4 percent of total tax revenues (Bs. 25.5 billion). This is relatively low compared with other LAC countries (Figure 1.11). In fact, customs and other duties as a share of tax revenues is lower only in Chile. While the recent increase in customs tariffs will drive the figure higher, it is unlikely to significantly expand customs revenues.

Figure 1.11. Customs and Other Duties on Imports as a Share of Tax Revenues (Percent)

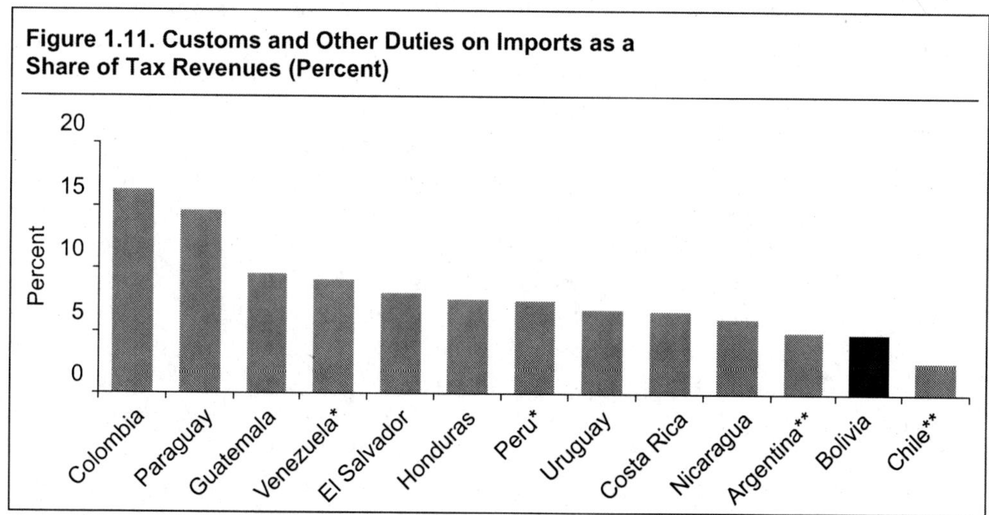

Source: World Bank WDI.

Notes: Data refer to 2006 unless otherwise noted.

* 2005, ** 2004.

FDI Evolution and Policies

A much-improved regulatory framework for FDI accompanied the trade liberalization. The 1990 Investment Law guaranteed the same rights to both local and foreign investment and prohibited any restrictions on foreign exchange. Consequently, throughout the 1990s the regulatory framework for FDI was one of the most open in the LAC region. In 1993, the Law for the Development and Tax Treatment of the Export Sector introduced the concept of tax neutrality and established a refund system for exporters.

High levels of FDI supported increased hydrocarbon export volumes. FDI in hydrocarbons and mining is linked with their (lagged) export volume (Figure 1.12). High FDI in the hydrocarbon sector in the late 1990s was associated with significant increases in export volume during the early 2000s. The relatively recent upsurge of FDI in the mining sector is having similar effects on export volumes. Vast investments in San Cristobal and San Bartolomé until 2007 promise a large rise in future export volumes. In the nontraditional sector, however, the link between investments and exports is unclear, owing to the low and variable levels of foreign investment. For example, there is no clear evidence of significant foreign participation in the upsurge of soya exports in the 1990s; FDI in this sector has behaved erratically. Soya exports were boosted by private investments, high international prices, and the absence of other dynamic economic alternatives because the traditional sector was only beginning to be reactivated.

Since 2000, FDI in most sectors has plummeted, even in traditional sectors such as hydrocarbons and utilities, as a result of the deteriorating investment climate. Despite changes to the regulatory framework in the 1990s that aimed to attract FDI, actual flows have decreased since the early 2000s, with the important exception of mining. The main reasons for this decline are the lack of pick-up in investment once the capitalization-related investment commitments were realized; the fact that the small size of the domestic market constrains private investment in nontradable sectors; the inability to ensure new markets for gas exports that require the development of identified reserves; significant political and social instability; and the nationalization process and changes to the tax burden on traditional activities. A number of factors related to the business environment also limit FDI flows, as well as the ability of firms to take advantage of export opportunities. (These can be seen in the Doing Business ratings for Bolivia, shown in Figure 1.13).

Weak investment in the traditional sector has also hurt nontraditional exports through lower power supply capacity and limited logistics expansion. Gross FDI in hydrocarbons is at its lowest despite contractual commitments to raise gas exports to Brazil and Argentina.[11] These shortcomings may affect Bolivia's overall economic performance because they prevent further expansion of logistical services and energy supply, which are required by all sectors including nontraditional exports. For example, power supply capacity is not projected to be able to satisfy demand even by 2010, because demand is growing while capacity has stagnated without further investment.

Figure 1.12. FDI and Export Volume in Selected Sectors

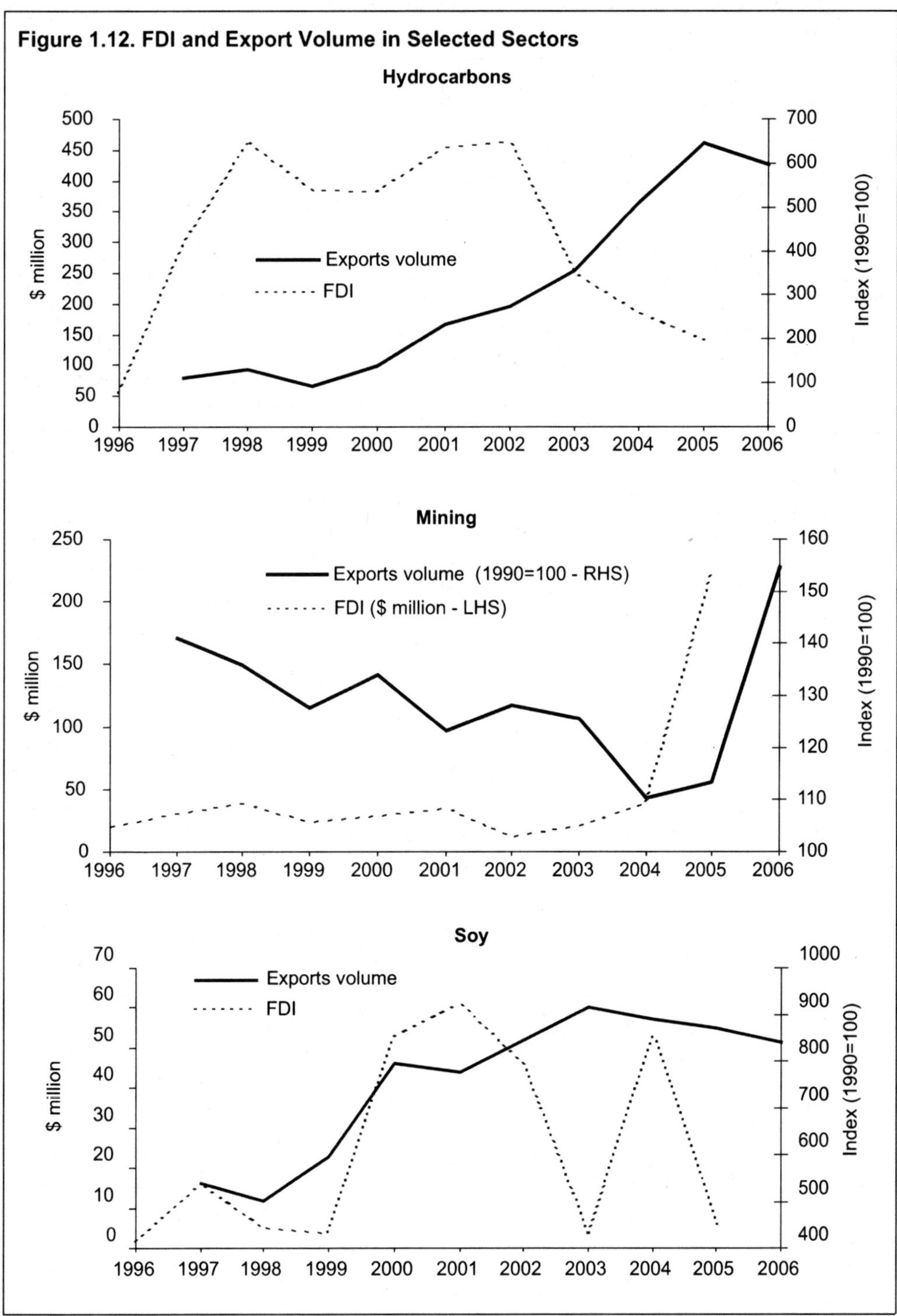

Source: INE.

Figure 1.13. Main Features of Bolivia's Business Environment

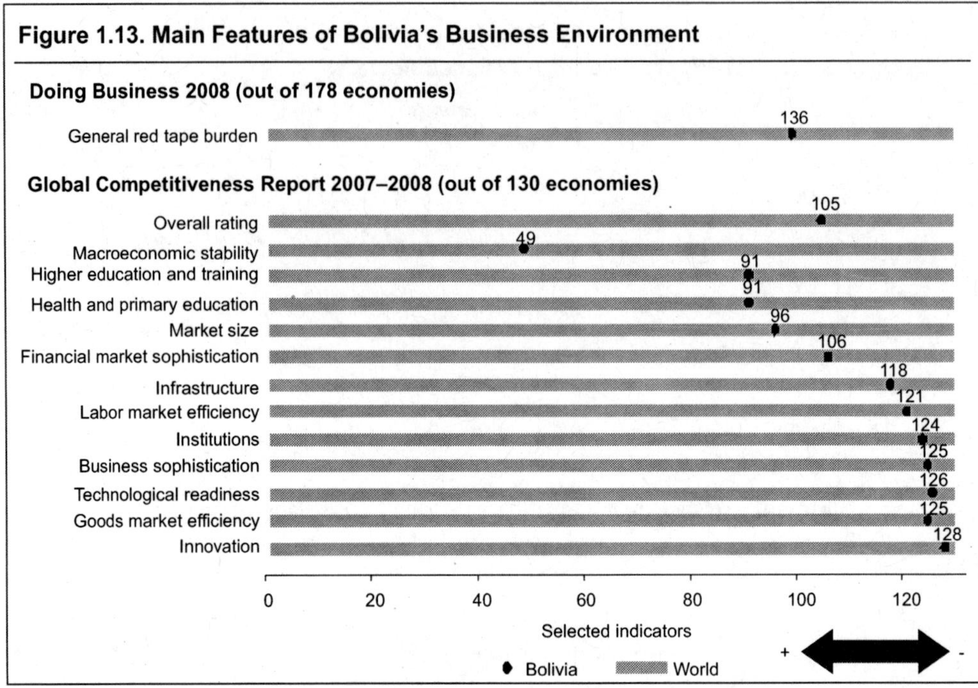

Source: Doing Business 2007 and Global Competitiveness Report 2007–2008.

The liberalization of capital flows led to record capital inflows in 1998, mostly benefiting traditional sectors. Capitalization, privatization, and other market-oriented policies triggered a significant FDI upsurge in nontradable utilities—telecom and energy, among others—and in traditional sectors [the gas pipeline to Brazil was built and the massive San Bartolome and San Cristobal mining projects were developed (Figure 1.14). Moreover, multilateral development banks—mainly the *Corporación Andina de Fomento* (CAF), Inter American Development Bank (IADB), and the International Finance Corporation (IFC)—have complemented these FDI initiatives, focusing in hydrocarbons, mining, utilities, and microfinance.

The manufacturing sector has attracted only 10 percent of total gross FDI since 1996, and minimal flows have gone to agriculture and tourism. FDI financed only a handful of successful products in the manufacturing sector, related to soya and jewelry exports. More specifically, soya-based vegetable oil received 40 percent and jewelry received 15 percent of all FDI in manufacturing. The remaining FDI flows have financed domestic market supply—oil refineries, milk, beer, and concrete industries (Figure 1.15).

Figure 1.14. FDI by Sector

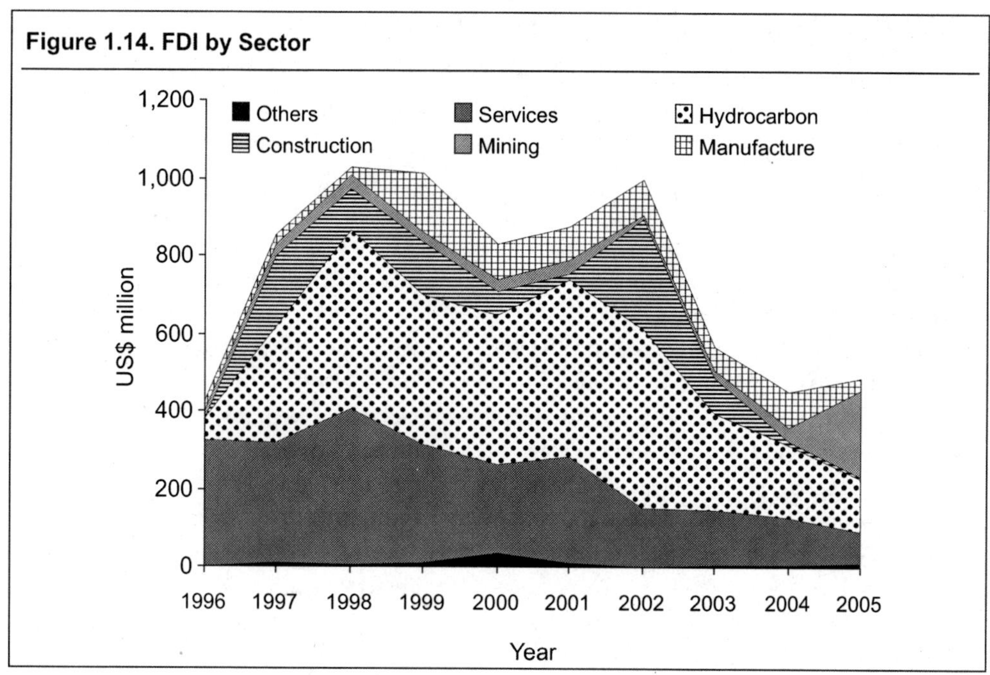

Source: INE.

Figure 1.15. FDI in Manufacturing Sector by Product, 1996–2005

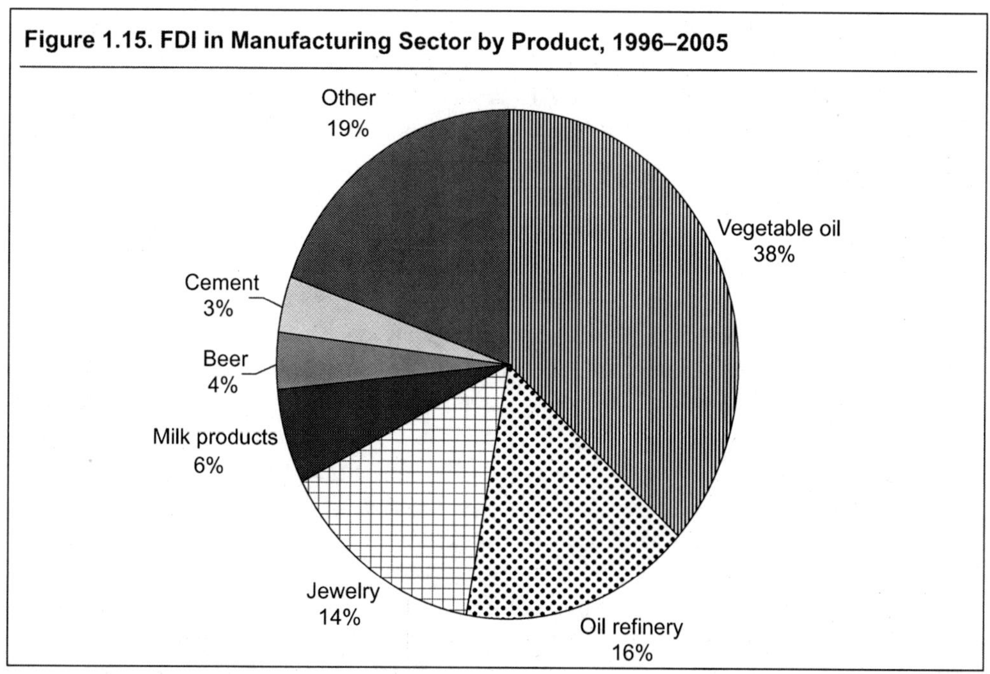

Source: INE.

Diversification and the Optimal Export Strategy for Bolivia

Diversification is a top priority for the government's export strategy as it implements its National Development Plan. The goal is to shift toward greater value-added exports, coupled with more balanced trade relations and diversified export markets and products.

The authorities' desire for diversification is well founded as adverse terms of trade and rent-seeking activities may make revenue from natural resources short lived. First, countries like Bolivia with a narrow export base concentrated in natural resources are more exposed to unfavorable terms of trade shocks.[12] Second, returns from commodities may be perceived as unstable, posing a threat to employment and output in the long run.[13] Windfall booms are temporary, underscoring the importance of planning and investing in new industries connected with the old industries in order to sustain economic development.[14] Ricardian Malthusian advocates also argue that non renewable resources are fated to diminish over time since they cannot be replenished. Thus, economic progress entails moving away from natural resources to sectors based on knowledge, capital, and technology. Third, the rate of technological change in resource-dependent activities is perceived to be lower than in manufacturing or services.[15] Finally, resource-intensive production may promote rent-seeking activities, lower the growth rate, and lead to civil wars.[16]

Targeted policies can help achieve diversification. The appropriate policy actions are likely to involve several things. First, the government will need to increase the accumulation of the types of physical and human capital needed for manufacturing and services and that are appropriate to Bolivia's comparative advantage and lay the foundation of a more diversified economic structure. Investing in activities related to hydrocarbons or minerals—such as in services, machinery, engineering product, or transport equipment—may be a first step.[17] Second, the authorities need to develop a trade regime that allows the emergence of new export activities, which will help Bolivia adjust as comparative advantage shifts. The policies should also promote technological change in the manufacture and services sectors. Finally, the policy actions should eliminate possible market failures that may prevent the production structure from shifting away from commodities.

Evidence from other countries indicates that diversification based on natural resource endowment can succeed. The experience of such Nordic countries as Sweden and Finland shows that natural resources can promote sustainable development and diversification. In their case, a few elements enabled a successful diversification strategy: First, strong institutions and institutional reform for growth and development enabled the introduction of new technologies to boost productivity and pave the way for industrialization. They also facilitate the sustainable use of land, raw materials, and resources. Second, the acquisition of relevant skills and knowledge enabled a greater role for public and semipublic institutions in promoting research and knowledge diffusion. In particular, FDI and the absorption of foreign technologies can be boosted through knowledge clusters. Third, the internationalization of the country through an open trade regime helped it acquire modern technologies (including patents) and helped adapt faster existing technologies to international standards. Finally, long-term investment in research and development increased the flexibility of the economy to create an environment where firms or entire industries are well positioned to adjust to changing conditions and benefit from innovation and market opportunities.[18]. See Box 1.1 for strategies beyond diversification for Bolivia.

Box 1.1. Beyond Diversification: The Export Strategy of Bolivia as a Resource-Rich Country

Natural resources are neither destiny nor curse for Bolivia. Exports of natural resources have been negatively correlated with total exports, which is referred to as the natural resources curse. But empirical evidence from cross-country regressions indicates that the curse is driven by the trade structure. A concentration of export revenues reduces growth by dampening productivity growth, thus determining the negative impact of natural resource exports relative to total exports. Once productivity effects are accounted for, natural resources are positively correlated with growth. But for natural resources to become destiny would depend on many factors, ranging from traditional endowments, comparative advantage, and public policies in education, knowledge infrastructure, trade policy, human capital, and innovation.[a]

Bolivia's low productivity growth suggests that the country has lost opportunities to make natural resources a greater driver of growth. Being far from the innovation frontier, Bolivia has the potential to catch up to countries at the frontier by adopting their technology and increasing its productivity. Bolivia's total factor productivity (TFP) growth has been lagging; indeed, it remained constant from 1950 to 2005.[b] Low productivity growth for many resource-rich LAC countries has been blamed on deficient national innovation and the lack of learning capacity to adopt new technologies. Rent seeking may also link natural resources with artificial monopoly power and anticompetitive forces, raising the barriers to technology transfer.

The empirical evidence also indicates that natural resources reduce economic growth in countries with very low human capital or high wealth inequality. Specialization in primary commodities for many developing countries has limited the benefit of industrial technical progress, and did not result in higher production or improved terms of trade.[c] But over the long term, commodity prices will decline; changes in comparative advantage will make developing countries more competitive in some manufacturing industries. In contrast, industrial countries will move toward producing services. Wealth inequality may also play a role in slowing the country's ability to adopt foreign technology as the marginalization of a large part of the population reduces access to franchises, financial institutions, and property rights.[d]

Achieving natural resource-based growth depends on many factors, ranging from trade policy to knowledge infrastructure. First, Bolivia's capacity to adopt new technologies can boost the potential returns to discovery and exploitation, with positive effects for growth. Second, countries with high innovation and effective human capital will be able to create new technologies, whereas those with lower stocks of human capital will adopt the technologies and those with even lower capital stock will not be able to adopt and will therefore stagnate.[e] Therefore, policies to promote innovation, increase the human capital stock and knowledge in infrastructure are influential in determining in which equilibrium a country may find itself. Third, more open economies, and those with a more developed knowledge infrastructure, grow faster. But the necessary degree of protection to preserve or jump start domestic industries is a function of the ability to innovate as fast as foreign competitors. Countries that also manage to avoid rent seeking are better able to benefit from their natural resources for higher growth.

Notes:
a. See Lederman and Xu (2001) as cited in Lederman and Maloney (2006).
b. Martin and Mitra (2001) as cited in Lederman and Maloney (2006) indicate that despite being far from the innovation frontier and hence having the potential to catch up on countries closer to the innovation frontier, the growth of TFP for LAC countries in agriculture and manufacturing has been lagging that of countries on the technological frontier.
c. See Prebish (1959) as cited in Lederman and Maloney (2006).
d. Blomstrom and Koko (2001) as cited in Lederman and Maloney (2006) find that knowledge networks, clusters of universities and public-private think-thank are crucial to growth in productivity and the development of new products.
e. See Howitt and Mayer (2005) as cited in Lederman and Maloney (2006).

Conclusion

Bolivia has opened up substantially, adopting a simple tariff structure and preferential access to developed markets and neighboring markets for a wide range of products. Despite a few successes—such as soya—FDI policy has not fostered investment in nontraditional sectors, on average, hindering the effective use of trade openness and preferential access to increase nontraditional exports. As a result, capital flows to nontraditional sectors, and thus their exports, have remained small.

Trade policy has been based on several preferential trade agreements with regional neighbors and developed markets (the European Union and the United States). The agreement with the United States is set to expire in December 2008. The high rate of preference utilization for both the European Union and United States underscores the importance for exporters to access these markets under preferential treatment.

Fiscal and trade surpluses have been expanding strongly, boosted by hydrocarbons prices and mining royalties. Customs and import duties have not been an important source of tax revenues; Bolivia is second to Chile in the region for smallest collection rates, which attest to the openness of the trade regime. The recent hike in import duties for more than 2,000 products may not change that significantly in the future.

The government's interest in export diversification is well justified since adverse terms of trade may jeopardize revenues from natural resource exports. International evidence suggests that it is possible to successfully diversify away from natural resources in Bolivia. It depends, however, on such factors as tapping new technologies to raise productivity and lay the foundation for industrialization; promoting research and knowledge diffusion for the acquisition of relevant skills; boosting FDI and the absorption of foreign technologies through knowledge clusters; and creating an open trade regime to acquire modern technologies (including patents) and adapt existing technologies to international standards.

Notes

[1] The 16 high performers are the group of non-oil exporting, nontransition countries that achieved more than 4.5 percent of average annual GDP growth since 1980—Botswana, Burkina Faso, Cambodia, Chile, China, India, Indonesia, Republic of Korea, Malaysia, Mauritius, Pakistan, Singapore, Sri Lanka, Taiwan Province of China, Thailand, and Uganda.

[2] Brenton and Newfarmer (2007) derive an index of export market penetration (IEMP) that measures the extent to which a country is actually exploiting its geographical market opportunities from the existing set of export products. For the given range of products that a country exports, the IEMP will be higher for countries that reach a large proportion of the number of international markets that import those products. The index for countries that only export to a small number of the overseas markets will have a low value.

[3] As of 2005, if exports of natural gas are excluded, the United States was already the largest market for Bolivian exports, accounting for about 22 percent of non-gas exports. The U.S. market was a particularly important market for manufactures: exports to the U.S. market accounted for almost 100 percent of jewelry exports, 70 percent of textile exports, 57 percent of leather manufactures exports, and 40 percent of furniture exports.

[4] WTO (2005).

[5] Lara and Soloaga, (2007).
[6] Giussani and Olarreaga (2006).
[7] WTO (2005).
[8] The utilization rate of preferences can be affected by different factors, including strict standards, restrictive rules of origin, lack of information, and burdensome procedures of eligibility. This low figure may imply some margin for improvement in preference utilization, associated with less restrictive rules of origin and possibly technical assistance for exporters to satisfy EU requirements related to certification, traceability, and administrative documentation.
[9] The OTRI corresponds to the uniform tariff that if imposed on all imports from partner countries would leave overall imports unchanged. The measure also makes it possible to disaggregate total barriers to trade into tariff and nontariff components (Kee, Nicita, and Olarreaga, 2006). The estimation is based on country-specific import demand elasticities at the detailed product level, which can result in differing restrictiveness estimates for countries that apply the same tariff schedule, such as Colombia, Ecuador, and República Bolivariana de Venezuela.
[10] The Dutch disease would refer to an erosion of competitiveness in nontraditional exports due to an appreciation of the exchange rate from higher natural resources exports
[11] Petrobras announced new investments but they have yet to be implemented. In mining, the San Cristobal and San Bartolome developments, initiated in 2000, were finished in 2007 and there are no other major private initiatives in the pipeline, except for iron ore deposits (El Mutun) to be exploited by the Indian company Jindal.
[12] See Prebish (1959) as cited in Lederman and Maloney (2006).
[13] See Cashin and McDermott (2002) as cited in Lederman and Maloney (2006).
[14] Australia, the United States, Sweden, and Finland adopted this approach.
[15] The Presbish-Singer argument is that countries that export commodities (such as most developing countries) would be able to import less and less manufactured goods for a given level of exports.
[16] See Sachs and Warner (1995) and Collier (2000) as cited in Lederman and Maloney (2006).
[17] Nordic countries' development growth is based on such a strategy: Sweden and Finland's main natural resources were timber and iron ore; today Swedish Ericsson and Finnish Nokia are the world leader in Telecom. In 1990, computer and telecom represented less than 7 percent of national exports; in 2000 the shares grew to over 20 percent in Sweden and 30 percent in Finland.
[18] See Blomstrom and Koko (2000) as cited in Lederman and Maloney (2006).

Annex 1.1. Restrictiveness of Bolivia's Trade Policy

Table 1.A.1. Import Tariffs Applied by Bolivia (Percent)

ISIC Rev.3	Description	MERCOSUR	Andean Community	Venezuela, R. B. de	Chile	Cuba	EU (27)	USA	Rest of the world
1	AGRICULTURE, HUNTING	0.6	0.0	x	1.4	10.0	3.8	5.6	5.8
2	FORESTRY, LOGGING	0.1	0.0	x	10.0	x	9.2	9.6	4.1
5	FISHING	2.3	3.6	x	10.0	x	x	10.0	10.0
10	MINING OF COAL AND LIGNITE	4.3	0.0	x	x	x	x	x	x
11	EXTRACTION OF CRUDE PETROLEUM	0.0	x	x	x	x	x	x	x
13	MINING OF METAL ORES	9.9	2.4	x	10.4	x	9.0	10.0	7.9
14	OTHER MINING AND QUARRYING	0.6	0.4	0.1	4.2	x	5.9	4.6	2.5
15	FOOD PRODUCTS AND BEVERAGES	1.0	0.1	0.0	3.7	10.0	9.6	5.1	4.8
16	TOBACCO PRODUCTS	0.0	0.1	0.0	x	x	10.0	0.1	0.2
17	TEXTILES	0.8	0.1	5.9	3.2	10.0	8.0	9.0	9.4
18	WEARING APPAREL	2.0	0.8	3.6	6.7	x	7.3	5.6	9.6
19	TANNING AND DRESSING OF LEATHER	5.9	1.1	0.1	10.0	x	7.9	9.1	9.7
20	WOOD AND OF PRODUCTS OF WOOD	4.9	3.9	10.1	10.0	x	5.3	1.4	9.5
21	PAPER AND PAPER PRODUCTS	0.3	0.1	0.0	4.0	x	9.5	9.5	8.9
22	PUBLISHING, PRINTING AND REPRODUCTION	0.8	0.3	2.2	6.4	0.0	1.1	3.3	3.2
23	COKE, REFINED PETROLEUM	0.4	0.4	0.0	3.8	x	8.8	9.9	8.2
24	CHEMICALS AND CHEMICAL PRODUCTS	0.8	0.3	0.2	2.7	0.0	7.5	7.7	5.7
25	RUBBER AND PLASTICS	2.3	0.2	1.4	6.8	0.2	9.5	9.6	9.6
26	OTHER NON-METALLIC MINERAL PRODUCTS	1.2	0.6	0.1	4.7	16.7	8.3	8.9	8.3
27	BASIC METALS	2.6	0.1	1.8	5.2	x	8.6	3.3	9.1
28	FABRICATED METAL PRODUCTS	1.6	0.1	0.1	3.1	x	6.7	9.3	8.2
29	MACHINERY AND EQUIPMENT	0.2	0.0	0.0	1.1	0.0	0.5	1.2	1.0
30	OFFICE, ACCOUNTING AND COMPUTING MACHINERY	0.0	0.0	0.0	0.0	0.0	0.0	0.0	0.0
31	ELECTRICAL MACHINERY	0.0	0.0	0.0	0.0	0.0	0.0	0.0	0.0
32	RADIO, TELEVISION AND COMMUNICATION EQUIPMENT	0.0	0.0	0.0	0.0	0.0	0.0	0.0	0.0
33	MEDICAL, PRECISION AND OPTICAL INSTRUMENTS AND CLOCKS	0.0	0.0	0.0	0.0	0.0	0.0	0.0	0.0
34	MOTOR VEHICLES AND TRAILERS	0.0	0.1	0.0	0.0	x	0.2	0.6	0.1
35	OTHER TRANSPORT EQUIPMENT	0.0	0.0	0.0	0.0	x	0.0	0.1	0.0
36	FURNITURE; MANUFACTURE N.E.C.	0.1	0.4	0.0	0.1	x	0.8	0.3	0.6

Note: These are trade weighted, applied tariff rates. Applied tariff rates are calculated as [tariff revenue / import value] so tariff exemptions and ad valorem equivalents of specific tariffs are taken into account. Calculations are based on Bolivian customs data for 2007. Fields with x indicate zero imports.

Table 1.A.2. Tariffs that Bolivian Exporters Face Abroad (Percent)

ISIC Rev.3	Description	MERCOSUR	Andean Community	Venezuela, R. B. de	Chile	Cuba	EU (27)	USA	Rest of the world
1	AGRICULTURE, HUNTING	0.0	0.0	0.0	0.1	x	0.0	0.0	18.6
2	FORESTRY, LOGGING	0.0	0.0	0.0	4.0	x	0.0	0.0	0.0
5	FISHING	x	x	x	x	x	x	x	x
10	MINING OF COAL AND LIGNITE	x	x	x	x	x	0.0	x	x
11	EXTRACTION OF CRUDE PETROLEUM	0.0	x	x	x	x	x	0.0	x
13	MINING OF METAL ORES	0.0	0.0	x	4.0	x	0.0	0.0	0.6
14	OTHER MINING AND QUARRYING	0.0	0.0	0.0	0.6	x	0.0	0.0	2.3
15	FOOD PRODUCTS AND BEVERAGES	0.0	0.0	0.0	0.0	12.4	0.0	0.0	7.0
16	TOBACCO PRODUCTS	0.0	0.0	x	x	x	0.0	x	0.0
17	TEXTILES	1.2	0.0	0.0	0.2	9.9	0.3	13.1	6.9
18	WEARING APPAREL	0.0	0.0	0.0	2.3	x	0.0	17.8	6.9
19	TANNING AND DRESSING OF LEATHER	0.0	0.0	0.0	0.9	x	0.3	1.4	2.9
20	WOOD AND OF PRODUCTS OF WOOD	0.0	0.0	0.0	0.7	x	0.0	0.0	0.8
21	PAPER AND PAPER PRODUCTS	0.0	0.0	10.2	0.0	x	0.0	0.0	14.4
22	PUBLISHING, PRINTING AND REPRODUCTION	12.3	0.0	0.0	1.3	x	0.0	0.0	5.6
23	COKE, REFINED PETROLEUM	0.0	0.0	x	5.4	x	x	x	x
24	CHEMICALS AND CHEMICAL PRODUCTS	0.0	0.0	0.0	3.9	2.6	0.0	0.0	0.2
25	RUBBER AND PLASTICS	4.0	0.0	0.0	5.9	x	0.0	0.0	7.7
26	OTHER NON-METALLIC MINERAL PRODUCTS	1.4	0.0	11.0	1.9	x	0.0	0.0	1.4
27	BASIC METALS	0.0	0.0	0.0	0.7	x	0.1	0.0	0.0
28	FABRICATED METAL PRODUCTS	0.0	0.0	0.0	4.2	x	0.0	0.0	2.2
29	MACHINERY AND EQUIPMENT	0.0	0.0	0.0	4.2	x	0.0	0.0	4.6
30	OFFICE, ACCOUNTING AND COMPUTING MACHINERY	1.8	0.0	0.0	4.0	x	0.0	0.0	0.2
31	ELECTRICAL MACHINERY	3.4	0.0	0.0	2.9	x	0.0	0.0	9.4
32	RADIO, TELEVISION AND COMMUNICATION EQUIPMENT	4.8	0.0	0.0	4.0	x	0.0	0.0	1.1
33	MEDICAL, PRECISION AND OPTICAL INSTRUMENTS AND CLOCKS	0.1	2.1	0.0	4.0	9.9	0.0	0.0	0.6
34	MOTOR VEHICLES AND TRAILERS	12.8	2.7	0.0	4.2	x	0.0	0.0	9.0
35	OTHER TRANSPORT EQUIPMENT	0.6	0.0	0.0	4.1	x	0.0	0.0	7.3
36	FURNITURE; MANUFACTURE N.E.C.	0.0	0.0	0.0	0.1	x	0.0	0.0	6.1

Note: These are trade weighted statutory tariff rates. Exemptions can not be taken into account and tariff rates are weighted by the share of Bolivia's exports to a country and the share of the export good in Bolivia's total exports in this category. Calculations are based on tariff and import data reported by Bolivia's trading partners in the TRAINS database for the latest available of 2005 and 2006. Fields with x indicate zero exports.

Table 1.A.3. Trade Taxes that Bolivia's Exports Face Abroad (Percent)

	Peru	Colombia	MERCOSUR*	U.S.	EU25	Rest of the world
Paddy rice	8.5	0.0	0.0	0.0	69.1	0.0
Wheat	0.0	0.0	0.0	0.0	0.0	0.0
Cereal grains nec	1.0	1.0	0.4	0.0	13.1	12.1
Vegetables, fruit, nuts	15.0	9.0	4.0	0.0	0.0	15.8
Oil seeds	5.8	5.7	2.6	0.0	0.0	47.5
Sugar cane, sugar beet	0.0	0.0	0.0	0.0	0.0	0.0
Plant-based fibers	7.7	6.6	0.0	0.0	0.0	0.0
Crops nec	7.8	5.6	4.3	0.0	0.0	9.0
Cattle, sheep, goats, horses	0.0	0.0	1.0	0.0	0.0	0.0
Animal products nec	10.3	0.0	3.3	0.0	0.0	7.7
Raw milk	0.0	0.0	0.0	0.0	0.0	0.0
Wool, silk-worm	8.9	0.0	0.0	0.0	0.0	8.4
Forestry	0.0	0.0	2.7	0.0	0.0	8.4
Fishing	0.0	0.0	0.0	0.0	0.0	0.0
Coal	0.0	0.0	0.0	0.0	0.0	0.0
Oil	0.0	0.0	0.0	0.2	0.0	0.0
Gas	0.0	0.0	0.0	0.0	0.0	0.0
Minerals nec	7.6	3.6	2.5	0.0	0.0	1.2
Meat: beef	13.4	0.0	0.0	0.0	0.0	0.0
Meat poultry, pig	15.8	0.0	7.2	0.0	0.0	0.0
Vegetable oils and fats	7.5	11.0	3.3	0.0	1.5	4.4
Dairy products	15.9	0.0	0.0	0.0	0.0	0.0
Processed rice	18.5	0.0	0.0	0.0	11.1	0.0
Sugar	8.3	6.2	5.1	0.0	19.3	172.4
Food products nec	12.3	12.4	5.7	0.0	7.8	27.2
Beverages and tobacco	8.9	10.5	3.6	0.0	0.0	9.7
Textiles	11.3	9.4	5.6	0.0	0.5	9.3
Wearing apparel	18.7	15.7	6.0	0.0	0.0	10.2
Leather products	14.2	12.4	4.7	4.0	0.2	10.6
Wood products	5.7	5.7	4.0	0.0	0.0	5.2
Paper products	8.4	8.9	6.2	0.0	0.0	1.7
Petroleum, coal products	7.8	5.2	1.6	0.0	0.0	0.7
Chemical, plastic prods	6.2	6.2	5.4	0.0	0.0	5.0
Mineral products nec	7.6	10.2	4.7	0.0	0.0	3.3
Ferrous metals	6.7	0.0	6.1	0.0	0.0	9.1
Metals nec	6.4	4.6	4.2	0.0	0.3	0.1
Metal products	7.5	10.3	8.6	0.0	0.0	4.5
Motor vehicles and parts	7.0	12.7	16.7	0.0	0.0	6.6
Transport equipment nec	6.0	6.2	4.1	0.0	0.0	1.8
Electronic equipment	7.6	5.9	7.4	0.0	0.0	3.9
Machinery and equipment	6.8	6.8	5.3	0.0	0.0	4.5
Manufactures nec	10.4	11.7	7.0	0.0	0.0	2.3

Source: Andriamananjara and Valenzuela (2008) based on GTAP database.

Note: These are destination's trade-weighted rates on tariffs (including tariff rate quotas) plus the ad valorem equivalents of specific tariffs.

* Includes Chile.

CHAPTER 2

Bolivia's Integration into the World Economy

Many argue that Bolivia's experience with trade liberalization, beginning in the mid-1980s, has had disappointing results. In this chapter, we look at Bolivia's integration into the world economy and discuss the concentration of its exports in products and markets and the amount that Bolivia trades relative to other countries.[1]

The Concentration of Exports and Potential for Diversification

Bolivia's exports are highly concentrated by markets. Bolivia's exports are highly concentrated geographically, with around 54 percent going to either MERCOSUR or CAN markets in 2007. Brazil is by far the largest market for Bolivian exports (Table 2.1). The United States' share of Bolivian exports was just 8.6 percent in 2007 In terms of the geographic composition of Bolivia's export markets the most notable development has been the rise of Brazil as a destination for exports, largely on account of exports of natural gas. Brazil went from accounting for just 2.6 percent of Bolivia's exports in 1998 to accounting for 36.5 percent in 2005. Significantly, however, Brazil has not increased its relative importance as a market for nontraditional Bolivian exports. Brazil accounted for only 2.8 percent of nontraditional exports in 2007, down from 3.6 percent in 1998. Exports of natural gas to Argentina have kept up the importance of Argentina as a destination for Bolivian traditional exports, but the relative importance of the Argentinean market for Bolivian nontraditional exports has declined. Around 10.1 percent of Bolivian nontraditional exports were exported to Argentina in 1998, while the figure was 3.8 percent in 2007. Among the most important markets for Bolivian nontraditional exports are República Bolivariana de Venezuela (accounting for 21.6 percent of nontraditional Bolivian exports in 2007) and the United States (16.4 percent), followed by Colombia (13.7 percent) and Peru (12.5 percent). In this regard, it is notable the sharp increase in República Bolivariana de Venezuela, which only accounted for 1.2 percent of Bolivian nontraditional exports in 1998. Overall, the top four destination markets for nontraditional Bolivian exports accounted for 74.2 percent of exports in 2007, up from 65.7 percent in 1998. This suggests that while the individual export markets may have shifted their relative importance, the geographic pattern of Bolivian exports remains highly concentrated—even when we only consider nontraditional exports.

Table 2.1. Bolivia's Main Export Markets (2007 and 1998)

	Share of... (in percent)	in total exports	in traditional exports	in nontraditional exports	Share of... (in percent)	in total exports	in traditional exports	in nontraditional exports
		2007				1998		
1	Brazil	36.5	46.7	2.8	U.S.	19.5	17.6	21.1
2	Argentina	8.8	10.3	3.8	UK	18.9	38.6	2.8
3	U.S.	8.6	6.2	16.4	Peru	12.6	3.6	20.0
4	Japan	8.5	10.9	0.7	Argentina	11.6	13.6	10.1
5	Venezuela, R. B. de	5.1	0	21.6	Colombia	8.1	0.2	14.5
6	Peru	4.7	2.3	12.5	Switzerland	8.0	17.7	0.1
7	Korea, Rep. of	4.1	5.3	0.4	Uruguay	4.8	0	8.7
8	Switzerland	3.3	4.3	0.1	Chile	3.1	0.7	5.1
9	Colombia	3.2	0	13.7	Brazil	2.6	1.4	3.6
10	Belgium-Luxembourg	2.7	3.4	0.3	Germany	2.0	1.7	2.2
11	UK	2.2	1.7	3.7	Ecuador	1.5	0	2.7
12	Canada	2.2	2.7	0.3	Venezuela, R. B. de	0.9	0.6	1.2
13	Panama	1.4	1.8	0	Italy	0.8	0.1	1.5
14	China	1.2	1.0	1.6	Netherlands	0.7	0.4	1.0
15	Chile	1.1	0.1	4.7	Spain	0.6	0.9	0.5
16	Netherlands	1.0	0.1	4.0	Mexico	0.6	0.4	0.7
17	Mexico	0.6	0.6	0.8	Canada	0.4	0.6	0.3
18	Italy	0.6	0	2.5	Korea, Rep. of	0.3	0.7	0
19	Paraguay	0.6	0	0.7	Japan	0.3	0.1	0.5
20	Spain	0.6	0.3	1.4	Malaysia	0.3	0.6	0

Source: INE.
Note: 2007 data is preliminary.

Bolivia's exports are also concentrated in products. More than 75 percent of all exports are accounted for by traditional exports (minerals and hydrocarbons). Despite recent diversification efforts, manufacturing exports represent only about 10 percent of the total. The importance of manufactured products in Bolivia's exports, however, is not the same across all markets. For instance, jewelry and apparel account for a higher-than-average share of exports to the United States, whereas exports to the European Union are essentially primary products. Exports to Andean markets are dominated by soya products, while exports to Brazil are dominated by natural gas (Figure 2.1).

Figure 2.1 Bolivia's Export Concentration

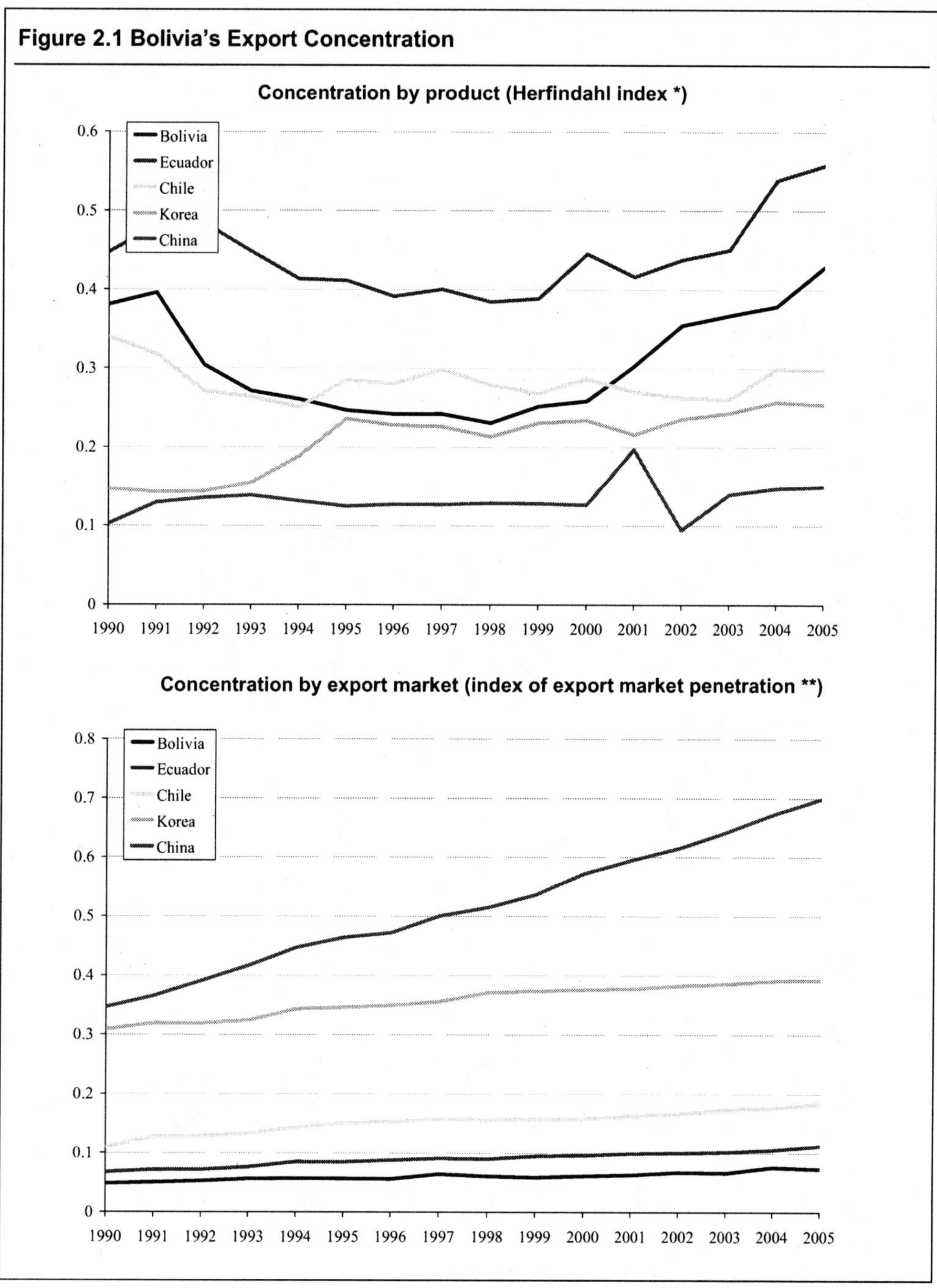

Source: World Bank staff based on UN Comtrade database.

Note: * Higher means more concentrated. ** The index is the ratio of all product/market export relationships a country has, divided by the potential number of trade relationships if the country was to export its products to all countries that import these products (higher means better market penetration).

Figure 2.2. Growth of Bolivia's Export Markets

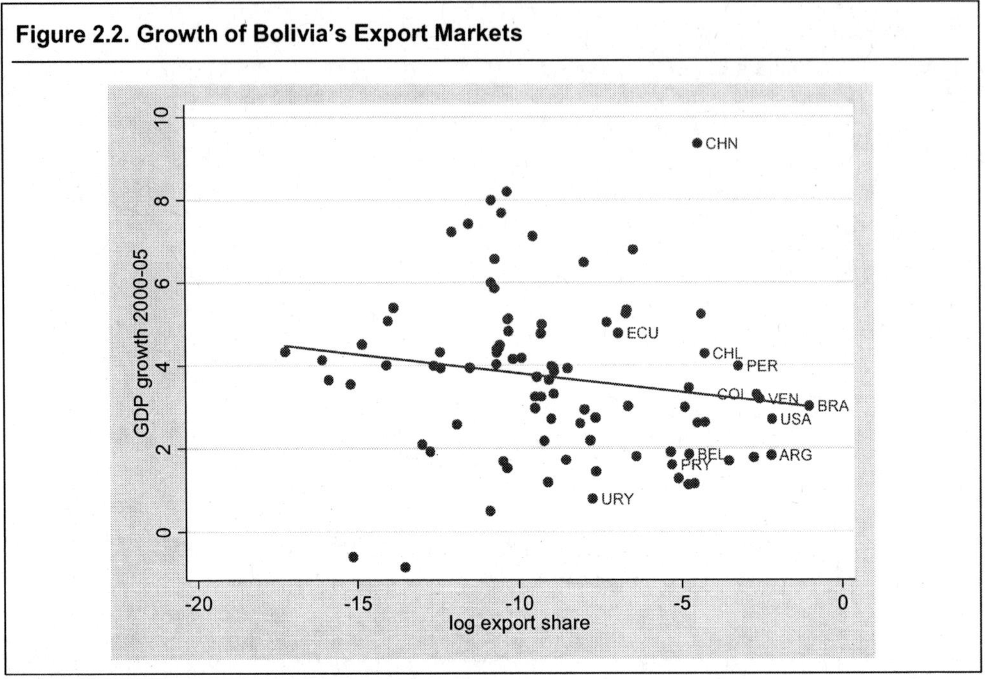

Source: Authors' calculations using COMTRADE data.
Notes: The vertical axis measures the average growth in the real GDP of countries to which Bolivia exports during 1992-2005. The horizontal axis measures the log of their share in Bolivia's exports over 1990-2005. Negative values on the horizontal axis are due to the fact that the log of a number below one (like a share) is negative.

Bolivia's export growth is limited by the fact that its main export markets are not growing fast. Demand for Bolivian exports depends in part on slower-growing traditional export markets, since more dynamic markets, such as China and India, are more distant. The correlation between the growth of Bolivia's export *markets* (in terms of real GDP) and their share in Bolivia's export portfolio is negative. (Figure 2.2 depicts a scatter plot of the GDP growth of Bolivia's export markets during 2000–05 against their average share in Bolivia's exports.)

The weak diversification of Bolivian exports mirrors its level of economic development. Indeed, product concentration is to be expected at low levels of income, and even more so for a country that is both landlocked and dependent on primary products.[2]

Bolivia's export concentration has recently increased. The share of traditional exports has risen in past years. In particular, soya and soya-based products still account for about one-third of nontraditional exports (although, as noted above, this share has declined in recent years). Since 2001, the concentration of Bolivia's exports has increased (Figure 2.3). The trend during 1992–2000 clearly showed shrinking concentration (rising diversification). Thus, despite the severe structural handicaps suffered by Bolivia's exporters, some diversification has occurred, which holds out the possibility that it can again in the future, with the right policies.

Figure 2.3. New Products and Concentration in Bolivia's Exports

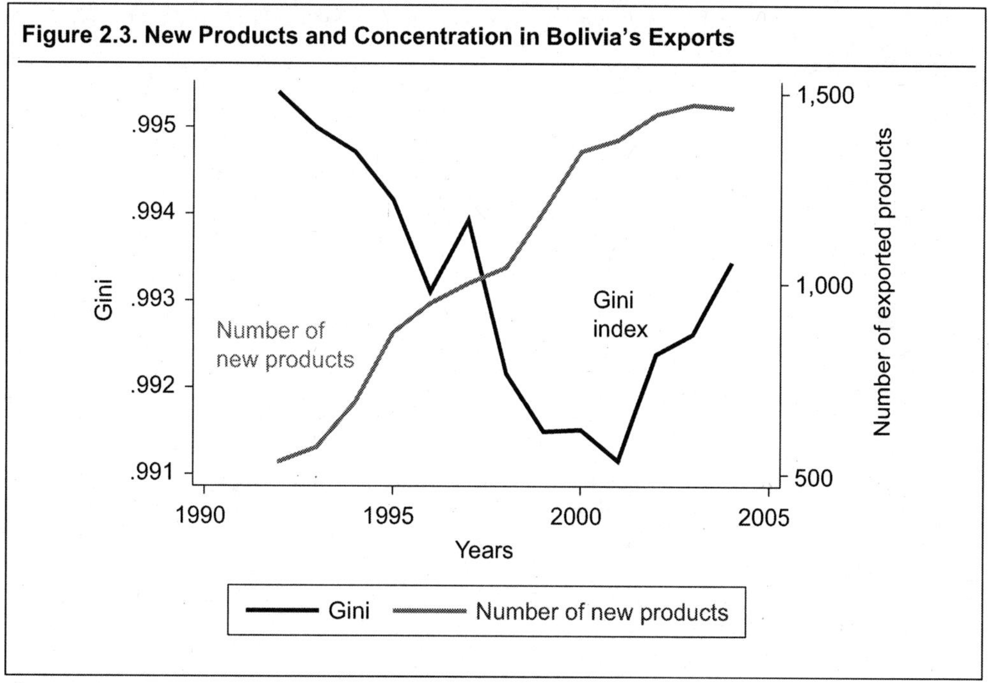

Source: Authors' calculations using COMTRADE data.

The increase in concentration has largely reflected price rises. The increase in the Gini coefficient during 2000–04 is a classic reflection of the effect of booming commodity prices on the export concentration of commodity exporters. Indeed, as commodity prices rise, their already dominant share in total trade also expands, boosting concentration measures.[3] For example, the export price index for traditional exports (base 1990=100) increased from 67 in 2003 to 157 in 2006.[4]

Bolivian export entrepreneurship is very high. Export entrepreneurship is typically high at low levels of income, reducing export concentration as income rises. Thus, active export entrepreneurship is to be expected at Bolivia's level of income. Still, Bolivia has 32 percent more export entrepreneurship—as measured by the number of new products—than its level of income would suggest (Table 2.2).[5] This performance is also higher than the Latin American average (19 percent) and bodes well for future export expansion if the policy environment is sufficiently conducive to export expansion. In Figure 2.3, the curve labeled "Number of new products" shows the number of new-product introductions in Bolivia's exports. Specifically, the curve records active product lines in year *t* that satisfy the following two criteria: the products were not exported in any of the previous two years (*t–1* and *t–2*); and they were exported for at least two years (*t* and *t+1*). The rise of the curve over the whole period suggests an expansion of Bolivia's trade attributable to exports of new products.

Table 2.2. New Products, Observed and Predicted Values: Bolivia vs. Other LAC Countries

	Number of available years	Observed number of "new exports"	Predicted number of "new exports" [a]	Ratio [b] (%)
Argentina	8	63.8	47.0	+35.6
Bolivia	9	86.1	65.0	+32.4
Brazil	12	60.3	78.2	-22.9
Chile	11	80.6	76.2	+5.8
Colombia	10	95.6	73.6	+29.9
Costa Rica	7	103.6	78.1	+32.6
Ecuador	10	82.0	68.4	+19.9
El Salvador	7	106.4	73.8	+44.2
Guatemala	8	131.0	71.2	+84.1
Honduras	6	99.8	64.4	+55.1
Mexico	11	49.0	71.4	-31.4
Nicaragua	8	77.5	62.5	+24.0
Paraguay	12	34.4	69.6	-50.5
Peru	7	117.6	73.7	+59.6
Uruguay	7	69.4	65.6	+5.9
Venezuela, R. B. de	7	76.4	74.9	+2.0
Latin America average	**8.8**	**83.4**	**69.6**	**+19.8**
East Asia average	**9.3**	**65.3**	**67.7**	**-3.6**

Source: Cadot and Dutoit (2008).
Notes: a. Computation based on the estimated coefficients reported in Table 3.
b. 100*((observed col.2 /predicted col.3) −1).

Export entrepreneurship is limited to a small number of products and is concentrated in differentiated products. Export entrepreneurship is limited to a small number of firms, approximately 700 in 2003, few of which revealed significant export values. The average length of Bolivia's "export spell"—the number of years in which a given product is exported without interruption to a given market—is shorter than for other LAC countries.[6] A decomposition of the number of new export products by Rauch's classification[7] shows that export entrepreneurship is particularly active in differentiated products where Bolivia has almost double the number of predicted new products (Table 2.3). Bolivia's pattern of expansion at the extensive margin (i.e., exports of new products) thus differs from that of Latin America. Indeed, the table suggests that the export activity at the extensive margin is in products that are not crude products (typically in the first two Rauch categories, homogenous and reference-price). In addition, the table shows that despite major structural handicaps, some Bolivian manufacturers manage to export. This information is crucial for the export promotion agency, as these small-scale export entrepreneurs may need assistance, judging by their short survival times.

Table 2.3. New Products, by Rauch Categories: Bolivia vs. Other LAC Countries

	Observed share in total new exports			Ratio observed/predicted		
	Homo.	Ref. price	Diff.	Homo.	Ref. price	Diff.
Argentina	0.32	0.27	0.42	53.5	21.2	51.9
Bolivia	**0.09**	**0.16**	**0.76**	**−53.5**	**−48.9**	**95.4**
Brazil	0.20	0.31	0.50	28.1	−19.6	−0.6
Chile	0.23	0.39	0.38	50.8	4.6	−22.6
Colombia	0.13	0.34	0.53	−21.9	−3.4	14.9
Costa Rica	0.17	0.15	0.69	10.9	−61.9	36.5
Ecuador	0.14	0.50	0.36	−23.8	52.9	−12.5
El Salvador	0.09	0.48	0.43	−42.7	34	−7.3
Guatemala	0.11	0.41	0.47	−32.8	20.8	7.4
Honduras	0.30	0.30	0.41	58.8	−3.2	6.6
Mexico	0.20	0.29	0.51	22.2	−15.2	11.2
Nicaragua	0.09	0.31	0.60	−53.9	5.4	63.8
Paraguay	0.26	0.34	0.40	50.9	1.1	−6.2
Peru	0.09	0.54	0.37	−46.7	52.6	−20
Uruguay	0.21	0.42	0.37	21.6	31.7	−9.6
Venezuela, R. B. de	0.12	0.37	0.50	−20.4	2.8	4
Latin America average	*0.17*	*0.35*	*0.48*	2.3	2.8	*10.1*
East Asia average	*0.13*	*0.35*	*0.52*	*−25*	*7.7*	*25.2*

Source: Cadot and Dutoit (2008).

Does Bolivia Trade Less than Other Countries Do?

Different factors determine how Bolivia's trade-to-GDP ratio compares with its regional neighbors. Bolivia's trade-to-GDP ratio approximates the average for Latin America (slightly above 40 percent) and is higher than other Andean nations. Beyond the usual determinants—such as size, factor endowment, and trade policies—international trade flows are affected by three additional factors: distance between trading partners, quality of infrastructure, and whether the country is landlocked. For Bolivia, all three factors loom large. Hence, the right counterfactual must be used in evaluating Bolivia's trade performance.

Bolivia's exports and imports are only marginally below those predicted by a gravity equation. Various techniques are available to assess whether countries trade more or less than they may be expected to, given their characteristics. These include a comparison of openness (such as exports and imports over GDP), the regression of openness indices on various country characteristics, and the estimation of gravity equations. Trade flows predicted using a correctly specified gravity equation can provide a good counterfactual to assess whether, and to what extent, Bolivia "under-trades" or "over-trades" relative to other countries.[8] This can be achieved by comparing actual trade with predicted trade for Bolivia (Figure 2.4).

Figure 2.4. Actual vs. Predicted Imports and Exports, Bolivia, 1992–2005

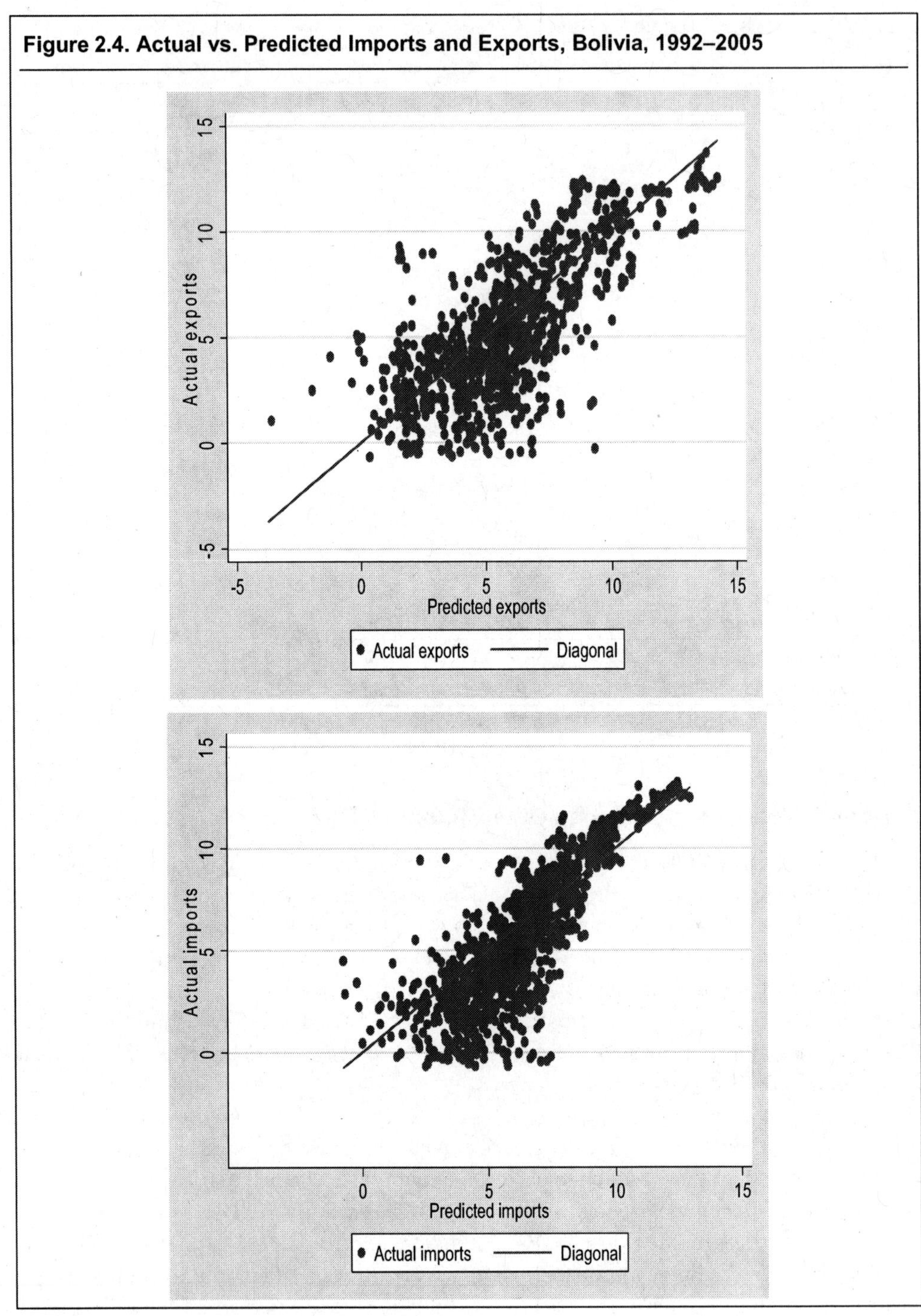

Source: Author calculations from COMTRADE.

The horizontal axis measures Bolivia's predicted exports to each trading partner using the gravity equation, and the vertical axis measures actual exports. Points above the diagonal indicate "over-exporting," while points under the diagonal indicate "under-exporting." Each point corresponds to aggregate trade between Bolivia and one of its trading partners in a given year. As points are fairly evenly scattered around the diagonal, it appears that there is no systematic pattern of under-exporting or under-importing. As points are fairly evenly scattered around the diagonal, there appears to be no systematic pattern of under-exporting or under-importing.

Bolivia tends to over-import and under-export by small margins—once its landlocked nature is accounted for. Figure 2.5 indicates that Bolivia imports more than predicted by about 3 percent and exports less than the predicted values by about 10 percent. This analysis takes into account Bolivia's being landlocked. If one does not account for being landlocked, Bolivia exports 43 percent less than predicted. The "under-exporting margin" seems to have widened until 2001, with an apparent reversal during 2001–05.

Bolivia's "over-trading" patterns indicate different behaviors depending on the trading partner: with lower performance with the United States and stronger integration with the CAN partners. Bolivia's actual trade versus predicted trade vis-à-vis its three largest partners in LAC (Argentina, Brazil, and Chile) shows a pattern of "over-importing" and "under-exporting," which is not surprising given their large share in Bolivia's trade (Figure 2.6). With regard to the United States, by contrast, the trend is toward increasing under-trading on both the export and import side (Figure 2.7). The decline in exports to the United States relative to predicted values highlights the limited success of preferences under the ATPA/ATPDEA to generate significant incentives for Bolivian exporters.[9] Finally, Bolivia over-exports to and over-imports from CAN members, suggesting a stronger economic integration with its Andean neighbors than with any other country (Figure 2.8).

Conclusion

Low rates of preference utilization in many product lines with the United States suggest a suboptimal use of preferential access. In addition, there is a substantial risk of preference erosion attributable to uncertainty surrounding the temporary renewals of ATPDEA preferences with the United States.

Bolivia's exports are highly concentrated geographically and by product. The price rise of commodities has particularly heightened concentration in recent years. But export entrepreneurship, as measured by the number of new products exported, is higher than one would expect given Bolivia's level of income. And trade resulting from the export of new products has been expanding. Bolivia has been able to export a diverse set of products, albeit intermittently and in small quantities, suggesting an unrealized potential for diversification through volumes-by increasing the volumes of the diversified set of products exported rather than increasing the number of products.

Figure 2.5. Over-Importing and Under-Exporting vis-à-vis the World, 1992–2005

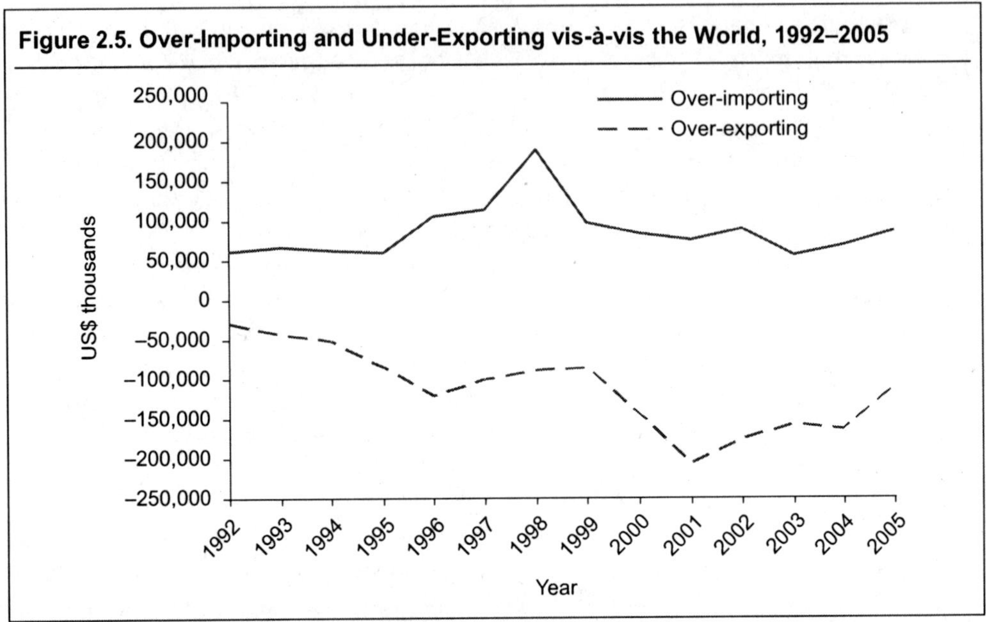

Source: Authors' calculations using COMTRADE.
Note: Thousand U.S. dollars (current).

Figure 2.6. Over-Importing and Under-Exporting vis-à-vis Brazil, Argentina, and Chile, 1992–2005

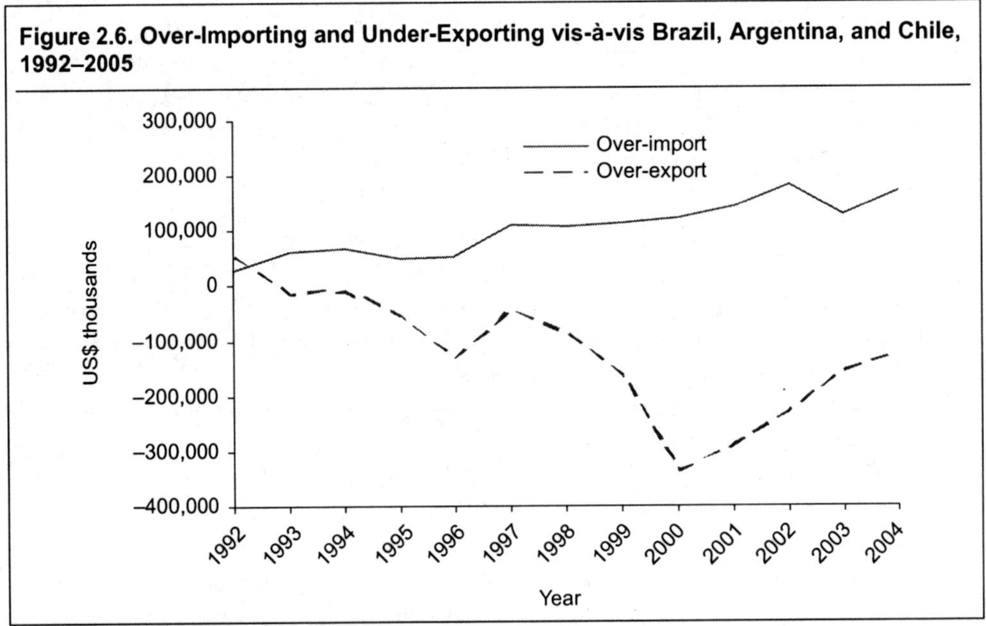

Source: Authors' calculations using COMTRADE.
Notes: Thousand U.S. dollars (current). Note that the values reported in Figure 2.5, as in Figure 2.6, are deviations from predicted values. Thus, they can be larger for a particular group of partners than overall, which is the case here since deviations from predicted values with LA-3 partners are larger than overall deviations. However, notwithstanding the higher volatility apparent in Figure 2.6, the pattern is roughly the same.

Figure 2.7. Under-Importing and Under-Exporting vis-à-vis the United States, 1992–2005

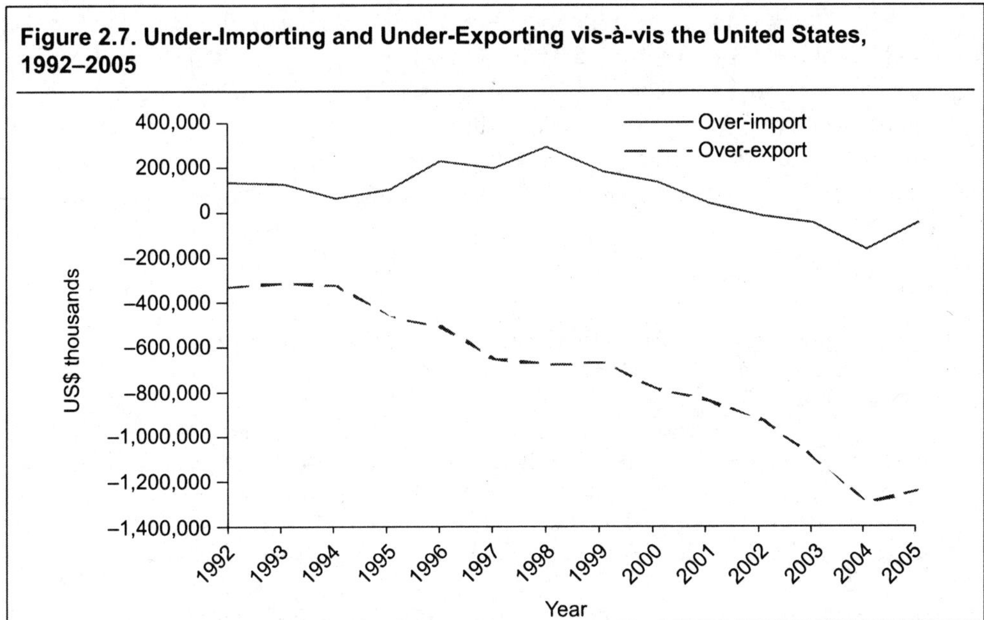

Source: Authors' calculations using COMTRADE.
Note: Thousand U.S. dollars (current).

Figure 2.8. Over-Importing and Over-Exporting vis-à-vis CAN, 1992–2005

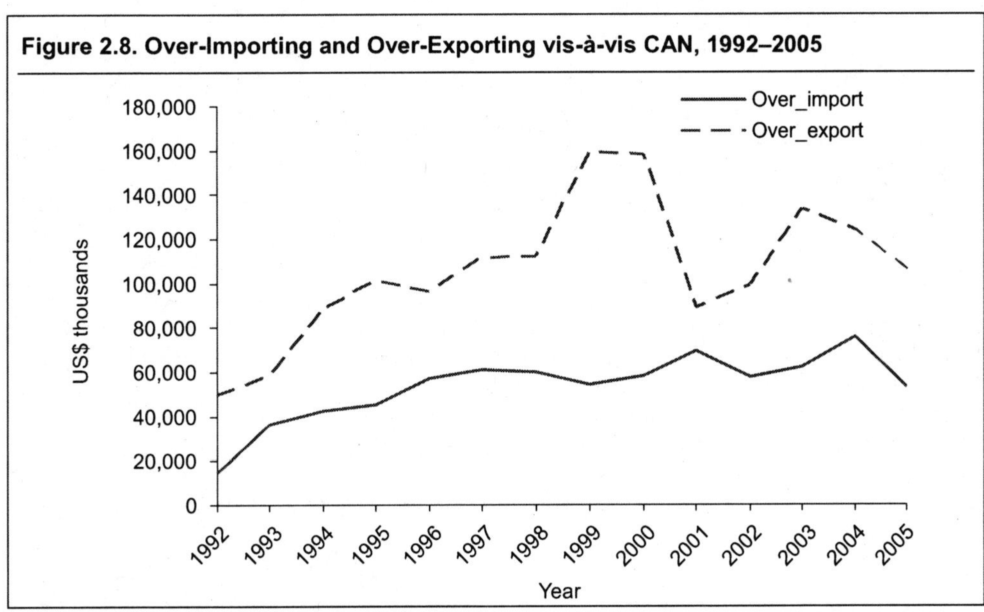

Source: Authors' calculations using COMTRADE.
Notes: Thousand U.S. dollars (current).

Bolivia's trade-to-GDP ratio approximates the average for Latin America, at slightly above 40 percent. The analysis of whether Bolivia trades more or less than other countries, given its characteristics, suggests that overall Bolivia tends to "over-import" and "under-export," although the margins are small: about 3 percent of predicted values on the import side and 11 percent on the export side. The analysis accounts for Bolivia being landlocked. If we do not account for this, Bolivian trade is 43 percent lower than predicted.

Notes

[1] Several sections of this chapter are drawn from a background paper prepared for the study by Cadot and Dutoit (2008), "Does Bolivia Undertrade?"

[2] Carrère and others (2007).

[3] Note that the very high values of the Gini coefficient are not peculiar to Bolivia. They are a general feature of export Gini indices calculated at the HS6 level (see Carrère and others 2007).

[4] Gini coefficients for exports are always very high, but evidence from other countries shows that their indices tell essentially the same story without the Ginis' clustering near one. Even though price effects are likely to dominate, the rising number of new products in Bolivia does suggest action at the extensive margin.

[5] We use predicted values from the regressions in Carrère and others (2007).

[6] See Giussani and Olarreaga (2006).

[7] Rauch (1999) distinguished between products traded on organized exchanges such as the London Metal Exchange, products with reference prices (listed in widely available publications like the Knight-Ridder CRB Commodity Yearbook), and differentiated products whose prices are determined by branding. He argues that finding markets for differentiated goods involves a sequential search for trading partners that can be long and costly and will in all likelihood involve networks based on ethnic, linguistic, or other factors of proximity. Exporting products listed in organized exchanges or reference-priced products involves anonymous markets and, hence, lower search costs.

[8] The gravity model used in the estimation includes time dummies, common language, common borders, and dummies for being landlocked. It also uses a time-varying measure of remoteness (a trade-weighted average of the distance vis-à-vis all trading partners). This measure of remoteness is (in principle) better than exporter and importer fixed effects. In order to control for unobserved bilateral influences at the country-pair level, the estimator is the Hausman-Taylor (1981) instrumental variable estimator with country-pair random-effect as in Carrère (2006). The interest of using random effects instead of fixed effects is to avoid colinearity with distance, but this creates a risk of correlation between the error terms with regressors, hence the need to instrument for potentially endogenous right hand side variables (e.g., GDPs). However, there is no attempt to deal with selection issues à la Helpman-Melitz-Rubinstein (2007).

[9] See the background paper on the impact of trade on employment by Cadot and Molina (2008).

Annex 2.1. Tests of Links between Exports and GDP Performance

Table 2.A.1. Contribution of Different Demand Components to Real GDP Growth in Bolivia

	Real GDP growth	Contribution of household final consumption to real GDP growth	Contribution of general government final consumption to real GDP growth	Contribution of investment to real GDP growth	Contribution of net exports to real GDP growth
	$\Delta Y / Y_{(t-1)}$	$\Delta C / Y_{(t-1)}$	$\Delta G / Y_{(t-1)}$	$\Delta I / Y_{(t-1)}$	$\Delta NE / Y_{(t-1)}$
1971	5.1%	2.7%	1.0%	2.2%	-0.8%
1972	8.0%	0.7%	1.3%	6.4%	-0.4%
1973	5.7%	5.8%	1.4%	-3.5%	2.0%
1974	2.9%	2.3%	1.2%	-2.7%	2.3%
1975	7.3%	2.9%	1.5%	8.2%	-5.3%
1976	4.6%	5.4%	0.8%	-4.0%	2.3%
1977	5.0%	3.7%	0.4%	1.1%	-0.2%
1978	2.1%	-2.0%	0.4%	5.1%	-1.5%
1979	0.1%	0.6%	2.2%	-3.2%	0.6%
1980	-1.4%	1.3%	-1.0%	-5.3%	3.7%
1981	0.3%	0.3%	1.3%	-0.1%	-1.2%
1982	-3.9%	-2.8%	-0.5%	-2.9%	2.3%
1983	-4.0%	-3.2%	-2.0%	-1.1%	2.3%
1984	-0.2%	0.0%	0.6%	3.6%	-4.4%
1985	-1.7%	2.8%	-1.2%	3.4%	-6.7%
1986	-2.6%	3.7%	-2.1%	-5.0%	0.9%
1987	2.5%	2.5%	-0.5%	2.1%	-1.6%
1988	2.9%	0.7%	0.5%	0.5%	1.2%
1989	3.8%	1.4%	0.1%	-2.1%	4.3%
1990	4.6%	2.6%	0.0%	2.0%	0.0%
1991	5.3%	2.6%	0.4%	3.7%	-1.4%
1992	1.6%	2.7%	0.4%	0.8%	-2.3%
1993	4.3%	2.6%	0.3%	0.0%	1.4%
1994	4.7%	2.2%	0.4%	-1.6%	3.7%
1995	4.7%	2.2%	0.8%	1.6%	0.1%
1996	4.4%	2.4%	0.3%	2.6%	-1.0%
1997	5.0%	4.0%	0.4%	4.8%	-4.2%
1998	5.0%	3.8%	0.4%	5.6%	-4.9%
1999	0.4%	2.0%	0.4%	-4.5%	2.6%
2000	2.5%	1.7%	0.2%	-1.4%	2.0%
2001	1.7%	1.0%	0.3%	-3.1%	3.5%
2002	2.5%	1.5%	0.4%	2.6%	-2.0%
2003	2.7%	1.4%	0.4%	-2.0%	3.1%
2004	4.2%	2.2%	0.2%	-1.7%	3.3%
2005	4.0%	2.4%	0.1%	2.4%	-0.8%
2006	4.6%	4.1%	0.8%	2.4%	-3.3%

Source: Staff calculations based on WDI data in constant local currency units.

Table 2.A.2. Results of Unit Root Tests of Real Exports and Real GDP

Series	ADF test t-statistic	Prob.	Interpretation
LX	0.72	0.991	We cannot reject the null hypothesis that the series has a unit root.
LY	1.17	0.997	We cannot reject the null hypothesis that the series has a unit root.
Δ *LX*	–5.24	0.000	We can reject at 1% level the null hypothesis that the series has a unit root.
Δ *LY*	–2.97	0.048	We can reject at 5% level the null hypothesis that the series has a unit root.

Source: Staff calculations based on data on exports and GDP from WDI in constant local currency units.
Note: Each ADF test uses an intercept and no trend and the lag length has been chosen based on minimizing the Akaike Information Criterion. Δ denotes series in first differences. Each p-value of the ADF statistic is reported for shortest lag length.

Table 2.A.3. Results of Johansen Cointegration Tests

Variables included: LX, LY, and dummy to capture trade liberalization from 1986 onwards

Hypothesized number of cointegration equations	Eigen Value	Statistic (Trace or Max. Eigen Value)	0.05 Critical Value	Prob.	Interpretation
Based on Trace Statistic					
None	0.53	48.0	42.9	0.01	
At most 1	0.32	21.2	25.9	0.17	We reject that there are no cointegration equations. We cannot reject that there is at most one such cointegration equation.
At most 2	0.20	7.7	12.5	0.28	
Based on Maximum Eigenvalue Statistic					
None	0.53	26.8	25.8	0.04	
At most 1	0.32	13.5	19.4	0.29	
At most 2	0.20	7.7	12.5	0.28	

Note: No restriction is imposed in the cointegration test; the test assumes linear deterministic trend. The lag length has been chosen based on minimum AIC (1 lag interval in first differences for both series).

Table 2.A.4. Pairwise Granger Causality Tests

Null hypothesis	F-Statistic	Prob.	Interpretation
LY does not Granger cause LX	0.92	0.41	We cannot reject the null hypothesis and, hence, there is no evidence that output Granger-causes exports
LX does not Granger cause LY	5.38	0.01	We can reject the null hypothesis and hence, *there is evidence that exports Granger-cause output*

Table 2.A.5. Results of Unit Root Tests of Real Exports and Real GDP

Series	ADF test t-statistic	Prob.	Interpretation
LX trad	−2.28	0.42	We cannot reject the null hypothesis that the series has a unit root.
LX nontrad	−2.67	0.25	We cannot reject the null hypothesis that the series has a unit root.
Δ *LX trad*	−5.72	0.000	We can reject at 1% level the null that the series has a unit root.
Δ *LX nontrad*	−4.32	0.008	We can reject at 1% level the null that the series has a unit root.

Source: Staff calculations based on UN COMTRADE breakdown for traditional exports (raw materials and minerals) and nontraditional exports (all other exports), in constant local currency units.
Note: Each ADF test uses an intercept and no trend and the lag length has been chosen based on minimizing the Akaike Information Criterion. Δ denotes series in first differences. Each p-value of the ADF statistic is reported for shortest lag length.

Table 2.A.6. Results of Johansen Cointegration Tests for Traditional Exports and GDP

Variables included: LX trad, LY, and dummy (1 for 1986 onwards)

Hypothesized number of cointegration equations	Eigen Value	Statistic (Trace or Max. Eigen Value)	0.05 Critical Value	Prob.	Interpretation
Based on Trace Statistic					
None	0.19	10.14	29.79	0.98	We cannot reject that there are *no* cointegration equations.
Based on Maximum Eigenvalue Statistic					
None	0.19	7.26	21.13	0.94	

Note: Changes in the assumptions about possible deterministic trends in the data do not alter the result.

Table 2.A.7. Results of Johansen Cointegration Tests for Nontraditional Exports and GDP

Variables included: LX nontrad, LY, and dummy (1 for 1986 onwards)

Hypothesized number of cointegration equations	Eigen Value	Statistic (Trace or Max. Eigen Value)	0.05 Critical Value	Prob.	Interpretation
Based on Trace Statistic					
None	0.46	32.10	29.80	0.02	We reject that there are no cointegration equations. We cannot reject that there is at most one such cointegration equation.
At most 1	0.29	10.67	15.49	0.23	
At most 2	0.01	0.20	3.84	0.65	
Based on Maximum Eigenvalue Statistic					
None	0.46	21.42	21.13	0.045	
At most 1	0.29	10.47	14.26	0.18	
At most 2	0.01	0.20	3.84	0.65	

Note: No restriction is imposed in the cointegration test; the test assumes linear deterministic trend. The lag length has been chosen based on minimum AIC (1 lag interval in first differences for both series).

Table 2.A.8. Pairwise Granger Causality Tests, GDP and Nontraditional Exports

Null hypothesis	F-Statistic	Prob.	Interpretation
LY does not Granger cause LX nontrad	2.30	0.12	We cannot reject the null hypothesis and, hence, there is no evidence that output Granger-causes nontraditional exports
LX nontrad does not Granger cause LY	0.50	0.61	We cannot reject the null hypothesis and hence, there is no evidence that nontraditional exports Granger-cause output

Annex 2.2. CGE Models

Comparative static models of national economies, known as computable general equilibrium (CGE) models are used to assess the economy-wide near-term economic impacts of trade policy reform. Among the CGE models, the GTAP model is a multi-region model, used prominently for trade analysis in national ministries, international public agencies, and academic research centers.

Standard assumptions of the model:

- On the production side:
  - Perfect competition and constant returns to scale.[1]
  - Land is specific to agriculture, and has imperfect mobility amongst alternative agricultural uses.
  - Labor and capital are mobile across all uses within a country and immobile internationally.
- On the demand side
  - Preferences: The regional representative household has a Cobb-Douglas aggregate utility function which allocates net national expenditures across private, government, and savings. Government demand across composite goods is also determined by a Cobb-Douglas assumption. Private household demand is represented by a Constant Difference of Elasticities functional form, which has the virtue of capturing the non-homothetic nature of private household demands.
  - Bilateral international trade flows are handled through the Armington specification by which products are differentiated by country of origin.
  - There is a constant aggregate level of land, labor, and capital employment reflecting the belief that the aggregate supply of factors is unaffected by trade-related shock.[2]

Advantage of CGE model: One of the great advantages of a CGE simulation is that impose consistency economy-wide, considering that changes in sectoral factor and product demands do not exceed supply, e.g. that the sum of sectors' employment does not exceed the labor force, or that all consumption be covered by production or imports. Thus, a CGE model provides unbiased estimates of national economic welfare, using Hicksian equivalent variation.[3] Moreover, the comparative static analysis is based on the current trade patterns of the country, thus a close-to-reality assessment of the short to medium term economic response to own country trade policy change can be elaborated. The greatest advantage of this regional household representation is the unambiguous indicator of welfare dictated by the regional utility function.

Drawbacks: The drawbacks of a standard CGE model are the absence of creation of "new trade", new investment patterns, and productivity growth resulting from the response to trade policy change. This implies that results are dependent on established trade patterns in the benchmark database.[4] Therefore, results must be assessed taking into consideration the absence of future gains derived from these potential gains to the economy.

Source: Based on Andriamananjara and Valenzuela (2008).

Table 2.A.9. Sectors Modeled

	Code	Description	Original GTAP sectors comprised
1	pdr	Paddy rice	Paddy rice.
2	wht	Wheat	Wheat.
3	gro	Cereal grains nec	Cereal grains nec.
4	v_f	Vegetables, fruit, nuts	Vegetables, fruit, nuts.
5	osd	Oil seeds	Oil seeds.
6	c_b	Sugar cane, sugar beet	Sugar cane, sugar beet.
7	pfb	Plant-based fibers	Plant-based fibers.
8	ocr	Crops nec	Crops nec.
9	ctl	Cattle, sheep, goats, horses	Cattle, sheep, goats, horses.
10	oap	Animal products nec	Animal products nec.
11	rmk	Raw milk	Raw milk.
12	wol	Wool, silk-worm	Wool, silk-worm cocoons.
13	frs	Forestry	Forestry.
14	fsh	Fishing	Fishing.
15	coa	Coal	Coal.
16	oil	Oil	Oil.
17	gas	Gas	Gas.
18	omn	Minerals nec	Minerals nec.
19	cmt	Meat: beef	Meat: cattle, sheep, goats, horses
20	omt	Meat poultry, pig	Meat products nec.
21	vol	Vegetable oils and fats	Vegetable oils and fats.
22	mil	Dairy products	Dairy products.
23	pcr	Processed rice	Processed rice.
24	sgr	Sugar	Sugar.
25	ofd	Food products nec	Food products nec.
26	b_t	Beverages and tobacco	Beverages and tobacco products.
27	tex	Textiles	Textiles.
28	wap	Wearing apparel	Wearing apparel.
29	lea	Leather products	Leather products.
30	lum	Wood products	Wood products.
31	ppp	Paper products	Paper products, publishing.
32	p_c	Petroleum, coal products	Petroleum, coal products.
33	crp	Chemical, plastic prods	Chemical, rubber, plastic prods.
34	nmm	Mineral products nec	Mineral products nec.
35	i_s	Ferrous metals	Ferrous metals.
36	nfm	Metals nec	Metals nec.
37	fmp	Metal products	Metal products.
38	mvh	Motor vehicles and parts	Motor vehicles and parts.
39	otn	Transport equipment nec	Transport equipment nec.
40	ele	Electronic equipment	Electronic equipment.
41	ome	Machinery and equipment	Machinery and equipment nec.
42	omf	Manufactures nec	Manufactures nec.
43	utilcons	Utilities and construction	Electricity; Gas manufacture, distribution; Water; Construction.
44	transcom	Transport and communication	Trade; Transport nec; Sea transport; Air transport; Communication
45	otherSvc	Other services	Financial services nec; Insurance; Business services nec; Recreation and other services; PubAdmin/Defence/Health/Education; Dwellings

Table 2.A.10. Impact of Different Trade Liberalization Scenarios on Bolivian Exports, Selected Sectors, Percentage Change

	Export Value, 2004 US$ million	Scenario 1- nonrenewal ATPDEA	Scenario 2- FTAs:U.S. with Peru and Colombia	Scenario 3- Alignment to CAN's Common External Tariff	Scenario 4- Deeper integration with Mercosur
Cereal grains nec	5.4	0.8	−0.5	0.1	−0.3
Vegetables, fruit, nuts	69.3	−2.5	1.6	0.2	1.2
Oil seeds	42.5	0.5	−1.3	0.1	3
Plant-based fibers	5.3	1.7	−17.9	0.0	−0.5
Crops nec	9.9	−4.7	3.5	0.4	0.8
Pigs, chicken	3.5	0.8	1	0.4	1.1
Forestry	1.3	2.4	0.9	−0.2	4.7
Oil	1	5	2.8	2.4	−1.7
Gas	221.5	0.4	0.2	−0.1	−0.2
Minerals nec	291.6	0.4	0.1	0.0	0.1
Meat: cattle, sheep	3.1	2	−18.2	0.1	−1.3
Meat: pigs, chicken	1.6	1.7	−0.6	1.4	−0.3
Vegetable oils and fats	535.4	1.1	−2.7	−1.0	−0.3
Dairy products	17.3	3	−7.9	0.5	−0.9
Processed rice	4.8	0.6	−11	0.5	−0.5
Sugar	35.1	−0.3	−1.4	0.0	−0.4
Food products nec	11.5	0.8	−0.6	−0.3	7.1
Beverages and tobacco	16.7	0.6	0.3	0.1	−0.1
Textiles	46.9	−12.2	−6.9	0.1	−0.1
Wearing apparel	35	−30.6	1.6	0.2	3.3
Leather products	20.3	−0.1	2.1	0.2	9.1
Wood products	69.1	−0.1	1.8	0.1	2.2
Paper products	3.9	2.3	−1.1	1.0	12.2
Chemical, rubber, plastic	24.3	−1.2	0.4	0.9	3.8
Mineral products nec	6.7	1.1	−1.3	−0.1	2
Ferrous metals	4.4	2.5	−4.8	0.3	1.8
Metals nec	116.6	−1.4	1.7	0.4	0.6
Metal products	5.9	−8.8	1.4	0.6	17.2
Motor vehicles and parts	3.4	−1.6	−0.1	0.4	43.7
Transport equip nec	9.1	−1.3	2.1	0.4	1.1
Electronic equipment	1.8	0.9	1.2	0.5	20
Machinery, equip nec	33.3	−2	1	0.7	14.1
Manufactures nec	69.8	−10.4	1.8	0.8	1
Util_cons	1.6	2	1.3	0.4	−0.3
Trans_comm	253.3	1.8	1.2	0.0	−0.6
OtherSvcs	116.1	1.9	1.3	−0.1	−0.6
Total	2098.8	−0.62	−0.45	−0.24	0.66

Source: Andriamananjara and Valenzuela (2008) based on GTAP model and database.

Table 2.A.11. Impact of Different Trade Liberalization Scenarios on Bolivian Imports, Selected Sectors, Percentage Change

	Import Value, 2004 US$ million	Scenario 1- nonrenewal ATPDEA	Scenario 2- FTAs:U.S. with Peru and Colombia	Scenario 3- Alignment to CAN's Common External Tariff	Scenario 4- Deeper integration with Mercosur
Cereal grains nec	3.6	−0.8	−1	0.3	1
Vegetables, fruit, nuts	11.6	−1.1	−1.3	7.6	0.6
Oil seeds	56.7	0.5	-3.2	−11.2	0
Plant-based fibers	15.4	-0.7	-1.2	-1.1	0.7
Crops nec	5	-1.7	-2.2	1.6	1.2
Pigs, chicken	3.5	-0.6	-0.8	-0.5	1.4
Forestry	0.7	-2	-0.5	3.2	1.4
Fishing	1.2	-1.2	-0.6	-0.9	2.2
Minerals nec	8.4	-1	0.5	2.3	0.8
Meat: cattle, sheep	1.5	-2.7	-2.1	5.3	13.8
Meat: pigs, chicken	2.3	-2.7	-2.8	2.1	9.6
Vegetable oils and fats	11.4	-0.9	-1.6	11.9	5
Dairy products	16.7	-2.2	-1.2	6.7	2.6
Processed rice	1.2	-1.6	-1.4	22.3	3.3
Sugar	4.8	-1.6	-0.6	-0.7	16.7
Food products nec	129.6	-0.5	-0.6	2.3	0.5
Beverages and tobacco	26.9	-0.7	-0.5	1.8	0.2
Textiles	107.1	-1.5	-0.5	0.9	0.2
Wearing apparel	19.7	-2.9	-0.8	-3.5	1.9
Leather products	26.8	-2.8	-1.3	-4.0	15.2
Wood products	16.7	-2.2	-0.9	4.3	5.1
Paper products	104.8	-0.8	-0.5	1.4	0.5
Petroleum, coal prod	63.2	-1.2	-0.7	3.7	1
Chemical, rubber, plastic	496.1	-0.7	-0.4	1.3	0.6
Mineral products nec	51.7	-1.9	-1	3.1	2.6
Ferrous metals	119.5	-1.6	0.1	0.4	1.4
Metals nec	28.6	-3.4	0.5	0.4	1
Metal products	82	-0.5	-0.5	0.8	0.6
Motor vehicles and parts	129.8	-0.8	-0.5	1.4	1.5
Transport equip nec	34.5	-0.9	-0.5	3.4	0.8
Electronic equipment	85.5	-1.1	-0.6	2.3	1
Machinery and equip	411.7	-0.8	-0.5	1.6	0.8
Manufactures nec	42.5	-1.4	-0.9	1.4	0.3
Util_cons	9.3	-1.9	-1.2	1.2	1
Trans_comm	200.4	-1.3	-0.9	-6.6	0.4
OtherSvcs	266.2	-1	-0.8	0.0	0.3
Total	2621.7	−1.00	−0.55	0.56	0.94

Source: Andriamananjara and Valenzuela (2008) based on GTAP model and database.

Table 2.A.12. Impact of Different Trade Liberalization Scenarios on Bolivian Output, Selected Sectors, Percentage Change

	Output Value, 2004 US$ million	Scenario 1- nonrenewal ATPDEA	Scenario 2- FTAs:U.S. with Peru and Colombia	Scenario 3- Alignment to CAN's Common External Tariff	Scenario 4- Deeper integration with Mercosur
Cereal grains nec	158.4	0	0	0.0	0
Vegetables, fruit, nuts	587.7	−0.3	0.3	−0.2	0.1
Oil seeds	501.9	1.3	−1.3	−0.2	−0.2
Sugar cane	82	−0.5	−0.3	−0.1	−0.3
Plant-based fibers	31.2	0.5	−2.6	0.5	−0.5
Crops nec	122.2	−0.3	0.4	−0.1	0
Cattle, sheep	138.9	−0.2	−0.2	0.0	0
Pigs, chicken	265	−0.2	0	0.1	0
Raw milk	51.6	0.3	−0.6	−0.5	−0.2
Forestry	109.5	−0.1	0.3	0.0	0.4
Fishing	23.2	0	0	0.0	−0.1
Oil	208.8	0	0	−0.2	0
Gas	290.6	0.3	0.2	0.0	−0.1
Minerals nec	489.2	0.3	0.5	0.1	0.1
Meat: cattle, sheep	359.4	−0.2	−0.2	0.0	−0.1
Meat: pigs, chicken	321	−0.2	0	0.0	−0.1
Vegetable oils and fats	590.3	1.3	−1.7	−1.4	−0.5
Dairy products	181.1	0.4	−0.7	−0.5	−0.3
Processed rice	465.4	−0.1	−0.2	−0.1	0
Sugar	161.8	0.1	−0.3	−0.1	−0.6
Food products nec	87.2	0.6	0.3	-3.1	0.3
Beverages and tobacco	390.5	0.1	0.1	−0.1	0
Textiles	74.1	-7.1	-3.9	−0.4	−0.4
Wearing apparel	189.8	-6.2	0.3	0.5	0.4
Leather products	117.3	−0.4	0.6	1.0	−1.6
Wood products	314.2	0.1	0.7	−0.1	0.5
Paper products	140.1	0.9	0.2	−1.6	0
Petroleum, coal prod	581.7	0	0	−0.2	0
Chemical, rubber, plastic	229.7	1	0.4	−2.8	−0.6
Mineral products nec	233.6	0	0	0.0	0
Ferrous metals	27.7	0.3	−0.3	−0.4	-2.1
Metals nec	128.5	−0.9	1.9	0.4	0.4
Metal products	12.6	-3	1	−0.9	6.9
Motor vehicles and parts	32	0.6	0.5	−0.6	2.5
Transport equip nec	15.6	0.3	1.9	−3.5	0.1
Electronic equipment	18.2	1.5	1.2	−3.6	1.5
Machinery and equip	58.6	−0.1	1.2	−1.9	7.2
Manufactures nec	124.2	−5.5	1.4	0.4	0.7
Util_cons	944	−0.6	−0.3	1.0	0.7
Trans_comm	3646.9	0.1	0.1	0.2	0
OtherSvcs	3711.4	0.1	0	−0.1	−0.1

Source: Andriamananjara and Valenzuela (2008) based on GTAP model and database.

Table 2.A.13. Impact of Different Trade Liberalization Scenarios on Labor Demand, Selected Sectors, Percentage Change

	Scenario 1- nonrenewal ATPDEA		Scenario 2- FTAs:U.S. with Peru and Colombia		Scenario 3- Alignment to CAN's Common External Tariff		Scenario 4- Deeper integration with Mercosur	
	Unskilled Labor	Skilled Labor	Unskilled Labor	Skilled Labor	Unskilled Labor	Skilled Labor	Unskilled Labor	Skilled Labor
Paddy rice	0	0	-0.3	-0.3	-0.1	-0.1	0	0
Wheat	0.4	0.4	0.3	0.3	-6.2	-6.1	-1	-1
Cereal grains nec	0.1	0	-0.1	-0.1	-0.1	-0.1	0	0
Vegetables, fruit, nuts	-0.2	-0.3	0.2	0.2	-0.2	-0.2	0.1	0.1
Oil seeds	1.5	1.4	-1.5	-1.5	-0.2	-0.2	-0.2	-0.2
Sugar cane	-0.4	-0.5	-0.4	-0.4	-0.2	-0.2	-0.4	-0.3
Plant-based fibers	0.6	0.6	-2.9	-2.9	0.5	0.5	-0.5	-0.5
Crops nec	-0.3	-0.3	0.3	0.3	-0.2	-0.2	0	0
Cattle,sheep	-0.2	-0.2	-0.3	-0.3	0.0	0.0	0	0
Pigs, chicken	-0.2	-0.2	-0.1	-0.1	0.1	0.1	0	0
Raw milk	0.3	0.3	-0.7	-0.7	-0.5	-0.5	-0.3	-0.3
Wool	-0.4	-0.4	-0.2	-0.2	0.5	0.5	0.2	0.2
Forestry	-0.2	-0.2	0.3	0.3	0.1	0.1	0.4	0.4
Fishing	-0.1	-0.1	0	0	0.0	0.1	-0.2	-0.2
Coal	0.5	0.5	0.3	0.3	0.0	0.0	-0.1	-0.1
Oil	0.1	0.1	0.1	0.1	-0.3	-0.3	0	0
Gas	0.5	0.5	0.3	0.3	-0.1	0.0	-0.1	-0.1
Minerals nec	0.3	0.3	0.6	0.6	0.2	0.2	0.1	0.1
Meat: cattle, sheep	-0.1	-0.2	-0.2	-0.2	0.0	0.0	0	0
Meat: pigs, chicken	-0.2	-0.2	0	-0.1	0.0	0.1	0	0
Vegetable oils and fats	1.4	1.3	-1.7	-1.8	-1.4	-1.4	-0.5	-0.4
Dairy products	0.4	0.4	-0.7	-0.7	-0.5	-0.4	-0.3	-0.2
Processed rice	0	-0.1	-0.1	-0.2	-0.1	0.0	0	0.1
Sugar	0.1	0	-0.3	-0.3	0.0	0.0	-0.6	-0.5
Food products nec	0.6	0.6	0.3	0.2	-3.1	-3.1	0.3	0.3
Beverages and tobacco	0.1	0	0.1	0	-0.1	0.0	0	0
Textiles	-7.1	-7.2	-3.9	-4	-0.4	-0.3	-0.4	-0.4
Wearing apparel	-6.2	-6.3	0.3	0.3	0.5	0.6	0.4	0.4
Leather products	-0.4	-0.4	0.6	0.5	1.0	1.0	-1.6	-1.6
Wood products	0.2	0.1	0.7	0.7	-0.1	0.0	0.5	0.5
Paper products	0.9	0.8	0.3	0.2	-1.6	-1.5	0	0.1
Petroleum, coal prod	0.1	0	0.1	0	-0.2	-0.1	0	0.1
Chemical, rubber, plastic	1	0.9	0.4	0.3	-2.8	-2.7	-0.5	-0.5
Mineral products nec	0.1	0	0	0	0.0	0.0	0	0.1
Ferrous metals	0.3	0.2	-0.2	-0.3	-0.4	-0.4	-2	-2
Metals nec	-0.9	-0.9	1.9	1.9	0.4	0.5	0.4	0.4
Metal products	-3	-3.1	1	1	-0.9	-0.9	6.9	6.9
Motor vehicles and parts	0.7	0.6	0.6	0.5	-0.6	-0.5	2.6	2.6
Transport equip nec	0.3	0.3	1.9	1.9	-3.5	-3.4	0.1	0.2
Electronic equipment	1.6	1.5	1.2	1.1	-3.6	-3.5	1.5	1.5
Machinery and equip	0	-0.1	1.2	1.2	-1.9	-1.8	7.2	7.3
Manufactures nec	-5.5	-5.6	1.4	1.3	0.4	0.5	0.7	0.8
Util_cons	-0.6	-0.7	-0.2	-0.3	1.1	1.1	0.7	0.7
Trans_comm	0.2	0.1	0.1	0.1	0.2	0.2	0	0.1
OtherSvcs	0.1	0	0.1	0	-0.1	0.0	-0.1	0

Source: Andriamananjara and Valenzuela (2008) based on GTAP model and database

Annex 2.3. Partial Equilibrium Analysis of ATPDEA Preferences

The United States granted free entry benefits to the exports from Andean Countries (Bolivia, Colombia, Ecuador, and Peru) as part of the Andean Trade Preference Act (ATPA) of 1991. These preferences were extended in the Andean Trade Promotion and Drug Eradication Act (ATPDEA) of 2002 to more products (basically apparel and tuna pouches).[5] In 2005–06 apparel and copper benefited the most from these preferences, followed by flowers and edible vegetables. Crude oil (basically from Ecuador and Colombia) has the highest value of total preferences utilized (almost two-thirds of the total value of ATPDEA preferences).

Figure 2.A.1. Andean Non-Oil Exports to the United States: Distribution of Preferences Granted by Product

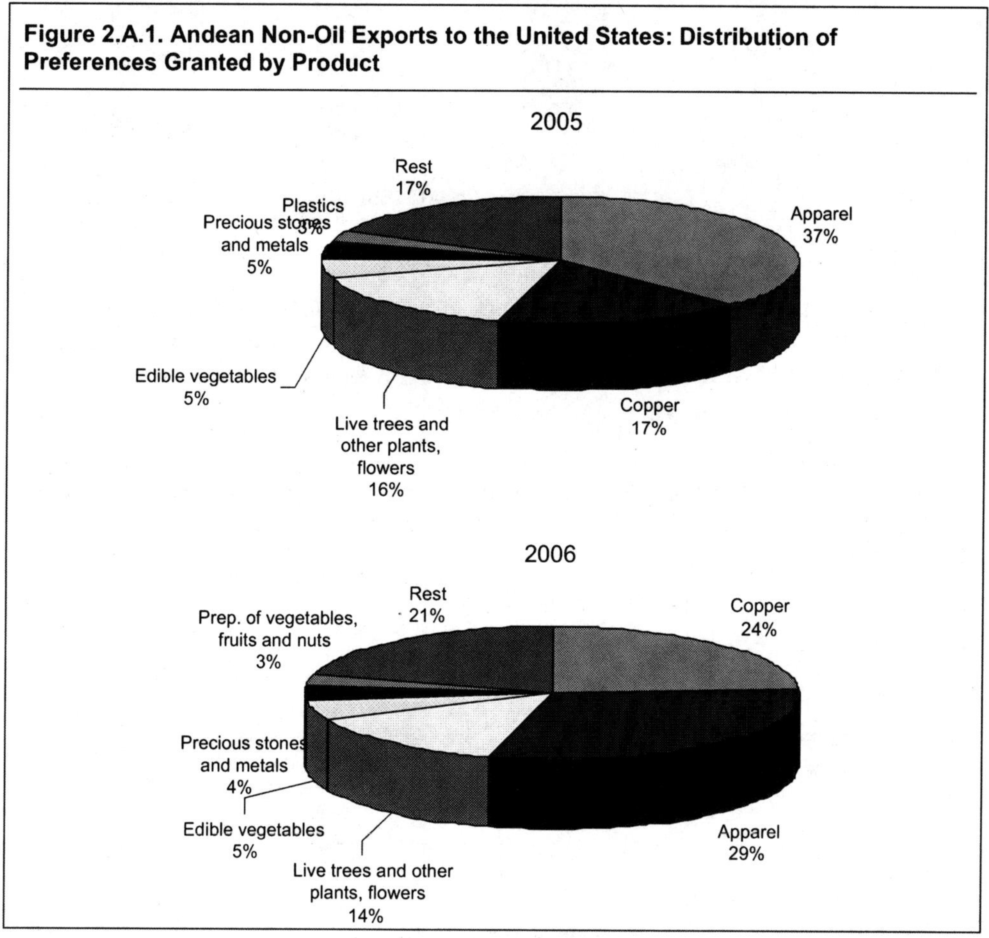

Source: USITC.

Taking into account the utilization rates for non-oil preferences by country, Bolivia on average seems to have benefited the most from the extension of preferences granted in 2002. Including crude oil exports, these average rates are higher for Ecuador and Colombia.

Figure 2.A.2. Average Utilization Rates of ATPA/ATPDEA Preferences, by Country

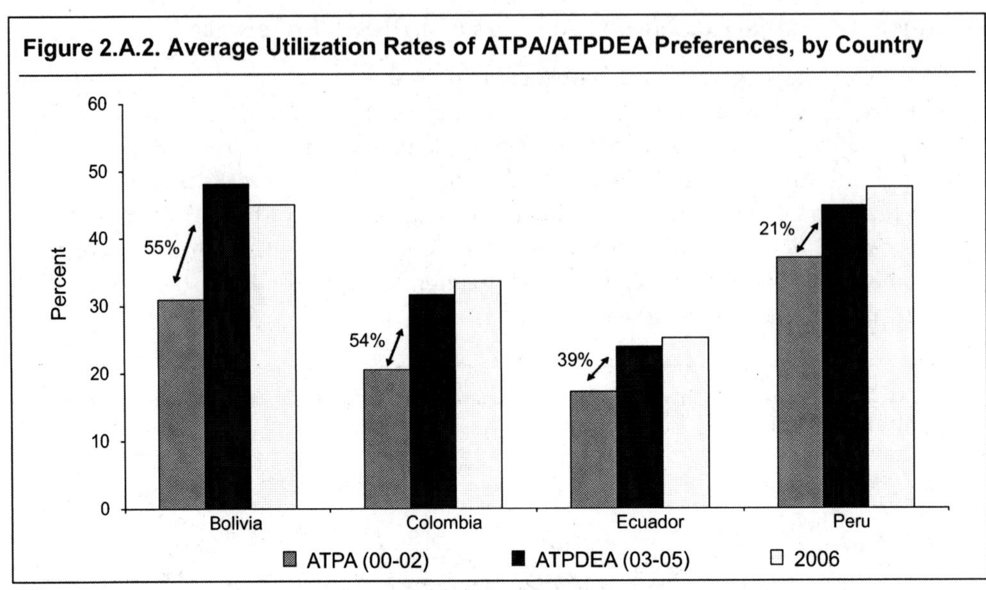

Source: USITC.

In Bolivia's case, 40 percent to 50 percent of Bolivian exports have entered into United States' markets under either the ATPDEA or GSP preferences. Although almost 50 percent of the exports entered not claiming preferences at all, only 6 percent were subject to tariffs, which on average are 6 percent.

Figure 2.A.3. Bolivia's Distribution of Exports to the United States, by Preferential Program

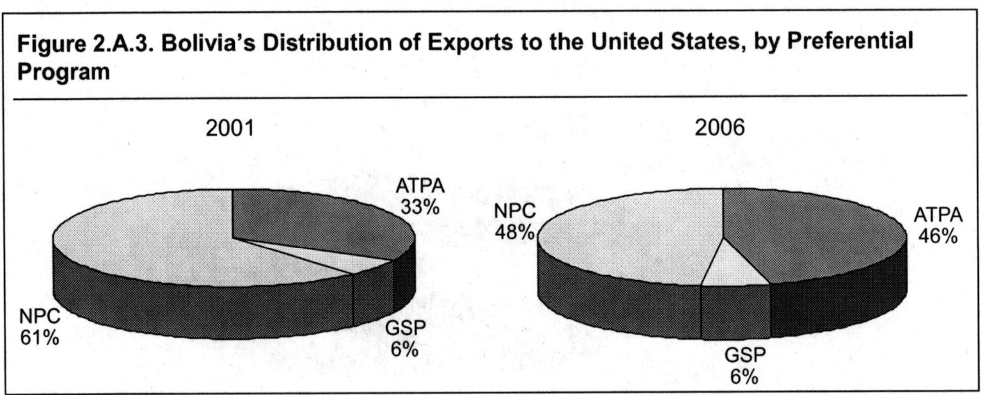

Source: USITC.

Analyzing the top ten Bolivian exports to the United States—which represented almost 80 percent of total exports in 2006—indicates that apparel, jewelry, and raw sugar are the products using the ATPDEA preferences the most.

Table 2.A.14. ATPDEA Utilization Rates for Top Ten Bolivian Exports 2000–06

		2000	2001	2002	2003	2004	2005	2006
711319	Jewelry of other precious metals	97%	92%	54%	94%	96%	95%	98%
800110	Tin, not alloyed							
270900	Petroleum oils and oils (crude)						100%	51%
261100	Tungsten ores and concentrates.	28%	3%		4%		6%	83%
441820	Doors and their frames	87%	76%	48%	82%	37%	37%	34%
080122	Brazil nuts :-- Shelled							
440724	Wood swan of tropical wood							
610510	Men's or boys' shirts of cotton				98%	100%	100%	100%
611020	Sweaters, pullovers, sweatshirts of cotton				93%	99%	100%	100%
170111	Raw sugar not containing added flavor	100%	100%	50%	100%		43%	100%
610910	T-shirts, singlets, tank tops of cotton				99%	100%	99%	100%
710812	Gold unwrought - Non-monetary	15%			1%			
150710	Crude oil, soy bean, degummed or not					100%		
610610	Women's or girls' shirts of cotton				75%	99%	97%	99%
	Percent they represent of the exports to US	**68%**	**74%**	**77%**	**77%**	**76%**	**78%**	**78%**
	Total exports to the US (in million dollars)	**198.3**	**173.1**	**166.8**	**192.0**	**273.1**	**307.7**	**377.6**
	Total exports to the World (in million dollars)	**962.5**	**1,067.9**	**1,187.1**	**1,496.0**	**2,101.7**	**2,558.1**	**3,418.5**

Source: USITC, COMTRADE.

Bolivian exporters have to face competition from Peruvian and Colombian exporters basically in five products: jewelry (Peru), apparel (Colombia and Peru), cane sugar (Colombia, Ecuador, and Peru), wood not-assembled (Colombia and Peru), and crude oil (Ecuador, Colombia, and Peru)

Figure 2.A.4. Exports' Evolution of Andean Countries in Main Bolivian Export Markets

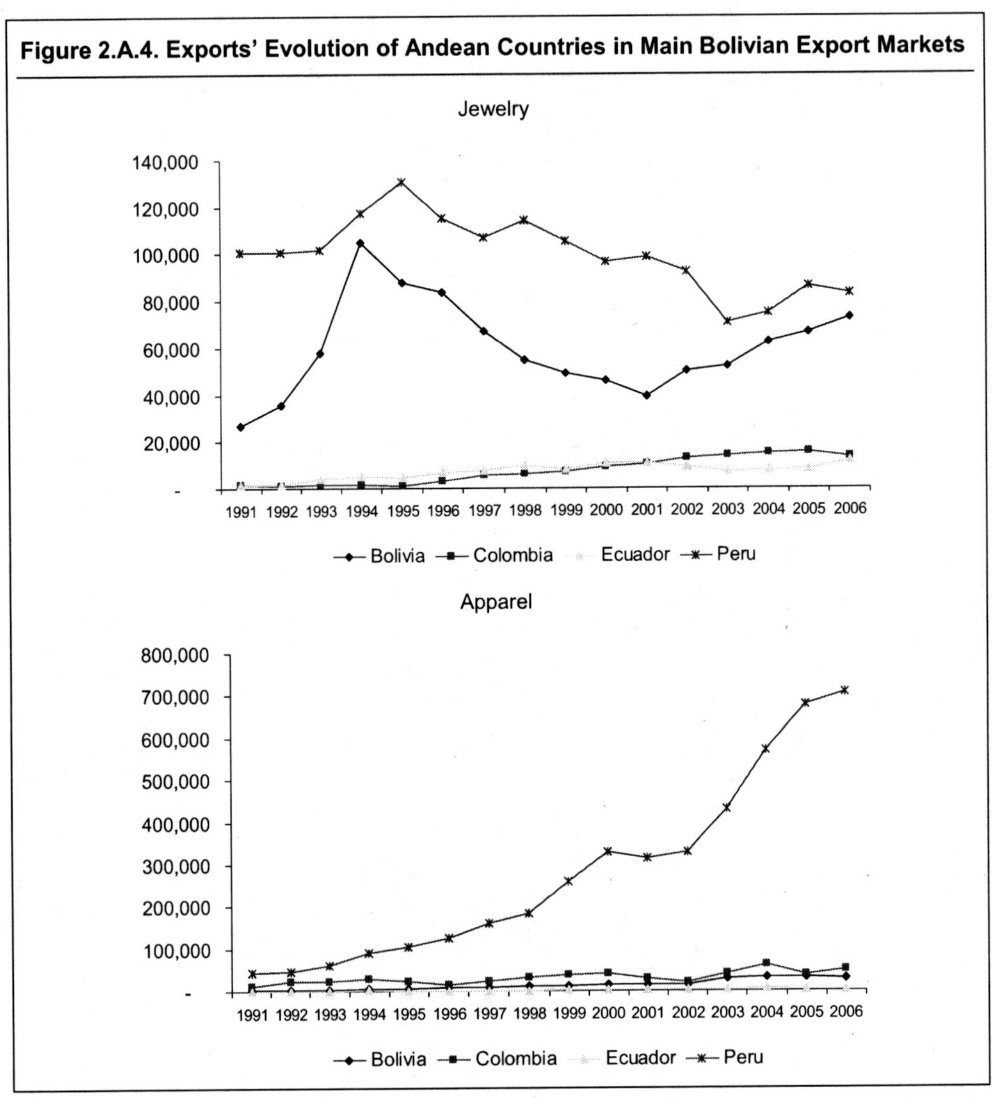

(Figure continues on next page)

Figure 2.A.4 (continued)

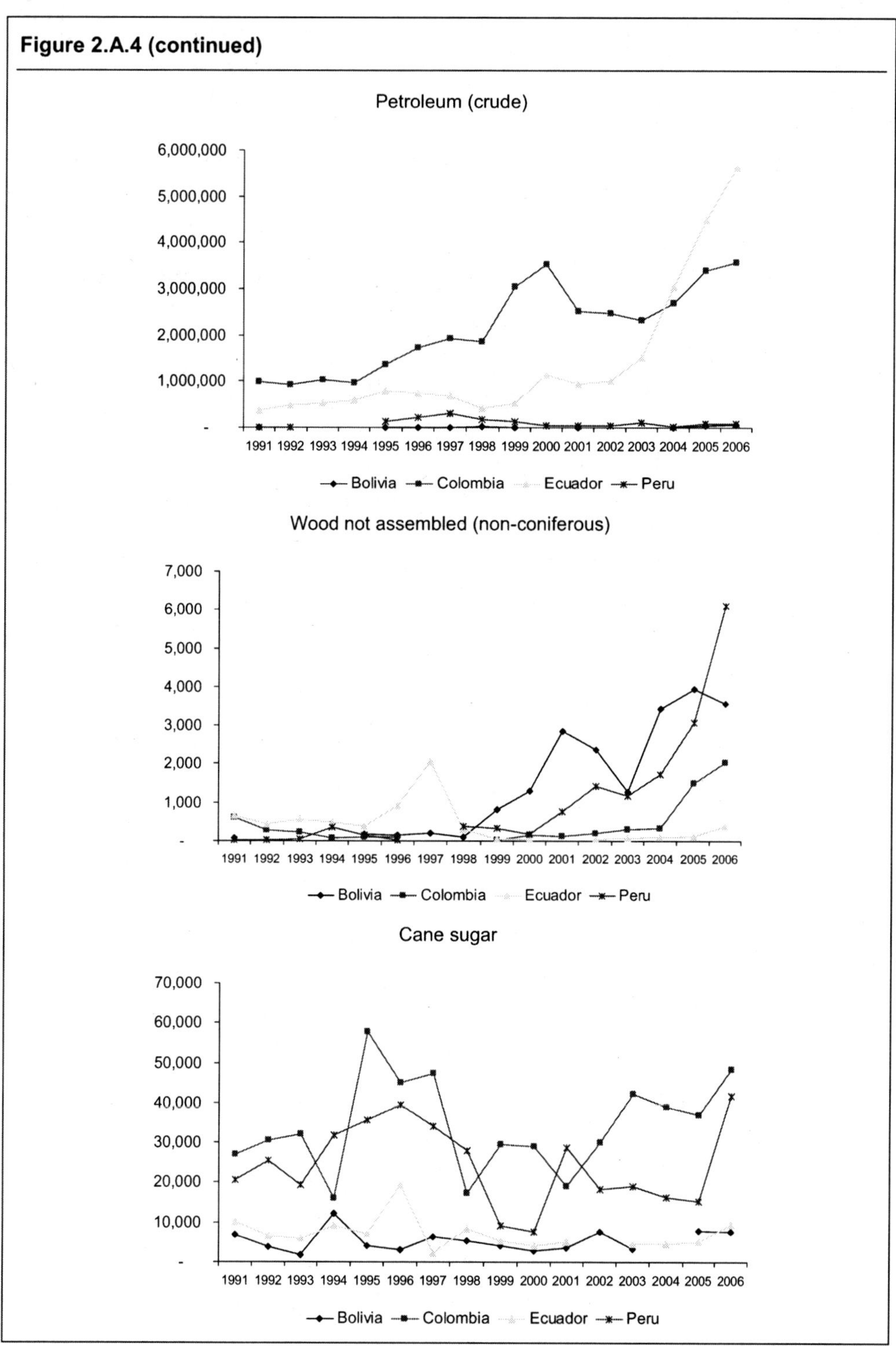

Source: COMTRADE.

Of all these products, jewelry and wood (not-assembled and non-coniferous) are the ones where Bolivian exporters offer a more comparable supply to the one from other Andean countries. In fact, the Bolivian supply of jewelry rivals the Peruvian supply very closely and it shows an upward trend between 2005 and 2006. Likewise, the Bolivian supply of not-assembled and non-coniferous wood is between the levels observed for Colombia and Peru, although in this case, it shows a downward trend between 2005 and 2006. In the case of apparel, crude oil, and raw sugar, Bolivian supply is significantly smaller than the one from the other Andean countries.

Table 2.A.15. Supply Comparison of Andean Countries in Jewelry, Apparel, and Crude Oil

Exporters	Imported value 2006 in US$ thousand	Share in USA's imports, %	Import growth in value between 2005-2006, %
Jewelry of other precious metals			
Peru	83,288	1.00	-4
Bolivia	72,897	1.00	10
Petroleum oils and oils (crude)			
Ecuador	5,619,048	2.00	25
Colombia	3,561,424	2.00	5
Bolivia	56,829	0.20	18
Men's or boys' shirts of cotton			
Peru	187,258	9.00	5
Bolivia	8,237	0.40	-4
T-shirts, singlets, tank tops of cotton			
Peru	149,394	4.00	-3
Colombia	24,133	1.00	117
Bolivia	5,311	0.10	-3
Sweaters, pullovers, sweatshirts of cotton			
Peru	308,117	4.00	7
Bolivia	8,029	0.09	81
Women's or girls' shirts of cotton			
Peru	61,833	6.00	8
Bolivia	6,740	0.62	-16
Wood (lumber) continuously shaped non-coniferous (hardwood)			
Peru	6,117	1.00	99
Bolivia	3,570	0.00	-10
Colombia	2,024	0.00	34
Raw sugar, cane			
Colombia	48,482	5.00	31
Peru	41,654	4.00	172
Bolivia	7,688	1.00	-3

Source: International Trade Centre.

Taking into account that the FTA between the United States and Peru has already been approved by both Congresses and the U.S.-Colombia FTA is following a similar process, we want to analyze how much Bolivian exports to the United States are affected if the ATPDEA preferences are not renewed (basically in these markets where they compete with Colombian and Peruvian exporters).

In principle, the losses in the five markets (jewelry, crude oil, apparel, wood, and cane sugar) would be mitigated by the fact that in three of these markets (jewelry, crude oil and wood non-coniferous), Bolivia could alternatively claim preferences under the GSP. However, even assuming the worst-case scenario (that Bolivia preference would go up to the MFN level observed) in the jewelry, crude oil, and wood markets, we observe that Bolivian export revenues' losses would be significant basically in the jewelry market ($22 million) and very modest in the case of crude oil ($0.4 million) and wood ($0.1 million). [6]. For these estimations, we have used the SMART Tool of WITS. [7]

Figure 2.A.5. Losses on Bolivian Export Revenues to the United States as a Result of Nonrenewal of ATPDEA Preferences (Partial Equilibrium Analysis)

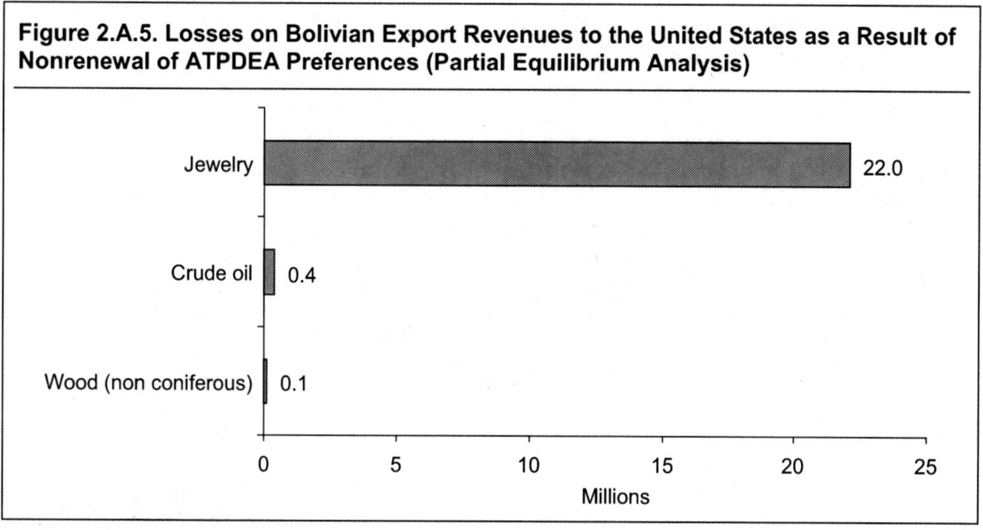

Source: WITS, OTRI dataset.

With respect to the other remaining markets with no GSP preferences (apparel and cane sugar), apparel would be the market mainly affected since, as we can see from the graph below, it is the market where preferences have been mostly exploited.

Figure 2.A.6. Bolivian Exports of Apparel and Raw Cane Sugar to the United States

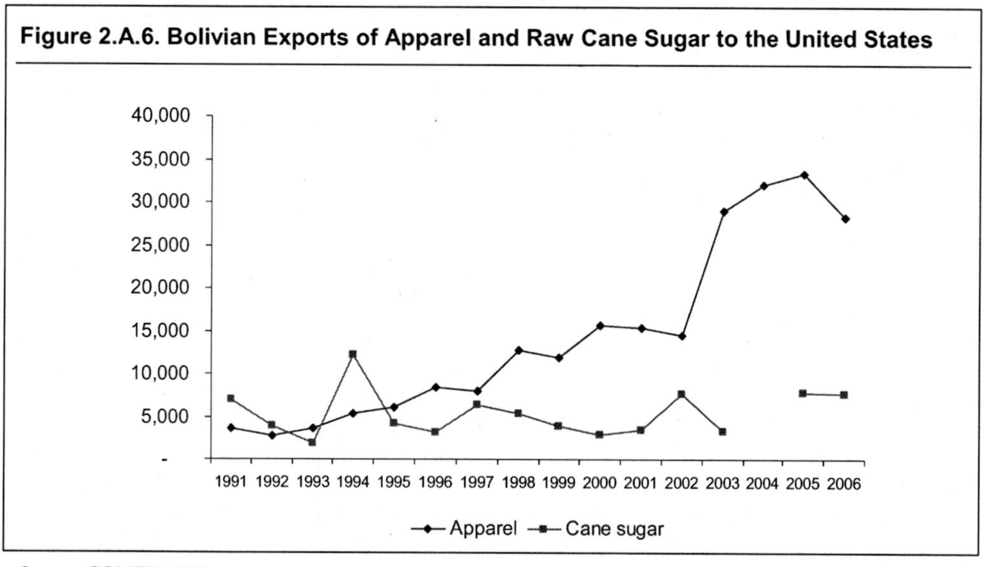

Source: COMTRADE.

We estimated the impact of trade deviation and trade creation on Bolivian exports in apparel to the United States (while Colombia and Peru maintain their preferential access to United States' markets), using the partial equilibrium model as before and assuming different elasticities of substitution between Bolivia versus Colombia and Peru: 0.5, 1.5 and 5. The results are presented below and as we can see, the total trade effect on Bolivian export revenues is not so significant for the apparel market. In the worst-case scenario (with a very high cross elasticity), Bolivia's losses in export revenues are above one million dollar which in 2006 only represented 4 percent of the total value exported in that industry.

Figure 2.A.7. Simulation of Impact of Tariff Change on Bolivian Export Revenues (in Apparel)

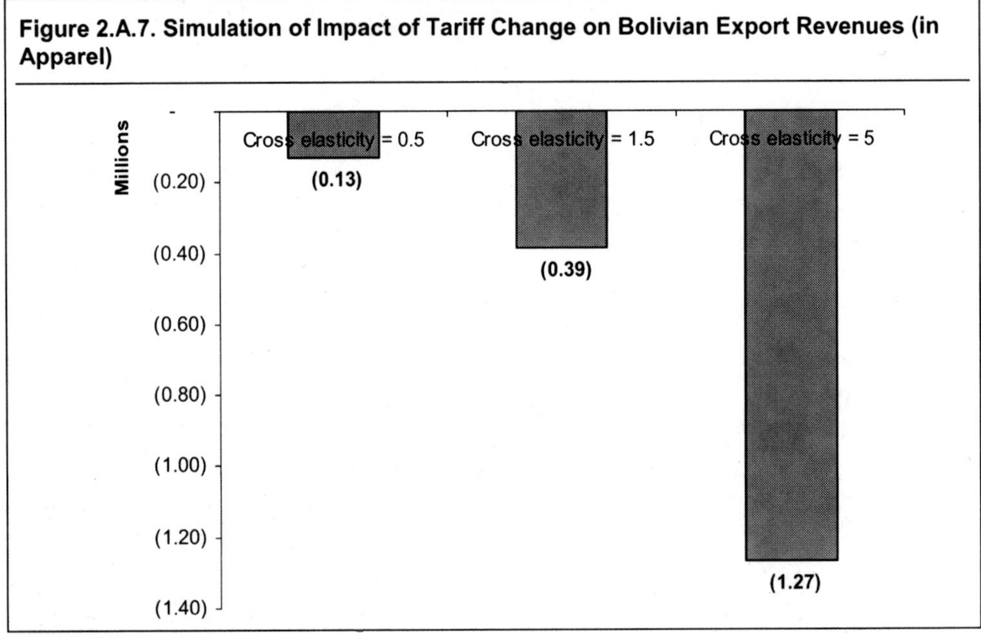

Source: WITS.

With regard to the losses from the increase of the tariff to MFN level in the cane sugar market (if the ATPDEA preference is not renewed), Bolivian exports revenues would be reduced in $4.6 million (assuming a substitution elasticity of 1.5 as it was assumed with the other products).

These results are somewhat consistent with previous results found on the overall effect that a nonrenewal of the ATPDEA preferences would have on Bolivia's export revenues to the extent that they reflect that the losses are modest (excepting the jewelry market). In fact, Guissari and Olarreaga (2006) find that if Bolivia is not a party of a FTA with the United States, its export revenues would drop by $5 million. The differences with respect to the results presented above could be due, on the one hand, to the fact that the GSIM model takes into account world market effects (basically that Bolivian exports of, for example, jewelry to different markets are substitutable). On the other hand, the difference could also be due to the use of more updated data for the current estimations with SMART, which reflect the increase in export flows from Bolivia in the last years especially in the jewelry market.

These results are also somewhat consistent with estimations obtained from general equilibrium models. Andriamananjara and Valenzuela (2008) find that the non renewal of the ATPDEA preferences would decrease Bolivian exports to the United States by almost $41 million annually. However, the results presented in this partial equilibrium analysis depart from their results to the extent that in their case, most of these losses come from the apparel sector, while in our case the sector explaining most of the losses is jewelry.

In fact, at this point, it is important to keep in mind that these results are just partial equilibrium approximations of the impact of losing preferences in specific markets. In this case, we have focused mainly on what Bolivia looses from a nonrenewal of the ATPDEA preferences in four markets where Bolivia stands to loose the most, and how United States's imports are deviated to Colombian and Peruvian supplies in apparel; however, these estimations do not take into account the gains that Bolivia could obtain from the shifting exports to other markets and which could more properly be evaluated with models of general equilibrium.

Annex 2.4. Impact on Employment Using Partial Equilibrium Analysis

Table 2.A.16. Impact of Deepening MERCOSUR Integration on Exports and Employment

MERCOSUR tariff=0	Initial exports to MERCOSUR	Exports change by Country *(in thousand US dollars)*						Employment		
		Argentina	Brazil	Paraguay	Uruguay	Total	In %of init. exports	Initial number of employees	LR empl. chge (% of initial empl.)	Absolute empl. chge
Food products	922.62	14.51	51.76	0.00	11.74	78.01	8.45	11,302	16.38	1,852
Food products	11.48	0.02	1.70	0.00	0.00	1.72	14.95	0	0.36	0
Beverages	17.89	3.66	0.00	0.00	0.00	3.66	20.48	5,752	0.77	44
Tobacco	0.14	0.04	0.00	0.00	0.00	0.04	0.04	195	0.01	0
Textiles	103.68	19.22	0.00	1.65	0.00	20.86	20.12	4,000	4.38	175
Wearing apparel except footwear	1,206.09	185.66	466.14	0.00	1.68	653.48	54.18	1,751	137.25	2,403
Leather products	2,963.47	42.44	175.41	0.00	72.71	290.56	9.80	948	61.03	579
Footwear except rubber or plastic	3.01	0.00	1.72	0.00	0.00	1.72	57.32	1,107	0.36	4
Wood products except furniture	2,078.54	47.03	0.00	190.01	13.02	250.06	12.03	2,502	52.52	1,314
Furniture except metal	0.70	0.48	0.00	0.00	0.00	0.48	68.47	1,958	0.10	2
Paper and products	198.65	4.94	0.00	0.00	18.88	23.82	11.99	3,297	5.00	165
Printing and publishing	10.81	0.04	0.17	4.14	0.00	4.34	40.13	3,321	0.91	30
Industrial chemicals	451.53	50.31	2.92	0.71	0.00	53.94	11.95	253	11.33	29
Other chemicals	77.74	0.28	0.00	20.79	0.00	21.07	27.11	2,604	4.43	115
Petroleum refineries	9,587.42	9.70	0.00	266.08	0.00	275.78	2.88	760	57.92	440
Miscellaneous products	0.00		0.00	0.00	0.00	0.00	0.00	0.00	0.00	0
Rubber products	0.22	0.12	0.00	0.00	0.00	0.12	56.16	114	0.03	0
Plastic products	305.77	147.70	12.75	8.24	0.00	168.70	55.17	2,803	35.43	993
Pottery china earthenware	4.69	2.10	0.75	0.00	0.00	2.85	60.84	5	0.60	0
Glass and products	0.26	0.05	0.00	0.00	0.00	0.05	17.58	475	0.01	0
Other non-metallic mineral products	88.71	19.02	0.00	0.00	2.44	21.46	24.19	4,001	4.51	180
Iron and steel	17.71	1.30	1.19	0.00	0.00	2.49	14.08	313	0.52	2
Non-ferrous metals	4,513.07	2.18	371.60	0.00	0.00	373.78	8.28	0	78.51	0
Fabricated metal products	164.08	5.91	45.03	0.00	0.00	50.95	31.05	1,411	10.70	151
Machinery except electrical	66.25	7.33	1.69	0.00	0.16	9.18	13.85	328	1.93	6
Machinery electric	661.81	91.96	0.54	2.20	161.52	256.22	38.71	715	53.81	385
Transport equipment	74.87	19.60	0.00	0.00	0.00	19.60	26.18	398	4.12	16
Professional and scientific equipment	19.04	1.33	3.39	0.00	0.00	4.72	24.77	105	0.99	1
Other manufactured products	211.34	13.75	44.25	0.00	0.00	58.00	27.44	950	12.18	116
TOTAL	*23,761.57*	*690.68*	*1,181.00*	*493.83*	*282.13*	*2,647.64*	11.14	*51,368*	5.56	*9,003*

Source: SMART-wits.

Table 2.A.16 (continued)

Bolivian tariff=0	(in $000)	Imports change *(in thousand US dollars)*						Employment		
	Initial Bolivian imports from the MERCOSUR	Argentina	Brazil	Paraguay	Uruguay	Total	in % of init. imports	Initial number of employees	LR empl. change (% of init. employ.)	Bounded job destruction
Food products	40,616.77	1,891.50	430.02	73.01	3.02	2,397.56	5.90	11,302	-100.00	-11,302
Food products	5,206.62	147.70	123.68	1.96	0.00	273.33	5.25	0	-57.41	0
Beverages	4,191.88	156.73	14.27	0.00	0.00	171.00	4.08	5,752	-35.91	-2,066
Tobacco	2,006.52		44.37	1.94	0.00	46.30	92.61	195	-9.73	-19
Textiles	4,208.64	42.25	154.29	2.71	1.00	200.25	4.76	4,000	-42.06	-1,682
Wearing apparel except footwear	1,644.09	31.65	134.54	6.59	2.89	175.66	10.68	1,751	-36.89	-646
Leather products	456.96	8.34	47.78	0.25	0.00	56.37	12.34	948	-11.84	-112
Footwear except rubber or plastic	2,200.85	115.41	719.50	5.51	0.64	841.06	38.22	1,107	-100.00	-1,107
Wood products except furniture	1,809.85	172.44	41.54	0.00	0.00	213.98	11.82	2,502	-44.94	-1,124
Furniture except metal	1,440.71	111.70	108.69	2.13	0.00	222.52	15.45	1,958	-46.74	-915
Paper and products	7,846.38	512.80	214.98	0.57	0.00	728.36	9.28	3,297	-100.00	-3,297
Printing and publishing	1,252.65	49.06	33.07	0.88	4.59	87.60	6.99	3,321	-18.40	-611
Industrial chemicals	50,501.25	742.05	1,249.30	46.74	8.47	2,046.55	4.05	253	-100.00	-253
Other chemicals	15,027.10	285.43	743.89	8.15	1.84	1,039.32	6.92	2,604	-100.00	-2,604
Petroleum refineries	89,091.95	681.56	109.52	0.28	0.00	791.36	0.89	760	-100.00	-760
Miscellaneous products	111.93	3.04	0.74	0.00	0.00	3.77	4.51	8.28	-0.79	0
Rubber products	8,628.52	89.62	1,239.06	0.00	0.00	1,328.67	15.40	114	-100.00	-114
Plastic products	9,293.75	581.08	1,455.79	139.81	7.65	2,184.33	23.50	2,803	-100.00	-2,803
Pottery china earthenware	480.41	10.53	41.21	0.00	0.40	52.14	10.85	5	-10.95	-1
Glass and products	6,280.22	70.87	180.94	64.41	0.00	316.21	5.04	475	-66.41	-315
Other non-metallic mineral products	6,160.03	158.26	419.49	0.25	0.15	578.15	9.39	4,001	-100.00	-4,001
Iron and steel	54,775.27	793.64	1,811.02	9.08	0.00	2,613.74	4.77	313	-100.00	-313
Non-ferrous metals	3,100.67	25.87	73.18	0.00	0.00	99.05	3.19	0	-20.80	0
Fabricated metal products	28,590.77	311.38	2,453.94	3.02	4.02	2,772.36	9.70	1,411	-100.00	-1,411
Machinery except electrical	56,809.95	551.89	1,214.83	0.91	2.87	1,770.49	3.12	328	-100.00	-328
Machinery electric	17,542.80	73.45	863.23	1.23	25.97	963.89	5.49	715	-100.00	-715
Transport equipment	41,447.99	499.67	2,541.15	0.93	2.98	3,044.73	7.35	398	-100.00	-398
Professional and scientific equipment	6,336.80	59.78	339.77	0.00	1.41	400.97	6.33	105	-84.21	-88
Other manufactured products	3,599.24	28.89	239.88	0.66	0.23	269.66	7.49	950	-56.64	-538
	470,660.58	*8,206.57*	*17,043.65*	*371.02*	*68.12*	*25,689.36*	5.46	*51,376*	*-54*	*-37,524*

Source: SMART-wits.

Annex 2.5. Effects on Poverty

Methodology to measure the impact of a trade shock on incomes

- **Step 1**: The effect of the assumed shocks on Bolivian trade flows (tariff changes in all simulations) are modeled using SMART, a highly disaggregated partial-equilibrium model. The model yields variations in trade values. These variations are essentially due to two forces: trade creation and trade diversion
- **Step 2**: Variations in trade values are "fed" into household survey data in order to obtain effects on real incomes. Real incomes are affected by so-called "first-order effects"-price changes and "second-order effects"-induced quantity changes. In both cases, the linkage from trade to household welfare is via prices and incomes; specifically, induced changes in consumer prices, producer prices, and wages. The following sections present the simulations:

In the simulations that follow, we restrict ourselves to first-order effects.

When the trade shock leads to job destruction, we estimate how changes in unemployment affect household incomes using a two-step procedure as follows:

(i) We run a probit of unemployment on individual and household characteristics:[8]

$$\lambda_i = \text{prob}(I_i = 1 | \mathbf{z}_i) = f(\mathbf{z}_i \alpha + u_i) \tag{0.1}$$

where $\mathbf{z}_i$ is a vector of individual and household's characteristics including, household head's age, education, household's composition, u_i is an error term with standard properties, and

$$I_i = \begin{cases} 1 & \text{if HH } i\text{'s head is unemployed} \\ 0 & \text{otherwise;} \end{cases} \tag{0.2}$$

(ii) We run a switching regression of household's income on household's characteristics of the following form. Let y_{i1} be the income of household i if the household head is employed and y_{i2} its income if he (she) is unemployed. Income in each status is determined by the following equation

$$y_{ei} = \mathbf{x}_{ei} \boldsymbol{\beta}_e + v_{ei} \tag{0.3}$$

if status is "employed" and

$$y_{ui} = \mathbf{x}_{ui} \boldsymbol{\beta}_u + v_{ui} \tag{0.4}$$

if it is "unemployed." Even though the sample split between employed and unemployed is observed, (0.3) and (0.4) cannot be estimated simply with two separate OLS regressions. To see this, suppose that unobserved individual characteristics (say, individual talent) affect both income and other individual characteristics (say, the level of education) while being also correlated with the probability of being unemployed. In that case, there would be a selection bias, even though the status is not a choice. We correct this bias using Heckman's two-step procedure, i.e. by running (0.1), retrieving the hazard rate, and using it to estimate "augmented" versions of (0.3) and (0.4).[9]

Tracking the impact of a trade shock on income in the manufacturing sector

From regression (0.1), we get propensity scores $\hat{\lambda}_i$ (estimated probabilities of being unemployed) for all household heads employed in the manufacturing sectors (for other households, this score would be meaningless); and we rank them by decreasing order of $\hat{\lambda}_i$ (from the most likely to be unemployed *among the employed ones* to the least likely). Then, knowing that *n* manufacturing jobs would be destroyed, we change the status of the *n* first household heads (the ones with the highest propensity scores) from employed to unemployed, and then recalculate their predicted incomes using the estimates from the income regression.

Predicted income is

$$\hat{y}_{ei} = E\left(y_{ei} \middle| \mathbf{x}_{ei}\right) = \mathbf{x}_{ei}\hat{\boldsymbol{\beta}}_e$$

when the household head is employed and

$$\hat{y}_{ui} = E\left(y_{ui} \middle| \mathbf{x}_{ui}\right) = \mathbf{x}_{ui}\hat{\boldsymbol{\beta}}_u .$$

when he/she is unemployed. The percent change in predicted income for an individual who loses his/her job is then

$$\delta_i = \frac{\Delta\hat{y}_i}{\hat{y}_{ei}} = \frac{\hat{y}_{ui} - \hat{y}_{ei}}{\hat{y}_{ei}} < 0 . \qquad (0.5)$$

We then apply this *predicted* percent income reduction to *observed* income, household by household:

$$\left.\frac{\Delta y_i}{y_i}\right|_{simulated} = \delta_i y_i . \qquad (0.6)$$

When the shock creates manufacturing jobs, the procedure is similar but slightly more complex. Switching from unemployment or from an existing job to manufacturing employment involves a choice which must be modeled as such, that is, the "switchers" must make more money by switching than by staying in the pre-shock occupation.

Tracking the impact of a trade shock on income in the agriculture sector

In agriculture, the effects of the trade shock were modeled differently from the manufacturing sector. In principle, things were simpler: the trade simulation gave us variations in the quantities of exports, by crop. Since we had export values but not domestic production, we did not know how much the reduction in U.S. import demand represented relative to Bolivia's initial production and, consequently, we could not use the share of each crop in the cash income of farm households to allocate the export cuts. Therefore we started instead from the price effect

$$\Delta p_k = \frac{-t_k^{US,MFN}}{1+t_k^{US,MFN}} < 0, \tag{0.7}$$

assuming full pass-through, and calculated the first-order effect for Bolivian farm households involved in the production of cash crop *k*. The effect for household *i* was calculated as

$$\frac{\Delta y_i^a}{y_i^a} = \sum_{k \in K} \omega_{ik} \Delta p_k \tag{0.8}$$

where $\omega_{ik} = y_{ik} / y_i^a$ was the share of cash income from the production of crop *k* in household *i*'s total income. We also assumed that:

1. Only cash income was affected by the export reduction.
2. All farmers producing cash crop *k* for export to the United States would be affected (the price decrease being transmitted backward to all sales of crop *k*, domestic or foreign).[10]
3. Farmers not producing crops exported to the United States would not be affected at all.

Tables of the impact of trade shocks on poverty

Table 2.A.17. Probit Regression Results, Selection Equation (Prob. Unemployed)

Dep. variable: unemployed = 1	
Male	-1.220
	(0.346)***
Age	-0.082
	(0.056)
Age squared	0.001
	(0.001)*
Education	-0.105
	(0.125)
Education squared	0.010
	(0.006)*
Indigenous	0.420
	(0.289)
# of children	-0.103
	(0.086)
Urban	-0.617
	(0.489)
depto==2	-1.142
	(0.491)**
depto==3	-1.257
	(0.569)**
depto==4	-0.319
	(0.562)
depto==5	-0.193
	(0.618)
depto==6	-1.152
	(0.580)**
depto==7	-0.938
	(0.514)*
depto==8	-1.245
	(0.592)**
depto==9	-0.594
	(0.871)
Constant	2.578
	(1.396)*
Observations	217

Table 2.A.18. Regression Results, Income Equation

	Employed	Unemployed
Age	0.0969	0.0604
	(0.0278)***	(0.0387)
Age squared	−0.0011	−0.0006
	(0.0003)***	(0.0004)
Education	0.0639	0.0840
	(0.0668)	(0.0738)
Education squared	0.0005	−0.0026
	(0.0032)	(0.0037)
Indigenous	−0.0663	−0.8695
	(0.1178)	(0.2735)***
Constant	4.1371	4.6144
	(0.8621)***	(0.9902)***
No. obs	156	61

Table 2.A.19. Income Effects for Deeper MERCOSUR Integration, Manufacturing (Income Change, %)

		Total	Indigenous	Nonindigenous
Percent variation	δ (mean over hhs)	−63.1	−70.4	−50.3
		(0.02)	(0.02)	(0.03)
Variation in money terms	δ*y (mean over hhs)	−1,266	−878	−1,982
		(308)	(96)	(643)
Aggregate variation	δ*y (sum all hhs)	−88,864	−48,614	−39,868
No. obs		87	57	30

Note: Standard errors in parentheses.

Table 2.A.20. Poverty Measures: MERCOSUR Integration, Manufacturing

	Poverty count (%)	Poverty gap index (%)
Before the trade shock	50.7	20.4
After the trade shock	69.6	33.7

Table 2.A.21. Income Effects for Deeper MERCOSUR Integration, Agriculture (Income Change, %)

		Total	Indigenous	Nonindigenous
Percent variation	δ (mean over hhs)	−7.5	−7.7	−6.8
		(0.004)	(0.004)	(0.006)
Variation in money terms	δ*y (mean over hhs)	−128.1	−121.1	−157.5
		(33)	(39)	(49)
Aggregate variation	δ*y (sum all hhs)	−155,318	−108,470	−46,848
No. obs		1269	921	348

Note: Standard errors in parentheses.

Table 2.A.22. Poverty Measures: MERCOSUR Integration, Agriculture

	Poverty count (%)	Poverty gap index (%)
Before the trade shock	69.5	42.1
After the trade shock	70.2	42.8

Annex Notes

[1] The functional forms are nested constant elasticities of substitution (CES) production functions. Land, labor (skilled and unskilled), and capital substitute for one another in a value added aggregate, and composite intermediates substitute for value added at the next CES level.

[2] This is not the 'full employment' assumption sometimes criticized by advocates of structuralist models of development, rather it assumes that aggregate employment is determined by factors such as labor market norms and regulation that are largely independent of trade policy in the long run (Hertel et al. 2007).

[3] In the benchmark year, the expenditure function is exactly equal to disposable income and reflects expenditures on goods and services, and savings. After the policy shock, the expenditure function reflects the value of expenditures required to achieve the new level of utility at benchmark year prices. Another different way of interpreting the national economic welfare estimate is to think that this is very closely approximated by the value of nominal disposable income deflated by the consumer price index.

[4] That is, the model is unable to estimate changes in trade in commodities that historically have not been traded.

[5] http://www.mincetur.gob.pe/COMERCIO/OTROS/Atpdea/ley_atpa_atpdea/resumen_ejecutivo.htm#resumen.

[6] These estimations have been made assuming an elasticity of substitution of 1.5 and using the tariff conversion of specific duties taken from the Overall Trade Restrictiveness dataset for the United States for crude oil.

[7] The SMART tool is based on a partial equilibrium model that estimates the impact of tariff changes on imports and in particular, it provides with estimates on trade creation and trade deviation as a result of these changes. The full explanation of the model used to estimate the trade creation/diversion under different scenarios of liberalization can be found in Jammes and Olarreaga (2005), "Explaining SMART and GSIM." In: http://wits.worldbank.org/witsweb/download/docs/Explaining_SMART_and_GSIM.pdf.

[8] Regional department controls as well as a dummy variable for urban or rural location were also used.

[9] See Maddala (1986) for a detailed description of the estimation method.

[10] Whether this is true or not depends on the curvature of the transformation surface between domestic and export sales. If it is flat, continued export sales to the United States require equality between domestic and export prices, so the former must adjust like the latter; if it is strictly convex, price differentials can be consistent with continued export sales.

CHAPTER 3

Linkages between Trade and the Economy

In this chapter, we examine the linkages between Bolivia's trade and its economy. We begin by documenting the link between foreign trade and economic growth and employment in the past. We then present a forward-looking analysis of the impact of different scenarios on growth, employment, trade flows, and poverty. The analysis relies on two different methodologies: a Computable General Equilibrium (CGE) approach and a partial equilibrium approach. The CGE approach allows us to examine economy-wide effects of different trade policy scenarios taking into account feedback effects across sectors. Therefore, the resulting effects reflect both the policy change considered and how the economy-wide response is modeled. In contrast, the partial equilibrium analysis does not account for economy-wide feedback effects but provides a straightforward interpretation of the direct impact of policy change through sectoral effects.[1]

Linkages between Trade, Growth, and Employment in the Past[2]

The Impact of Foreign Trade on Bolivia's Economic Growth

Many argue that foreign trade has contributed only moderately to economic growth in Bolivia. As noted in the World Bank's Country Economic Memorandum (2005), Bolivia's GDP growth has traditionally been high when export growth was low, and vice-versa. This pattern is attributed not only to the small share of GDP accounted for by exports, but also the few links between the export sector and the rest of the economy. Most assessments agree that the development of the export sector and its links with the rest of the economy has been relatively modest (see, for example, Rodríguez 2004 and Zambrana 2002).

In a growth-accounting sense, the contribution of net exports to real GDP growth in Bolivia has been relatively modest. This simple calculation is based on the identity that relates GDP to its expenditure components (private consumption, government consumption, investment, and net exports). The contribution of net exports to real GDP growth has remained volatile and—as will be discussed further below—modest, without a significant change in its pattern before and after the trade reforms of the mid-1980s (Figure 3.1).

Figure 3.1. Contribution of Net Exports to Real GDP Growth, 1971–2006 (Annual Growth Rates)

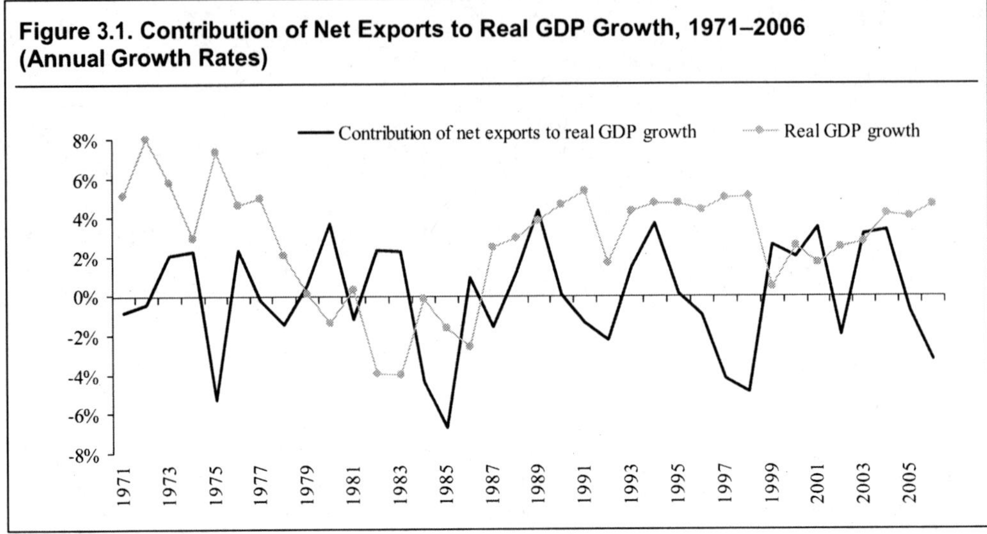

Source: Staff calculations based on WDI data. See Appendix 2.1 of this study for details of calculations and breakdown of the contribution to real GDP growth by demand component.

The volatile contribution of net exports to real GDP growth stems from sharp fluctuations in both exports and imports. Bolivian export and import growth rates have exhibited sharp accelerations and slowdowns (Figure 3.2), partly driven by the composition of trade flows (which are heavily concentrated in commodities). The persistent concentration in commodities helps explain why volatility has remained high also during the two decades or so after the trade reforms of the mid-1980s. Note, however, that trade reforms did help reverse the secular trend of slow and even negative export growth. Thus, while export growth has been volatile in recent years, exports have contracted in a lot fewer years.

Figure 3.2. Export and Import Growth, 1971–2006 (Annual Growth Rates of Exports and Imports of Goods and Services in Real Terms)

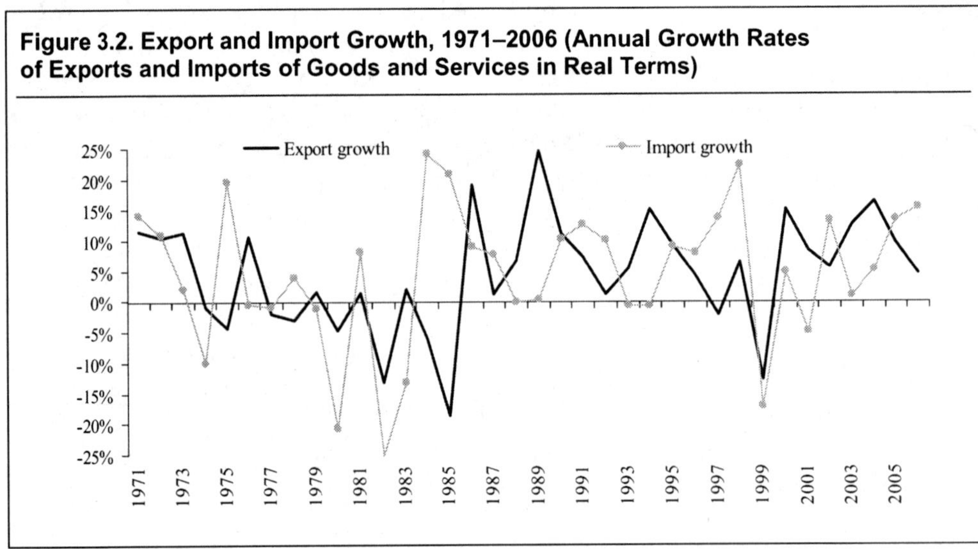

Source: Staff calculations based on WDI data.

Figure 3.3. Long-Run Evolution of Real Exports and Real GDP (Variables in Natural Logarithms)

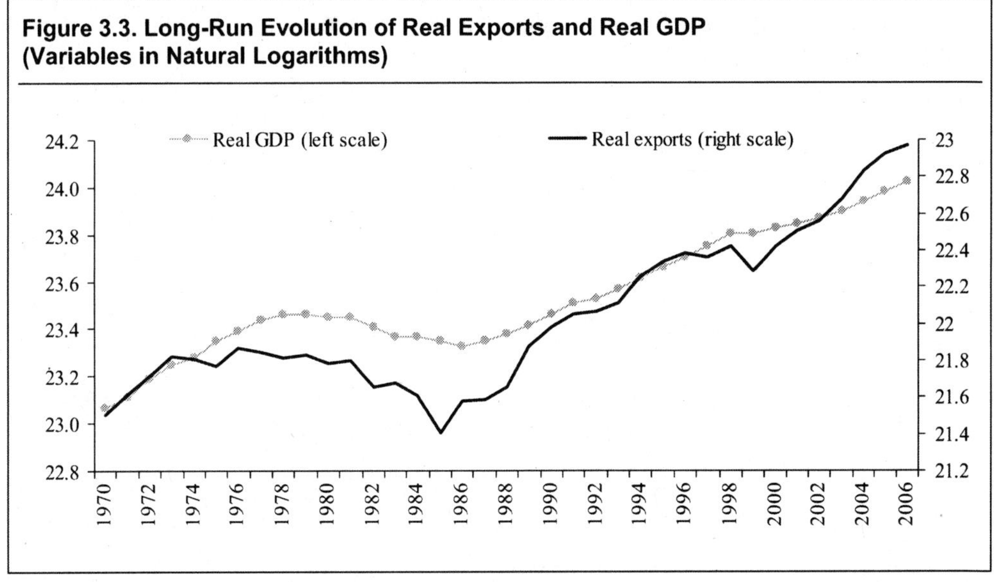

Source: WDI.

But analyzing the impact of net exports on economic growth through the GDP accounting framework has serious limitations, and should be supplemented by time-series analysis.[3] Time-series analyses can help to explore the extent to which exports and economic growth are causally linked. Empirically, the key question is whether causality runs from exports to growth (the export-led growth hypothesis) or from growth to exports (growth-led exports hypothesis). Establishing this causality has important policy implications, as evidence of export-led growth is often interpreted as calling for a renewed focus on facilitating trade. In practical terms, most single-country analyses seek to find a long-run equilibrium relationship between exports and GDP using the cointegration framework suggested by Engle and Granger (Figure 3.3).[4]

The tests suggest that exports *cause* GDP growth, while there is no evidence that GDP growth *causes* exports. Cointegration implies correlation between the two series, but it does not indicate the direction of the causal relationship. The results from running pair-wise Granger causality tests indicate that there is unidirectional causality. Exports appear to cause GDP, because exports help explain the future evolution of the GDP time series. In contrast, there is no evidence that GDP causes exports, since the GDP time series does not help predict the future evolution of exports.

We repeated the above analysis, but this time disaggregating between traditional and nontraditional exports. The analysis of aggregate real exports may mask important underlying differences between different export categories.[5] This argument is relevant for Bolivia, where it is commonly argued that traditional export sector has had few links with the rest of the economy, and nontraditional exports (exports that exclude raw materials, minerals, and fuels) have grown much more modestly than traditional exports. The time series of exports of raw materials and minerals and the time series of all other exports show in fact rather different patterns, suggesting that a disaggregated analysis may indeed be appropriate (Figure 3.4).

Figure 3.4. Bolivian Exports by Groups of Products, 1962–2006 (US$ Millions)

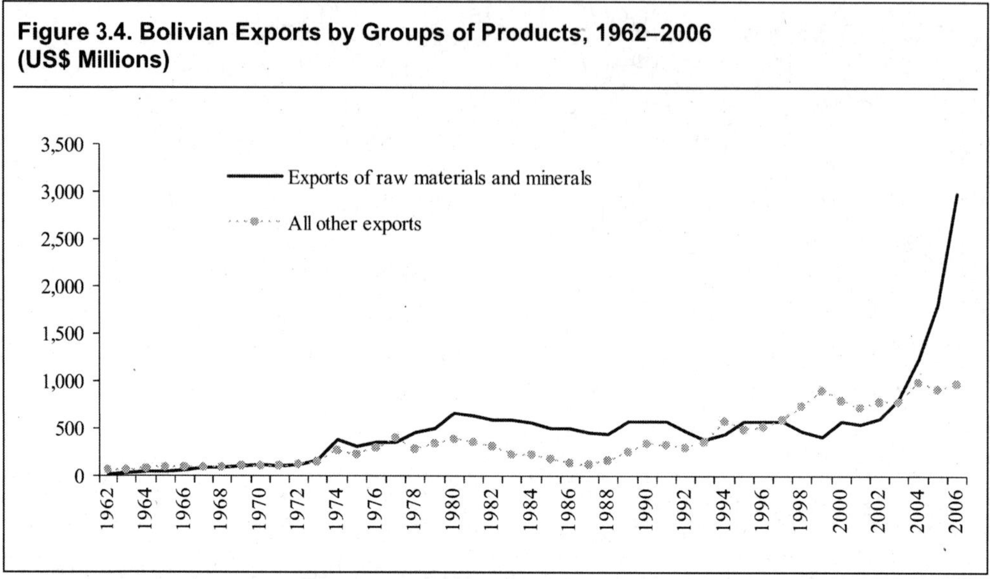

Source: Staff calculations based on UN COMTRADE data.
Note: Exports of raw materials and minerals includes SITC 1-digit groups no. 2 (crude materials, inedible, except fuels) and no. 3 (mineral fuels, lubricants, and related materials).

The analysis reveals no long-run relationship between traditional exports and GDP, while nontraditional exports are linked to GDP. For traditional exports, the test results suggest a failure to find a cointegrating relationship, perhaps because of the explosive nature of the growth of traditional exports in recent years. Nontraditional exports (all exports other than raw materials, minerals, and fuels) do show evidence of a long-run relationship.

However, pair-wise causality tests failed to provide evidence of causality from nontraditional exports to growth. These disaggregated results suggest that perhaps the evidence of a long-run relationship found at the aggregate level, and of causality running from exports to growth, is heavily influenced by the large weight of traditional exports.

Overall, the contribution of net exports to GDP growth has been modest, with weak causal links from exports to GDP. But the analysis cannot capture structural changes in the relationship between exports and the rest of the economy that may have occurred since 2006. Such changes may arise from the increase in government revenues of the traditional sector and the implementation of the National Development Plan to direct those revenues to the productive and social sectors of the economy.

The Impact of Foreign Trade on Bolivia's employment[6]

The linkage between export growth and employment is likely to be limited, given the concentration of exports and the modest size of the manufacturing sector. Bolivia's exports are highly concentrated in the mining and oil sectors, both of which are capital-intensive rather than labor-intensive. Despite recent diversification, manufacturing exports represent about only 10 percent of total exports. Thus, the linkage between overall export growth and employment is likely to be tenuous. Employment growth in Bolivia's manufacturing sector has been small over the sample period (Figure 3.5).

Figure 3.5. Distribution of Employment Growth, by ISIC Industry

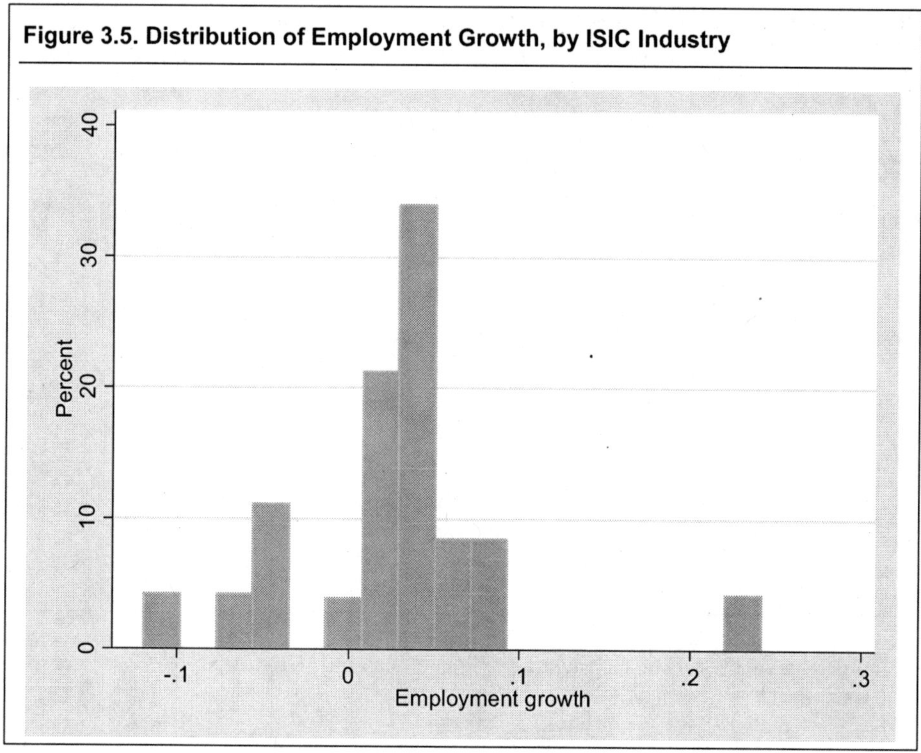

Source: Authors' calculations from UNIDO data.

The figure shows the distribution of industries over a range of employment growth rates going from –15 percent to +30 percent. The highest frequency is about 4 percent of average annual growth, and the bulk of Bolivia's industries have seen their employment grow at annual rates between zero and 10 percent.

The importance of manufactured products in Bolivian exports is not the same across all destinations. Jewelry and apparel account for a higher than average share of exports to the United States, for example, while exports to the U.S. market overall represent less than 13 percent of Bolivia's exports. By contrast, exports to the European Union are essentially primary products, and exports to Andean markets are dominated by soya products. Bolivia's imports are also highly concentrated and dominated by capital goods (60 percent of the total). The United States represents 14 percent of the total. Thus, whether on the export or import side, activity in the trade relationship with the United States is likely to have relatively small effects on Bolivia's total trade.

Employment in the export sector accounts for 40 percent of manufacturing employment. Despite a weak past performance and the dominance of primary products in Bolivia's portfolio exports, employment in the export sector is critical.[7] Exports to the United States have the highest labor content, followed by exports to Andean countries. Exports to MERCOSUR are about half as labor-intensive.

Table 3.1. Regression Results Using Import and Export Values

	(1) RE	(2) FE	(3) FD	(4) GMM	(5) GMM system	(6) GMM system
Real wage	93.816	84.409	−26.891	−49.833	−13.444	−22.244
	(1.59)	(1.53)	(0.55)	(0.85)	(1.03)	(1.03)
Real investment	0.030	0.011	0.003	0.012	0.015	0.014
	(4.26)***	(2.01)**	(0.93)	(2.92)***	(1.98)**	(1.92)*
Real imports	−0.002	−0.002	−0.000	−0.001	−0.000	−0.001
	(1.71)*	(2.00)**	(1.12)	(0.62)	(1.83)*	(1.41)
Real exports	0.009	0.009	0.001	0.007	0.001	0.002
	(4.75)***	(6.03)***	(1.11)	(4.05)***	(2.16)**	(2.78)***
L. Number of employees				0.370	0.949	0.938
				(3.20)***	(18.85)***	(15.69)***
Constant	1,048.95 1	1,279.63 1	80.470	49.598	113.972	209.665
	(3.53)***	(6.73)***	(2.55)**	(2.57)**	(1.54)	(1.26)
Observations	*160*	*160*	*135*	*113*	*138*	*138*
Number of industries	*25*	*25*		*24*	*25*	*25*
R-squared		0.48	0.03			

Source: Cadot and Molina (2008).
Notes: Absolute value of z statistics in parentheses. * Significant at 10 percent; ** at 5 percent; *** at 1 percent, respectively.

Estimates of the link between export and employment growth indicate that $1 million worth of exports creates 1,000 manufacturing jobs in Bolivia (Table 3.1). Thus, a 10 percent ($50 million) increase in manufacturing exports would generate 50,000 jobs. The implied elasticity at the mean (10) is too high to be plausible if we take the (low) initial value of 50,000 jobs. However, using the more reasonable number of 500,000 jobs, the implied elasticity is consistent with earlier estimates quoted in Lara and Soloaga (2007) (Box 3.1).

Box 3.1. Estimating Manufacturing Jobs in Bolivia: 50,000 or 500,000 Jobs?

According to UNIDO data, manufacturing employment in Bolivia amounts to 50,000 jobs. This is a small number when one considers that Bolivia's labor force was 3.5 million in 2000 and 4.2 million in 2006. Of that, 28 percent worked in industry (mining and manufacturing) in 2000 (the most recent figure available), or about one million. If only 50,000 jobs were in manufacturing, 950,000 would be in mining, which is not plausible. Nevertheless, only about 50,000 manufacturing jobs are accounted for in official statistical sources, including United Nations Industrial Development Organization UNIDO and the World Trade Organization WTO's latest country report, which quotes Bolivian official sources. By contrast, based on the national survey for living conditions-ENCOVI 2002, Lara and Soloaga (2007) estimate manufacturing employment at 13 percent of total employment, which currently stands at about 4 million, according to the World Bank's WDI. This would mean about 500,000 jobs. They estimate manufacturing job creation resulting from the Doha Round at about 50,000, which is of course incompatible with an initial estimate of 50,000 jobs. Given the uncertainty about the number of manufacturing jobs, we give results in percentage terms rather than actual numbers.

Figure 3.6. Export Growth and its Correlation with Employment

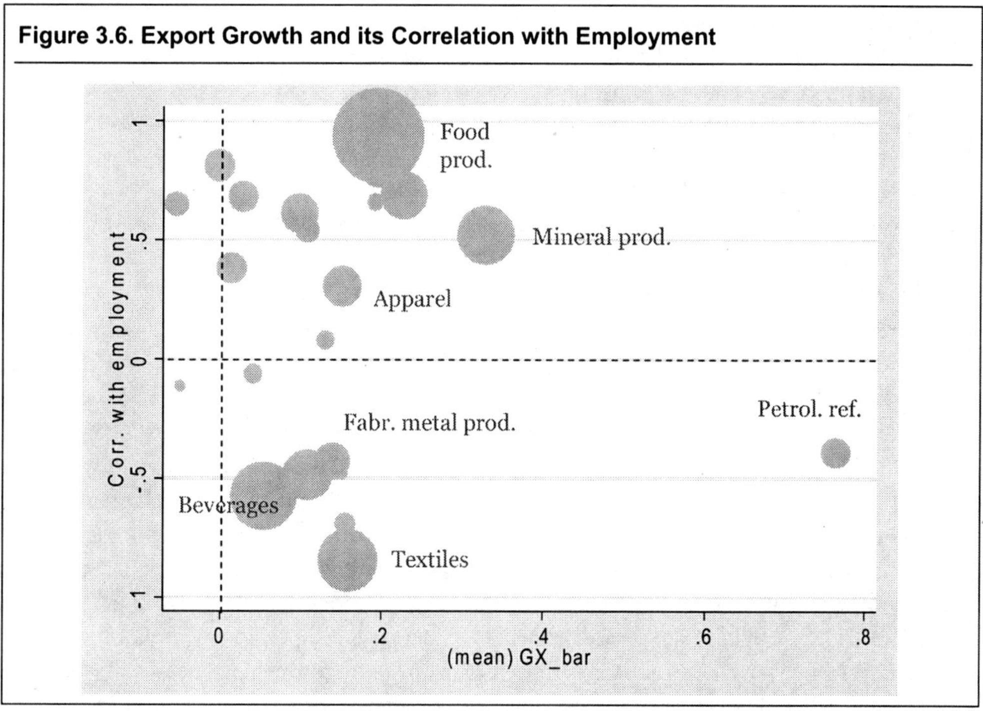

Source: Authors' calculations from UNIDO and COMTRADE data.
Note: Cumulated export growth on the horizontal axis, partial correlation between export and employment, calculated from estimation results on the vertical axis. The size of the bubbles is proportional to total employment in the industry, averaged over the sample period.

A correlation between export growth and employment reveals that export growth was a contributor to employment growth in some industries, while in others it was not (Figure 3.6). Industries in the northeast quadrant of the figure—essentially food products, minerals, and apparel—displayed both positive export growth and positive association with employment, meaning they contribute to employment growth. Industries in the southeast quadrant—textiles, beverages and metal products—had positive export growth but negative association with employment, so their growth in export markets was apparently accompanied by changes in labor-saving technology. These simple results suggest that the food-products industry (especially soya derivatives) stands out in terms of both the growth of its exports and its high labor content, making it a good target for promotion programs aimed at fostering employment growth in the export sector.

Forward-Looking Analysis of the Impact of Trade Shocks on the Economy

Here, we assess the impact of different trade shock scenarios on the Bolivian economy. The country today faces several trade-related policy choices and potential shocks. We use both computable general equilibrium CGE and partial equilibrium approaches to estimate the economic costs, with a view to helping both public policy makers and private economic agents make informed decisions on preempting adjustment costs and designing the right policy responses. We present the two methodologies because each has different strengths and weaknesses. While the partial equilibrium method ignores how the rest of the economy reacts to the initial change in trade flows or prices, it has the advantage that one can identify impacts at the sectoral level. In contrast, the CGE methodology accounts for how the entire economy reacts, but this strength is also its weakness as the precise modeling of how the economy works becomes critical (see Annex 2.2 for a detailed discussion of the pros and cons of CGE modeling). We briefly discuss the trade implications of each scenario in the first subsection, and then present the main results of the scenario analysis under two approaches: CGE analysis of the overall impact of trade, and partial equilibrium analysis of the impacts of trade on employment and on poverty. The pros and cons of each methodology are discussed in the annex.

Many trade-related developments facing Bolivia can affect its trade and domestic economy. These developments relate to changes in the trade policy of key trading partners, progress in regional or subregional integration processes, and changes in global economic prospects. The most prominent challenge is the expiration of the ATPDEA agreement with the United States. Another important development is the implementation of the U.S.-Peru FTA and the signature of the U.S.-Colombia FTA. Bolivia has signaled its intention to pursue market opening through consolidation and intensification of its participation in various trading blocs, especially in the CAN and MERCOSUR. Lastly, the U.S. subprime crisis has triggered a global economic slowdown that may hurt Bolivia, whereas the surge in commodity prices may benefit its exports. The final scenarios investigate the impact of a U.S. slowdown and of rising commodities prices on Bolivia's trade flows.

Different scenarios analyzed

In the near term, the Bolivian economy is likely to be affected by three types of trade-related shocks, as noted above:

- trade policy changes in its key trading partners
- progress in regional or sub-regional integration process
- changes in global economic prospects.

While the scenarios analyzed do not cover all the possible developments facing Bolivia,[8] they do offer informative criteria of the likely (relative) order of magnitude of the potential economic consequences of important trade-related developments.

SCENARIO 1: NONRENEWAL OF ATPDEA

If the preferences are not renewed, Bolivia may still enjoy preferential access to the U.S. market on a number of products under the Generalized System of Preference (GSP), for which all developing countries are eligible, and which is less generous and covers much fewer products than the ATPDEA.[9] A worse-case scenario is the loss of all preferences, and a reversal to a Most Favored Nation (MFN) treatment of Bolivian exports by the United States. This scenario assumes that the counterfactual of a nonrenewal of the ATPDEA would be for Bolivia to face MFN tariffs. However, even at the MFN level, U.S. tariffs are still relatively low, averaging 5 percent for agricultural and food products and 2 percent for all other nonagricultural products.

SCENARIO 2: RATIFICATION OF U.S.-PERU AND U.S.-COLOMBIA FTAS

By definition, these agreements are preferential and thus discriminatory. The economic evidence exposes the negative effects of these types of trading blocs on excluded non-member countries.[10] As an "innocent bystander" to these agreements, Bolivia is likely to be hurt, especially because of the participants being important export destinations for Bolivian products. The main channels are through a dilution of preferences in U.S. markets, or through more intense competition from U.S. exporters in Peruvian and Colombian markets. The simulation quantifies both effects. While the FTAs do not grant any significant additional market access for Peru and Colombia into the U.S. market—above what they already benefit from with the ATPDEA—the FTA may bring more U.S. products in these two countries. This may ultimately affect Bolivian producers through increased smuggling of merchandise, bypassing the customs system.

SCENARIO 3: REALIGNMENT OF BOLIVIA'S TARIFF SCHEME TO CAN COMMON EXTERNAL TARIFF

Since April 2008, Bolivia has aligned its tariff schemes with those of the common external tax of CAN countries. This would imply an increase of import duties for almost 2,000 products with respect to the current (2007) tariffs regime. This is likely to further distort economic incentives. As this policy discriminates against non-CAN regional trade, it may lead to harmful trade diversion. The simulation quantifies the economic implications of this policy by using the new import tariff scheme resulting from Bolivia's recent increase of its imports duties.

SCENARIO 4: FURTHER INTEGRATION WITH MERCOSUR

Bolivia is an associate member of MERCOSUR. The four MERCOSUR countries were recently granted associate membership to the CAN. While quite extensive preferences are granted to goods circulating in the CAN-MERCOSUR region, substantial barriers (albeit much lower than the MFN rates) remain for a large number of products. The simulation quantifies the impact on Bolivia of further economic integration with MERCOSUR by modeling a (hypothetical) complete reciprocal removal of the remaining quantifiable barriers between Bolivia and MERCOSUR.

SCENARIO 5: IMPACT OF A U.S. ECONOMIC SLOWDOWN

The IMF recently projected that global economic growth will slow to 4.1 percent in 2008, down from a 2007 estimate of 4.9 percent, and that U.S. growth will slow to 1.5 percent in 2008 from 2.2 percent in 2007. To the extent that the United States is an important market for a number of Bolivian export sectors, such a slowdown can undermine Bolivia's trade prospects and its economy. For this scenario, a counterfactual state of the world is simulated in which U.S. GDP was 1 percent lower than in the baseline.

SCENARIO 6: CHANGES IN COMMODITY PRICES

As noted in the latest Country Economic Memorandum (World Bank, 2005), Bolivian export performance in the past seems to have been driven primarily by exogenous factors beyond the control of Bolivian public policymaking. This scenario examines the responsiveness of Bolivia's export and output of soya products (soybeans and soya oil), natural gas, and other minerals to changes in world prices. These three sectors account for more than 55 percent of Bolivia's total exports.

CGE analysis of trade impact under different scenarios[11]

This section assesses the macroeconomic and sectoral effects of trade-related shocks on the Bolivian economy using a CGE model. The potential impact of various trade-related developments are quantitatively assessed for a number of economic variables, including the volume of trade in goods and services, the GDP and economic welfare, sectoral output, wages and employment across industry sectors, and the final prices paid by consumers. The main results are summarized in Table 3.2, while more detailed sectoral results are shown in the Appendix. The modeling framework is a multi-country CGE, which includes the most complete global database for trade policy analysis.[12] Boxes 3.2 and 3.3 briefly describe the modeling framework as well as its underlying database. The GTAP model used here is a static model that allows for comparisons of the global economy in two "states of the world": one (observed) in which the base values of policy instruments and other exogenous variables are unchanged, and another in which the model attained a new equilibrium after some variables were changed, or shocked, to reflect the simulation being studied. The model is thus purely static, and does not capture typical "dynamic" gains from trade, such as capital accumulation, technological changes, productivity gains, or product discovery. The model is also deterministic in that it does not account for the credibility (or lack of uncertainty) effects that may result from various trade agreements.

Table 3.2.Impact of Different Trade Policy Scenarios on Bolivia's Macro Indicators

	Scenario 1: Nonrenewal ATPDEA	Scenario 2: FTAs: Peru-U.S., U.S.-Colombia	Scenario 3: Alignment to CAN's Common External Tariff	Scenario 4: Further integration with MERCOSUR	Scenario 5: Slowdown of the U.S.
Change in rental and wage rates (%)					
Land	−0.2	-2.1	−0.5	0.1	0.1
Unskilled Labor	−0.8	−0.5	0.3	0.3	0
Skilled Labor	−0.7	−0.5	0.2	0.3	0
Capital	−0.8	−0.5	0.3	0.3	0
Natural Resources	0.7	0.9	−0.1	0.2	0.2
Change in consumer prices (%)	−0.6	−0.5	−0.1	0.1	0.3
Change in Total Exports (%)	−0.6	−0.5	−0.2	0.7	−0.2
Change in Total Exports (US$mil.)	−13	-9.4	-5	13.9	-4
Change in GDP (%)	−0.7	−0.53	−0.2	0.15	0.01
Equivalent variation (US$ mil.)	**−13**	**-8.8**	**-3.3**	**2.7**	**1.4**
Due to:					
Allocation effects	−1.6	−1	−1.7	0.1	0.7
Terms of trade	−11.4	-7.8	−1.6	2.6	0.7

Source: Andriamananjara and Valenzuela (2008) based on GTAP model and database.

Box 3.2. The GTAP Model

The GTAP model (Hertel 1997) has the advantage of being a relatively conventional, multi-region model, which is used prominently for trade analysis in national ministries, international public agencies, and academic research centers. The GTAP model has also been tested as a whole against historical experience (Valenzuela and others 2007).

We use the most standard assumptions of the model in this analysis. On the production side, we assume perfect competition and constant returns to scale. Land is specific to agriculture and has imperfect mobility among alternative agricultural uses. Labor and capital are mobile across all uses within a country and are immobile internationally. On the demand side, there is a regional representative household whose expenditure is governed by a Cobb-Douglas aggregate utility function, which allocates net national expenditures across private and government expenditure, and savings. The greatest advantage of the regional household representation is the unambiguous indicator of welfare dictated by the regional utility function. Government demand across composite goods is determined by a Cobb-Douglas function. Private household demand is represented by a Constant Difference of Elasticities functional form, which has the virtue of capturing the non-homothetic nature of private household demand. Bilateral international trade flows are handled through the Armington specification, through which products are differentiated by their country of origin. We assume a constant aggregate level of land, labor, and capital employment, reflecting the belief that the aggregate supply of factors is unaffected by trade-related shocks.

One of the advantages of using a CGE simulation is that it imposes consistency economy-wide, such as changes in sectoral factor and product demands do not exceed supply. That is, the sum of sectors' employment does not exceed the labor force and all consumption is covered by production or imports. Therefore, a CGE model provides unbiased estimates of national economic welfare, using Hicksian equivalent variation. Moreover, the comparative static analysis is based on the current trade patterns of the country, and thus permits a close-to-reality assessment of the short- to medium-term economic response to own-country trade policy changes.

The drawbacks of a standard CGE model are the absence of the creation of "new trade," new investment patterns, and productivity growth resulting from trade policy changes. It also does not account for potential technology transfers or "learning by trading" that may happen between trading partners. Results are dependent on established trade patterns in the benchmark database. Hence, results must be analyzed taking into consideration the absence of future gains derived from these potential gains to the economy. The perfect competition and constant returns to scale assumptions made in the GTAP model tend to produce conservative estimates of the impact of trade liberalization relative to models making different assumptions.

Source: Andriamananjara and Valenzuela (2008).

Box 3.3. The GTAP Database

The analysis makes use of the most complete global database for trade policy analysis, the GTAP database. In its latest release (October 2007, version 7p3), the database contains information for 105 countries/sub-regions and 57 production sectors, with a base year of 2004. In addition to the data on trade in each of the sectors between each pair of economies or regions in the model, there are data on the domestic production and use of each commodity, including the use in the production of other commodities (based on national input-output tables); the supply and use of land, labor, and capital; and GDP. The database also contains information on tariffs, some nontariff barriers, and other production and export taxes. Import tariff equivalents contained in the GTAP database for 2004 are sourced from the United Nations MAcMap database by CEPII. These protection data are maintained at the HS-6 digit level and encompass a comprehensive treatment of trade preferences as well as the conversion of specific tariffs and tariff rate quotas into their ad valorem equivalents (Bouët and others 2008). Bolivia is included in this version as an individual country, relying on information from the Supply and Use tables for 2004 from the Bolivian National Institute of Statistics (Ludeña and Telleria 2006). In order to provide reasonable detail, this analysis is conducted by focusing on an aggregation of 45 production sectors and 25 trade partners (Table A1 in Andriamananjara and Valenzuela [2008] shows the sectoral aggregation). The base tariff data for Bolivia was updated using the Bolivian Tariff Schedule 2007 collected from Bolivian Customs. The analysis also imposes zero tariffs on intra-CAN exports.

Source: Andriamananjara and Valenzuela (2008).

SCENARIO 1. NONRENEWAL OF ATPDEA

A nonrenewal of the ATPDEA is estimated to reduce Bolivian exports to the United States by almost $42 million, or 13 percent. This shock would cause a small redirection of Bolivian exports to other important markets in the Andean region, MERCOSUR, and the European Union. For example, exports to the European Union and the CAN markets would each rise by 2 percent (Table 3.3). Given the somewhat offsetting effects, the net change in total Bolivian exports would be a decline of about $14 million (less than 1 percent).

Table 3.3. Scenario 1—Impact on Bolivian Exports to Selected Partners

	Percent change	Value change in US$ million
United States	−12.6	−41.9
Brazil	0.6	1.6
Chile	1.8	1.0
Colombia	1.1	2.0
Peru	1.4	2.0
Venezuela, R. B. de	1.1	2.0
EU	1.9	6.3
Total	−0.6	−13.6

Source: Andriamananjara and Valenzuela (2008) based on GTAP model and database.

Removal of ATPDEA preferences would affect the textiles and clothing sectors most, and would trigger a redeployment of exports to other markets. The sectoral impact of a nonrenewal of the ATPDEA is highly influenced by the initial value of trade, as well as the level of the counterfactual (MFN) tariff that would be applied to replace the preferential rate. The most affected sectors would be textiles and clothing, for which the drop in exports is estimated at $6 million (12 percent) and $10 million (30 percent), respectively. Despite a relatively low alternative tariff, some manufacturing categories are also hit by a large (11 percent) fall in exports. Regarding trade markets, the analysis suggests that exports of oilseeds and vegetable oils (mainly soya-related) to the CAN economies would increase substantially.

The overall effect on GDP is modest, a 0.7 percent drop, while the overall welfare cost is estimated at $13 million, of which $11 million is due to worsening terms of trade.[13] The shock affects incentives to trade and hence output at the sectoral and aggregate levels. GDP is estimated to fall slightly, by 0.6 percent. At the sectoral level, fewer incentives would reduce export output. For instance, the domestic production of textiles and clothing is estimated to drop by 7 percent and 6 percent, respectively. As productive resources are reallocated across sectors, demand for different factors of production (land, unskilled labor, skilled labor, capital) is altered. In this scenario, as workers are released from the contracting textiles and apparel sectors, they move to such other productive sectors as transport and electronic equipments, and to oilseeds, vegetable oil, natural gas, and paper products.[14]

SCENARIO 2. RATIFICATION OF U.S.-PERU, AND U.S.-COLOMBIA FTAS

The simulations indicate that being excluded from the U.S. FTAs would have a negligible effect on Bolivian GDP. The welfare cost of the shock is small, at $9 million, driven by the worsening of Bolivia's terms of trade. A Colombia-U.S. and Peru-U.S. FTA would affect Bolivia mainly through the dilution of preferential access to CAN countries. Indeed, since the United States does not substantially grant any additional preferential access to Peru and Colombia beyond what they received under the ATPDEA, Bolivia's terms of access into that market are not likely to be reduced. But Bolivia's exports to its two Andean neighbors will face additional competition from U.S. exports as these countries preferentially liberalized with the United States.

Bolivian exports to Peru and Colombia would fall by 4 percent ($6 million) and 10 percent ($17 million), respectively. While most of these exports would be shifted to other markets, especially the United States ($5 million), the European Union ($4 million), and MERCOSUR ($3 million), the net impact on Bolivia's total export would be a very small drop ($9 million). At the sectoral level, the impact of the FTAs on domestic production closely matches the impact on exports. The production of vegetable oils (Bolivia's main export products to Peru and Colombia) would drop by almost 2 percent. Oilseeds (soya) output is dampened by two variables. First, preference dilution in the Peruvian and Colombian market reduces incentives to exports, and hence to produce. Second, as the incentives to produce vegetable oils weaken, the demand for oilseeds (which serve as the main input in oil production) would also weaken. On the whole, the production of oilseeds would shrink by almost 1.3 percent. Production of textile is expected to decline by almost 4 percent, with a 7 percent decline in exports.

Table 3.4. Scenario 2—Impact on Bolivian Exports to Selected Partners

	Percent Change	Value Change in US$ million
Ecuador	2.1	0.6
Peru	−4.0	−5.9
Colombia	−9.9	−17.4
MERCOSUR	0.8	2.9
United States	1.7	5.5
EU	1.3	4.2
Total	−0.5	−9.4

Source: Andriamananjara and Valenzuela (2008) based on GTAP model and database

Employment in the plant-based fiber and textiles sectors is most affected by the FTAs. Because of declining demand for labor in a number of important labor-intensive sectors, the equilibrium wage rate in Bolivia is expected to fall slightly following the establishment of the FTAs. Employment would increase in a few sectors, such as metal products and a number of manufacturing sectors. The decline in the production of oilseeds and soya-related products would lead to a decline in the demand for land, which would lower the rental rate for that production factor.

SCENARIO 3. ALIGNMENT OF BOLIVIA'S TARIFF SCHEME TO CAN COMMON EXTERNAL TARIFF

Adoption of the CAN CET would entail an increase in Bolivia's import tariffs in a number of important sectors, as well as a "complication" of its simple uniform tariff schedule. [15] For those sectors with increased tariffs (oilseeds, clothing, and leather products), imports are expected to decrease. On the other hand, many sectors would have their tariffs on non-CAN members decreased—for these, imports would likely increase. On balance, total Bolivian imports are expected to rise slightly, by $15 million (0.56 percent). The changes are small at the sectoral level: Imports of the category-machinery and equipment, and the category chemical, rubber, and plastic are the most affected, with imports increasing by 7 percent and 6 percent, respectively.

The increase in tariff protection in some sectors could generate an "anti-export bias" in Bolivia's incentive structure. That is, as a result of increased protection, productive resources tend to shift to the newly protected import-competing sectors, and away from exporting ones. Furthermore, exporting firms would face higher production costs from imported inputs. In particular, the vegetable oil sector is among the most affected (with exports and output declining by $5 million and $7 million, respectively) following a ($6 million) decline in soya import. Overall, Bolivian total exports will be $5 million lower than in the baseline following the CET adoption.

At the macro level, the impact of adopting the CET is relatively small. The net aggregate impact on national welfare is a decline of $3.3 million, which is equally divided between a negative allocative efficiency effect and deterioration in the terms of trade. GDP is estimated to drop slightly by 0.3 percent. The effect on GDP is a very small reduction, as well on wage rates.[16]

SCENARIO 4: DEEPER INTEGRATION WITH MERCOSUR

Further integration into MERCOSUR would increase trade flows. The potential increase in exports from improved access to the MERCOSUR market is estimated to be $14 million (0.7 percent). This relatively modest effect owes to the fact that Bolivia already enjoys favorable access to the MERCOSUR market. The main export impacts are concentrated in a few sectors in which MERCOSUR tariffs are relatively important; sectoral level, machineries, motor vehicles and parts, metal products, and paper products would experience double-digit export expansion.

Since Bolivia is also already providing some preference to imports from MERCOSUR, the extent of further import liberalization by Bolivia is limited. On the whole, more trade is created than diverted, and total Bolivian imports are expected to increase by $25 million (1 percent). Imports of leather products, meat, and sugar would expand significantly as a result of the policy experiment.

At the macro level, the impact of further integration with MERCOSUR is relatively small. A full removal of bilateral trade taxes between Bolivia and MERCOSUR countries yields a limited change (0.15 percent in GDP). The deal would also yield a small welfare gain equivalent to $2.7 million (driven by the improved terms of trade attributable to better access to the MERCOSUR market).

SCENARIO 5. SLOWDOWN IN THE U.S. ECONOMY

The overall impact of a slowdown in the U.S. economy on Bolivia's economy is relatively low. The main channel through which Bolivia would be affected is on the export side. Bolivian exports to the United States can be expected to decline for all the sectors in the model. But the magnitude of these declines tends to be very small. The reasons for the low impact are that the United States accounts for just 10 percent of Bolivia's total exports; the assumed decline in U.S. growth itself is small;[17] and that a substantial fraction of exports to the United States are primary products, for which demand tends to be highly inelastic. The most affected sectors would be manufactures, transport equipments, clothing and wood products. Nonetheless, although the United States are an important trading partner for Bolivia, important export commodities such as soya products or natural gas are mainly destined for neighboring economies and are not really affected by the U.S. slowdown.

At the aggregate level, exports to the United States would drop by $4.2 million (1.3 percent), which would lead to a $4.2 million (0.2 percent) decline in total exports. Owing to decreased demand in the U.S. economy, U.S. products that were previously destined for the U.S. domestic market are being shifted to other export markets (including Bolivia). As a result, Bolivia's imports would rise slightly (0.11 percent). The experiment does not yield any significant changes in Bolivia's GDP (about 0.01 percent).

SCENARIO 6. CHANGES IN WORLD PRICE OF MAJOR EXPORT COMMODITIES

The responsiveness of Bolivian sectoral output and exports to changes in the world price for Bolivia's key exports commodities: soya (oilseeds), soya oil (vegetable oil), natural gas, and minerals are investigated.[18] For all four considered sectors, the impact on GDP is positive but limited (less than 0.05 percent). The main results are presented in Table 3.5. Gas production and exports are shown to be rather inelastic to changes in world price. This is consistent with the production technology and production structure of gas extraction. If the world price of natural gas rises steadily, then Bolivia would expand its exports and output by 6 percent ($13 million) and 4 percent ($13 million), respectively.

Table 3.5. Impact of a Hypothetical 10 Percent Increase in the World Price in Selected Commodities

	Sectoral export (%)	Sectoral export (US$ mil.)	Sectoral output (%)	Sectoral output (US$ mil.)	GDP (%)	Equivalent variation (US$ mil.)
Soya	23.12	9.87	23.31	117.55	0.04	124.61
Vegetable oils	28.11	151.07	25.58	151.51	0.03	89.8
Gas	5.78	12.91	4.37	12.73	0.03	38.13
Minerals	16.38	47.89	8.26	40.56	0.02	29.56

Source: Andriamananjara and Valenzuela (2008) based on GTAP model and database.

The other three sectors (soya, soya oil, and minerals) tend to be more elastic to changes in world prices. For instance, an increase in the price of soya and soya oil is estimated to lead to a sectoral export and output increase of more than 20 percent. Furthermore, there appear to be strong intersectoral linkages: the 25 percent production increase in vegetable oil attributable to a rise in world price also leads to an 18 percent increase in soya production, but a 13 percent decline in soya exports.[19]

An increase in the world price of minerals is estimated to raise Bolivia's exports and output by 16 percent ($48 million) and 8 percent ($41 million), respectively. Among the four sectors, this is the one that leads to the most modest GDP and welfare impact.

Conclusions and Policy Implications

The simulated effects tend to be modest, especially at the macro level. This is partly because of the specifications of the model, which do not take into account such dynamic potential gains from trade as attracting investment or increasing production and trading. There may, however, be a number of valid reasons to believe that the economy-wide impacts of the considered scenarios would be relatively small. For example, the existing levels of tariff protection being imposed (for example, in the case of nonrenewal of the ATPDEA) or liberalized (for example, in the case of MERCOSUR, or U.S.-Peru/U.S.-Colombia FTAs) are low, limiting the impact. In some case (for example, the U.S. slowdown), the simulated shock is itself small and does not significantly affect the key Bolivian export sectors.

The reported results help increase understanding of the relative importance of the different experiments. For instance, the exercise reveals that the losses from a nonrenewal of the ATPDEA preferences to U.S. markets are relatively more important than those from the U.S. FTAs with Peru and Colombia, or from the CET adoption. In terms of exports, a nonrenewal of the ATPDEA decreases Bolivia's exports by about $13 million, while further integration in MERCOSUR would increase them by $14 million.

The experiments are also useful in identifying the sectoral distribution of the effects of each scenario. The loss of ATPDEA would affect mainly clothing and textile exports, the U.S. FTAs with other Andean economies influence exports of oilseeds and vegetable oil, and the effects of an FTA with MERCOSUR would be concentrated in the manufacturing sectors (such as machinery, motor vehicles and parts, and paper products). The analysis also finds that exports and output of natural gas are inelastic to changes in the world price, while those of soya-based products are highly responsive.

The prospects for exploiting the potential gains from trade may lay in the "nontariff" areas, given that the estimated impact of these "tariff-based" experiments is rather limited and that Bolivia's geography as a land-locked country with extensive borders. For example, it may be more important to reduce the costs of trading, in terms of document processing and actual transportation costs. By pursuing trade-facilitating investment mechanisms, Bolivia's tradability would be enhanced, and so too would be opportunities for gains from further trade liberalization. Moreover, our modeling ignores services trade reform (because of the lack of data). Yet, such reform may yield significant gains, not only directly via the services sector but also indirectly through lowering the cost of backbone services inputs into goods production and exports.

Box 3.4. Methodology Used for the Partial Equilibrium Analysis of the Impact on Employment

The model is based on the "Armington assumption" in which products are differentiated by country of origin, generating monopolistic competition between differentiated national varieties. Consumer preferences have a nested structure that allows to apply "two-stage budgeting," the upper-stage allocation being between goods (such as shirts) and the lower-stage between national varieties of those goods (such as Bolivian vs. Mexican shirts).

The trade analysis follows the traditional Vinerian approach and distinguishes between trade-creation and trade-diversion effects. The magnitude of the former is determined by interaction between the price elasticity of the exporter's supply, μ_k^{BOL}, [a] and that of the importer's demand, ε_k^{US}. [b]

The estimation procedure follows the steps:

(i) Replacing tariff-free treatment for eligible (and preference-requesting) Bolivian exports by GSP treatment at the U.S. border;
(ii) Generating the implied changes in trade flows using a highly disaggregated partial-equilibrium framework; and
(iii) Calculating the long-run employment effect of these variations in trade values onto sectoral employment using the panel estimates.

Notes:
a. The elasticity estimates are from Kee, Nicita and Olarreaga (2006), kindly shared by Marcelo Olarreaga.
b. The magnitude of the latter is determined by interaction between the exporter's elasticity of supply, again, and the importer's elasticity of substitution. No reliable estimates of elasticities of substitution are available at the product level so the conventional approach is to use a plausible across-the-board value.

Partial Equilibrium Analysis: Impact of Different Scenarios on Employment and Trade[20]

This section looks at the effect of various trade shocks on job creation using partial equilibrium analysis, which—in contrast to the CGE methodology—allows us to focus on the effects of different trade shocks for specific sectors of activity. The analysis considers four scenarios: the nonrenewal of ATPDEA preferences, the establishment of a reciprocal Bolivia-U.S. FTA, the signing of FTAs by the United States with Peru and Colombia, and a deepening of the MERCOSUR integration. The results indicate that exports have not been a main source of employment in Bolivia, except for the soya-based food industry, and that the different scenarios show limited impact on employment.

SCENARIO 1. NONRENEWAL OF THE ATPDEA

The analysis suggests that the elimination of the ATPDEA would decrease Bolivian exports to the United States by 20 percent, but overall exports by only 3 percent. Bolivia loses about $16 million in textile and apparel (the largest loss) and $5 million in food products. The total loss is $32.8 million. The effect of the elimination is more important for some products, such as jewelry and tin. A scatter plot of post-ATPDEA elimination against initial exports to the United States (Figure 3.7) shows that most values are along or close to the diagonal, which is the "no-change" locus. However, some exports values are highly skewed, such as the exports of jewelry and tin those dominate Bolivia's U.S.-bound trade.[21]

Figure 3.7. Change in Exports to the U.S. Attributable to the Elimination of ATPDEA

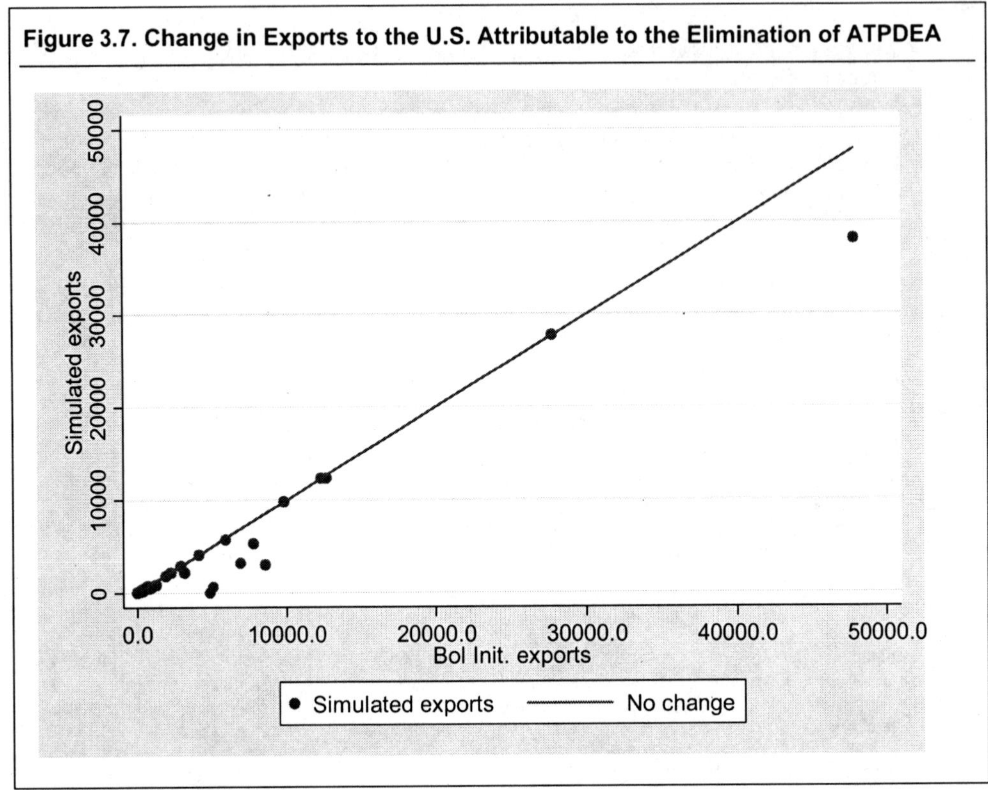

Source: Authors' calculations.
Notes: Export values are in US$ thousands.

The overall effect of the trade shock on employment is small, with the textile and apparel sector most affected (Table 3.6). The effect on the textile and apparel sector is 1.9 percent of initial employment. But because the employment data cover only the manufacturing sector, the trade shock's simulated effect on employment can be evaluated only for that sector.[22] The low impact of the nonrenewal of ATPDEA is in large measure due to low utilization rates of preferences, as discussed in Chapter 1.

Scenario 2. Transformation of ATPDEA into a Reciprocal FTA

A reciprocal FTA would eliminate tariffs on U.S. imports and modestly increase imports from the United States. The simulated rise in imports from the United States adds up to $8.75 million—2.9 percent of initial imports from the United States and 0.4 percent of overall initial imports. The small size of the shock reflects the fact that Bolivia's MFN tariffs are low and the United States accounts for only about 15 percent of Bolivia's imports. By comparison, Argentina, Brazil, and Chile together account for about three quarters of Bolivia's imports.

Table 3.6. Trade and Employment Effects of ATPDEA Elimination

ISIC 3 code		Bolivian exports (thousand US$) to U.S.				US tariffs		Export variation		Employment variation	
		To world	Total	Eligible to ATPDEA	Shipped under ATPDEA	MFN	ATPDEA	Value (US$ ooo)	Percent of initial exports	Initial number of employees	Variation (% of initial employment)
311	Food products	399,648	5,140	5,133	0	6.1	0.3	-4,896	-95.2	11,302	-0.09
312	Food products	10,731	1,923	1,923	0	5.5	0.0	-131	-6.8	-	-
313	Beverages	775	151	151	0	5.8	1.1	-43	-28.8	5,752	0.00
314	Tobacco	0	0	0	0	6.0	0.0-	-		195	0.00
321	Textiles	14,587	379	168	18	7.1	3.6	-21	-5.6	4,000	0.00
322	Wearing apparel exc. footwear	38,566	26,246	26,246	3,808	10.2	0.4	-16,000	-61.0	1,751	-1.92
323	Leather products	22,893	841	841	718	6.0	0.7	-177	-21.0	948	-0.04
324	Footwear exc. rubber or plastic	377	22	22	0	12.4	0.0	-5	-20.6	1,107	0.00
331	Wood products except furniture	44,225	25,267	15,315	0	5.3	1.3	-562	-2.2	2,502	-0.05
332	Furniture except metal	15,795	6,929	2	0	1.3	0.3	0	0.0	1,958	0.00
341	Paper and products	2,731	18	18	0	2.9	1.5	0	-1.5	3,297	0.00
342	Printing and publishing	600	75	68	0	4.0	3.1	-15	-20.0	3,321	0.00
351	Industrial chemicals	14,334	1,486	1,486	0	4.4	0.7	-266	-17.9	253	-0.22
352	Other chemicals	2,365	0	0	0	4.1	1.4-	-		2,604	0.00
353	Petroleum refineries	4,176	1,270	1,270	0	3.9	2.5	-439	-34.6	760	-0.12
354	Miscellaneous products	0	0	0	0	3.8	3.3-	-		-	-
355	Rubber products	80	4	4	0	4.1	2.1	0	-4.1	114	0.00
356	Plastic products	2,581	312	257	0	5.3	0.0	-17	-5.5	2,803	0.00
361	Pottery china earthenware	168	22	22	0	4.3	0.0	-1	-4.5	5	-0.04
362	Glass and products	2,363	70	70	0	5.7	0.0	-6	-8.1	475	0.00
369	Other non-metal. min. prod.	2,173	427	393	0	3.5	1.1	-100	-23.4	4,001	-0.01
371	Iron and steel	2,026	3	3	0	3.2	0.8	0	-4.7	313	0.00
372	Non-ferrous metals	75,265	34,166	6,079	0	1.6	0.0	-230	-0.7	-	-
381	Fabricated metal products	1,739	114	114	0	2.6	0.0	-3	-2.6	1,411	0.00
382	Machinery except electrical	7,994	1,618	707	0	1.2	0.4	-35	-2.2	328	-0.02
383	Machinery electric	5,929	591	570	0	2.8	0.8	-35	-5.8	715	-0.01
384	Transport equipment	20,110	1,041	974	0	1.8	0.1	-22	-2.1	398	-0.01
385	Prof. & scientific equip.	2,209	265	257	0	2.1	0.2	-7	-2.6	105	-0.01
390	Other manufactured prod.	50,789	48,433	48,283	0	2.9	0.3	-9,802	-20.2	950	-2.17
Total		*745,230*	*156,812*	*110,377*	*4,544*			*-32,814*	-20.9	*51,368*	*-0.13*

Source: Authors' calculations. See Cadot and Molina (2008)

The effects vary by industry and are dominated by machinery, textile and apparel, and food products. Machinery ($1 million), textile and apparel ($1.6 million), and food products ($1.2 million) record the largest increases in absolute value. Taken together, these products account for about half of Bolivia's imports from the United States, but only 9 percent of its total imports. In terms of relative increase, footwear, textile and apparel, and sugar are the steepest. However, these products account for less than 1 percent of Bolivia's imports from the United States.[23] The industries experiencing a negative (though very modest) change in employment are food products, textiles, apparel, chemicals, and machinery; and those expanding the most were the U.S. export categories. Indirect export expansion effects are very modest—a mere $2.2 million, even assuming total market access.

SCENARIO 3. RATIFICATION OF U.S.-PERU, U.S.-COLOMBIA FTAS

Trade diversion effects attributable to enhanced competition of U.S. products on Andean markets are more substantial. The most notable effect is a trade diversion owing to enhanced competition posed by U.S. products on Andean markets. Such FTAs would not necessarily involve much trade diversion on the Andean side. The total loss is $4.9 million. Change is largely confined to food products on the Colombian market, which is an outlet for Bolivian soybeans. Export and employment changes are again negligible. This study assumes unchanged market access for Bolivia's products to Andean countries, as tariffs are already zero and nontariff barriers are unlikely to be significantly affected in the short run

CONCLUDING REMARKS ON THE IMPACT ON EMPLOYMENT

Partial-equilibrium simulation results for the four scenarios show that the trade shock is in all cases very small. The simulations reflect the choice of elasticity values, underestimating results if the elasticity of supply is too low.[24] As such, the trade diversion effects identified are large rather than small. The transmission of those effects to employment data on long-run relationships and short-run effects are quite small.

The evidence indicates that redesigning the incentives of preferential trade arrangements with the United States could have a greater effect for Bolivia. Experience in other parts of the world suggests that when well-designed preferences can generate new exports—such as textile and apparel for some sub-Saharan African countries under the U.S. African Growth and Opportunity Act (AGOA)—that were not even part of those countries' initial "portfolio" of exports. This is probably the most relevant source of underestimation of the trade and employment effects of preferences. But for U.S. preferences to affect Bolivia in a way comparable to AGOA, they would have to be drastically redesigned with a relaxation of rules of origin comparable to AGOA's special regime so as to induce both a better use of preferences and a potential effect on FDI in Bolivia. This might be an important topic for Bolivia in the ATPDEA's renewal negotiations.

Partial Equilibrium Analysis: Impact on Poverty under Different Trade Shock Scenarios[25]

We now look at the effect of various trade shocks on poverty using partial equilibrium analysis, with the same four scenarios as in the previous section. See Box 3.5 for Methodology and Box 3.6 for an overview of Poverty from the Household survey.

Box 3.5. Measuring Income Changes for Households Resulting from a Trade Shock

Trade shocks affect individual households through two channels: earnings and the cost of living. We trace the transmission of trade shocks through these two channels with a multi-step methodology that combines simulation and econometrics. The first step analyzes both transmission channels (earnings and cost of living) by using a partial-equilibrium model to track the effects of tariff changes on the value, volume, and unit value (that is, price) of exports and imports, product by product, at a disaggregated level (1,000 goods). The analysis takes two routes.

- For cost-of-living effects, we use a household survey to characterize the expenditure basket of households, differentiating them by income level and indigenous status. So-called "first-order" effects (which do not take account of the rebalancing of consumption baskets triggered by price changes) are obtained by feeding price changes into household expenditure data. Summing these changes over all goods for each household gives the change in real income generated by the price shock on the expenditure side.
- For earnings effects, the analysis is different in agriculture vs. manufacturing. For agriculture, the methodology is the same as that used for the calculation of expenditure effects except that we apply the price changes on the basket of farm *sales* rather than expenditures. The second step uses panel-data to assess how changes in export and import volumes translate into employment changes at the industry level for households employed in the manufacturing sector. The estimated coefficients can be thought of as long-run elasticities of employment to trade. A trade shock can then be translated into the creation or destruction of *n* jobs in each industry.

The third step estimates simultaneously how household (HH) income varies with the household head's individual characteristics, and the probability, for each household, of being employed vs. unemployed. The effect of HH head characteristics on HH income depends on whether the HH head is employed or unemployed. In a fourth step, we rank employed HHs by decreasing order of their probability of being unemployed, on the basis of their individual characteristics. Typically, low-education households rank high, meaning they are vulnerable to job destruction.

When steps 1 and 2 indicate that a trade shock destroys, say, *n* jobs, we allocate the job-destruction across employed households on the basis of their probability of being unemployed. When the shock creates manufacturing jobs, the procedure is similar but slightly more complex since switching from unemployment or from an existing job to manufacturing employment involves a choice which must be modeled.

The final step brings together cost-of-living and earnings effects to calculate overall real-income changes for all households and aggregate these changes across households to obtain the trade shock's effect on the poverty headcount and poverty gap.

Box 3.6. Poverty in the 2005 Household Survey

About two-thirds of Bolivia's population is in poverty, of which half are in extreme poverty.[a] As in most low-income countries, poverty affects rural households more than urban ones, with poverty rates of 80 percent and 53 percent, respectively. Poverty is also unevenly spread geographically. Of Bolivia's three ecological regions (the Altiplano, the Valley, and the Plain) the poorest is the Altiplano, where farmers are isolated from world markets by difficult terrain and poor infrastructure. Poverty and remoteness translate into low use of fertilizers and low productivity, creating a vicious circle of poverty. As a result, the rate of self-consumption is highest in the Altiplano—the expenditure budget for the poor is dominated by food. By contrast, the share of export-oriented agriculture is highest in the Plain, which produces most of the country's output of soybeans. Poverty also affects ethnic groups differently. The indigenous population represents about 60 percent of the population and is generally poorer,[b] less educated, less urbanized, and more heavily affected by unemployment. The probability of being unemployed is 24.5 percent for indigenous against 21.3 percent for nonindigenous people.[c] Considering the entire labor force, these numbers fall to 3.9 for indigenous and 7.1 for nonindigenous.

Notes:

a. See Lara and Soloaga (2007).

b. Average income is almost twice as large, at Bs. 1,975 for nonindigenous people vs. 1,018 for indigenous ones

c. These unemployment probabilities were calculated using a sample of manufacturing workers and unemployed people so they should not be compared to unemployment rates.

The analysis indicates that ATPDEA's elimination or transformation into a reciprocal FTA would have almost no effect on poverty in Bolivia. The main reasons are:

- The little scope for improvements in market access from tariff reductions only, since Bolivia already enjoys tariff-free access on the U.S. market.
- The rate of utilization of U.S. preferences where they could matter (in textiles and apparel) is very low.
- Bolivia's preferential liberalization could have only very small effects given the limited number of products that the United States exports to Bolivia and the small volumes involved.

Scenario 1. Nonrenewal of the ATPDEA

Replacing duty-free status by MFN status for Bolivian exports to the United States triggers a reduction in the dollar value of Bolivian exports.[26] In a partial-equilibrium setting, the effects are more concentrated. In the manufacturing sector, the trade shock affects industry wages and employment. This simulation is restricted to employment effects, owing to data limitations to estimate wage pass-through equations.[27] In the agricultural sector, the trade shock affects income from the production of cash crops.[28]

The end of the ATPDEA is estimated to lead to a reduction of 0.13 percent in manufacturing employment. The textile and apparel sector would be the most affected, with a 2 percent drop.[29] The very small effect is due to low preference utilization rates. Hence, the loss of preferential status only applies to those exports that requested preferences in the first place, which is very limited. As these utilization rates have been consistently low since 2000, the loss of preferential status is barely perceptible. If the baseline manufacturing employment is assumed to be 50,000 jobs (Box 3.1), the number of individuals losing their jobs as a result of the ATPDEA's termination is very small—about a hundred—and the aggregate income loss is negligible. A "smoother regression curve" estimate supplies no evidence that the income changes resulting from the trade shock are more positive for the wealthier part of the population than for the poorer.[30] For the agricultural sector, the income effects were estimated to be negligible because of the extremely small price effect that resulted from the tariff shock.

Scenario 2. Transforming the ATPDEA into a Reciprocal FTA

The transformation of the ATPDEA into a reciprocal FTA has a very small effect on the import side. Bolivia's MFN tariffs are generally low (about 10 percent) and the United States represents barely 15 percent of its imports, with many zero trade lines. So even assuming an infinite elasticity of U.S. supply to Bolivia, the effects are very small. But the analysis does not consider action at the extensive margin, that is, if the United States starts to export products that it currently does not export to Bolivia. An FTA would also have a very small effect on consumption, and the effect shows no correlation with an individual's status as indigenous (Table 3.7)

Table 3.7. FTA: Simulated Expenditure Change

	Total	Indigenous	Nonindigenous
Change in percentage terms	−4.0	−4.2	-3.7
	(0.001)	(0.001)	(0.001)
No. observations	4,047	2,417	1,630

An FTA with the United States is not likely to boost Bolivian exports to the United States. Bolivia already enjoys duty-free access on the U.S. market except for ATPDEA's exceptions, but in 2002 these exceptions were reduced relative to the ATPA vintage 1991. As a result, improvements in market access for Bolivian producers would be very limited. The only substantial effect comes from trade diversion on Andean markets.

SCENARIO 3. RATIFICATION OF U.S.-PERU, U.S.-COLOMBIA FTAS

Soybean exports to Colombia are the most affected by the signing of U.S.-Peru and U.S.-Colombia FTAs. The change, relative to the current arrangement, is that U.S. products are granted tariff-free access, which means added competition for Bolivian products. The only product where this trade-diversion effect is substantial is soybeans, for which Colombia is a significant outlet. Simulations suggest that Bolivia would lose about $4 million in sales of soybeans to Colombia if Colombia signed an FTA with the United States. The export reduction on Andean markets represents a loss of 2.5 percent of Bolivia's initial exports. With an export elasticity of 3.5, this translates into a 0.7 percent decrease in the price of Bolivian soybeans. Income changes for soybeans exporters owing to trade diversion in soybeans on the Colombian market are minimal. Consumption effects could not be calculated since data on soybean consumption are not available. In manufacturing, there is almost no effect for the same reason: market access is unchanged.

SCENARIO 4. DEEPENING INTEGRATION WITH MERCOSUR

Estimates indicate that deepened integration with MERCOSUR would result in a modest increase in poverty. The overall results from MERCOSUR integration are modest. With the income decrease caused by job loss and the decrease in the prices of agriculture products, only a small number of households switch status from non-poor to poor and, as a consequence, the poverty headcount increases slightly by 1.2 percentage point. There is no evidence that changes in poverty incidence are different for indigenous and nonindigenous people. The poverty gap index indicates an increase in poverty intensity that is more evident among indigenous households.[31] The estimated effects of the trade shocks on poverty are shown in Table 3.8.[32]

Table 3.8. Total Effects on Poverty and Welfare-MERCOSUR Integration

	Total	Indigenous	Nonindigenous
Poverty headcount (%)			
Before the trade shock	41.8	47.4	33.1
After the trade shock	43.1	49.2	33.4
Poverty gap index (%)			
Before the trade shock	19.4	23.1	13.6
After the trade shock	20.2	24.2	13.9
Welfare change (%)	4.9	4.9	5.0

Concluding Remarks on the Impact on Poverty

The simulation results suggest that ATPDEA's elimination or transformation into a reciprocal FTA, as well as deeper MERCOSUR integration, would have virtually no effect on poverty in Bolivia. Among all the scenarios analyzed, the only substantial channel is trade diversion on Andean markets in soybeans resulting from a U.S.-Peru and a U.S.-Colombia FTA but even that effect is limited. The main reasons are:

- There is little scope for improvements in market access from tariff reductions only, since Bolivia already enjoys tariff-free access on the U.S. market and preferential low tariffs on MERCOSUR countries.
- Even if there were, the rate of utilization of U.S. preferences where they could matter (in textiles and apparel) is very low.
- Bolivia's preferential liberalization could have only very small effects given the limited number of products the United States exports to Bolivia and the small volumes involved.

As always with this kind of simulation, trade adjustments are considered at the intensive margin rather than the extensive margin—and the analysis cannot capture the signaling effects that trade agreements can have for investment. Hence, there may be scope for expanded trade in new products rather than existing ones following the trade shock. Well-designed preferences could trigger inward investment and the emergence of new export items, as the AGOA did for East Africa. But whether this occurs depends on many internal and external factors that lie beyond the scope of this paper.

Notes

[1] Annex 2.2 of this study presents the pros and cons of each methodology and the steps used.

[2] The growth section is based on contributions from Oscar Calvo.

[3] To see why, consider a one-off increase in consumption (or investment) consisting solely of imported goods. The calculation of the contribution of demand components to real GDP growth would show an increase in the contribution of consumption to growth and a decrease in the contribution of net exports to growth. But the one-off increase in consumption of imported goods had no impact on economic activity. Only if we assume that imports displace domestic

consumption would the domestic economy be affected. In any case, the negative correlation between GDP growth and the contribution to growth of net exports will necessarily arise by virtue of the GDP accounting identity: as demand components like consumption and investment increase, they will contribute to higher GDP figures but—since they have a certain 'import content'—they will also necessarily bring down the contribution of net exports.

[4] For recent examples see Dawson (2006), Love and Chandra (2005), and Awokuse (2003). Some of these include other variables such as the terms of trade, though, as discussed in the text, the issue of misspecification is not likely to be significantly reduced. More novel contributions include Awokuse (2006), and Bahmani-Oskooee and Oyolola (2007), which use cointegration coupled with bounds-testing as a way to establish causality.

[5] As Ghatak and others. (1997) maintain for the case of Malaysia.

[6] This section is based on a background paper by Cadot and Molina (2008), "Sunset over the ATPDEA: Implications for Bolivian Employment."

[7] Giussani and Olarreaga (2006).

[8] For instance, no attempt is made to analyze the prospects for an EU-Bolivia FTA. A (hypothetical) U.S.-Bolivia FTA is considered in the Partial Equilibrium Scenarios and the poverty analysis.

[9] While the ATPDEA provides duty-free access to U.S. markets for approximately 5,600 products, the GSP program covers only about 4,650 products.

[10] See Hoekman and Özden (2007).

[11] This section on CGE is based on a background paper for the study Andriamananjara and Valenzuela (2008)

[12] The static model by design does not produce information about the speed with which changes occur, about what happens to various dimensions of the economies in the meanwhile, or what may have happened to change some of the underlying dynamic structures of the economies, such as specific patterns of foreign direct investment or technological changes that may alter the future growth pattern of economies.

[13] In economic terms, national welfare can be measured by the "equivalent variation" metric. A positive figure for equivalent variation implies that the policy change would improve economic welfare. The equivalent variation of a policy change can be decomposed into allocative efficiency and terms-of-trade effects. Allocative efficiency effects derive from re-allocation of factors of production (resources) into more rentable production activities. Terms-of-trade effects relate to the relative cif/fob prices paid/received with respect to world average prices, for example, gains in terms of trade arise from an improvement in the prices received from Bolivian exports relative to the prices paid for Bolivian imports.

[14] The assumption is that the supply of factors of production is constrained, therefore expansion of one sector sometimes imply contraction of another. An expansion across all sectors is also possible when factors have been allocated efficiently in the absence of distorting policies.

[15] Compared to Bolivia's simple and uniform 2007 tariff schedule, the CAN CET scheme has 4 levels of import taxation at 5, 10, 15, and 20 percent for all tariff lines. Out of the 5,136 product lines (with non zero trade flows) in the Bolivian tariff schedule, tariffs would decline for 1,108, stay the same for 2,185, and increase for 1843, following the adoption of the CET. Moreover, (simple) average tariff would increase from 8 percent to 10 percent.

[16] Note that a true integration of CAN market may entail an elimination of the CAN's mechanism for price stabilization in agricultural products (SAFP). Some recent estimates of the extent of the protection delivered by the SAFP scheme in Colombia and Ecuador (Guterman 2008; Valenzuela and others 2007) suggest a doubling of the effectively applied tariff in agriculture as an aggregate and four- to seven-fold in some individual commodities. The results reported here focus on the impact of the adoption of CAN CET and do no address the elimination of intra-CAN barrier to

trade. It is highly likely that the elimination of the SAFP would grant Bolivia important gains in terms of trade and economic welfare.

[17] The experiment conducted here is to exogenously simulate a counterfactual state of the world in which the U.S. GDP was 1 percent lower than in the baseline.

[18] For each sector, the world demand is exogenously shocked so as to yield a 10 percent increase in the sectoral world price. The model is then used to determine the general equilibrium impact of the price increase on Bolivia's incentive to export and produce.

[19] In a separate simulation, the economic implication of the imposition 15 percent export tax on Bolivian soybean exports is studied. The use of export tax as a trade policy instrument has increased recently as a policy response to the on-going food price crisis. It is estimated that imposing a 15 percent tax on soya exports would decrease those exports by 28 percent and would increase vegetable oil export by a mere 1 percent. Output of soya would decline by 1.7 percent, while that of vegetable oil increase by 1.9 percent. An export tax on soya would decrease Bolivian GDP by a limited amount (0.06 percent).

[20] This section is based on a background paper for the study by Cadot and Molina (2008).

[21] This observation is, however, sensitive to aggregation. Once exports are aggregated at the section level, textile and clothing, where tariff preferences matter much more, is equal to base metals as an export item on the U.S. market.

[22] An analysis of the trade shock's poverty effects covering the agricultural sector is provided in the background paper Cadot and Fonseca (2008).

[23] The large size of the United States makes it possible to treat the U.S. export supply elasticity as infinite, so that the appropriate framework is SMART's "small-country" version. The analysis proceeds in three steps that parallel those of the previous, but the results must be interpreted much more carefully since the simulation results are affected by a larger uncertainty on the import side than on the export side.

[24] The mean value of the export elasticity used is 7, a high value for an export elasticity (in a small manufacturing sector like Bolivia's, bottlenecks are very likely to appear quickly). If anything, reality is likely to involve smaller supply elasticities. On the demand side, a standard elasticity of substitution (5) is used, which is probably on the high side given the substitutability between Bolivian and U.S .products on Andean markets.

[25] This section is based on a background paper for the study by Cadot and Fonseca (2008).

[26] This is modeled using SMART; see Annex 2.5 for details.

[27] Cadot and Molina (2008) treated the endogeneity of wages in the employment equation by using Blundell and Bond's system-GMM estimator.

[28] This is a contrast from the general-equilibrium setting, where the trade shock would trigger a chain of resource-reallocation effects in the domestic economy potentially affecting all wages (through Stolper-Samuelson elasticities), prices, and quantities.

[29] The very small size of our simulated effects is due to the fact that we use preference utilization rates reported by the U.S. ITC to apply the loss of preferential status only to those exports that requested preferences in the first place. Because these utilization rates have been consistently low since 2000, the loss of preferential status is barely perceptible.

[30] That is, a series of non-parametric regressions, one per observation (percentile of the income distribution), and run over samples centered on the observation in question. The curve generated is a smooth curve that can accommodate any nonlinear relationship between the variable plotted on the horizontal axis (income centiles) and that on the vertical axis (income change due to the trade shock). If it is upward-sloping, the change is regressive (more positive for richer centiles than for poorer), and vice versa. The curve is flat, suggesting no bias either way.

[31] This is similar to the finding using the CGE approach. However, export expansion is much smaller than under GTAP analysis, as the partial equilibrium analysis here covers only manufacturing, and export expansion is likely to be in soya products.

[32] The poverty headcount indicates poverty incidence and is calculated as the proportion of households who are living below the poverty line. The change in the poverty headcount is obtained by putting together the income changes experienced by manufacturing workers and farm households and comparing household per capita income to the Bolivian poverty line before and after the shock. The poverty gap index, which measures the depth of poverty, is the mean distance separating the households from the poverty line (with the non-poor being given a distance of zero), expressed as a percentage of the poverty line. Adapting from the methodology described by McCulloch (2005), we combine the income effects from manufacturing and agriculture and the consumption effects to get an approximation of the percentage change in welfare resulting from the trade shocks.

Annex 3.1. Transports and Logistics

Border Control Management and Other Customs Issues

The following section is the result of field research by a Bank team to gather information on the functioning of Bolivia's border control management. Bolivian Customs—*Aduana Nacional de Bolivia* (ANB) has 11 border stations: four with Chile, three with Argentina, and four with Brazil. Working hours vary in accordance with the traffic volumes, but even Tambo Quemado (the border crossing en route to Arica port and the second busiest) has only one shift, 8 a.m. to 8 p.m. with 2 hours off for lunch, midday to 2 p.m. It is open 7 days per week. At inland Customs clearance facilities, the working hours are normal office hours, Monday-Friday and Saturday morning. The shorter working hours may help explain why importers prefer to declare at the border, even in inconveniently remote locations like Tambo Quemado, rather than near their destination.

The TIT convention (*Acuerdo de Transporte Internacional Terrestre*) is the general legal instrument governing the registration of road transport operators for carrying cargo to and from Bolivia to neighboring countries. This registration can be either permanent or occasional (specific trips or short periods). Bolivia's bilateral treaty with Chile of 1904 gives Bolivia additional rights in connection with Bolivian cargo passing through the Chilean ports. Only Bolivian trucks may carry Bolivian cargo in transit to and from Arica port, whereas only Chilean trucks may carry bilateral traffic from elsewhere in Chile into Bolivia. Loaded Bolivian trucks on arrival at Arica report to the port administration. Both Chilean and Bolivian Customs have offices in the port. Cargo owners and trucking firms make their own contracts for haulage between Bolivia and the port and back, without recourse to any queuing system. It is common practice for export sales contracts to be FOB Arica.

The Ministry of Transport (MoT) is responsible for legislation and regulations governing the transit services, with the Superintendencia de Transporte responsible for enforcing the regulations, notably as regards qualifying truck firms to perform international haulage. The registry for such vehicles has hitherto been held solely in La Paz, but is now being decentralized to the five largest cities: La Paz, Santa Cruz, Cochabamba, Oruro, and Potosí. There is room for simplifying the registration process, which today involves duplication of procedures by MoT and ANB, and for extending the validity period of the authorization to operate.

The two basic documents for export by road are the DUE (*Documento Único de Exportación*), covering the purchase/sale of the cargo, and the MIC (cargo manifest), covering the contents of the truck, both modeled on the UN Standard Administrative Document. A DUE can cover a single large shipment carried by many trucks.[1] In Arica port a truck delivers the MIC/DTA (*declaracion de transporte aduanero*), as well as the waybill (*carta de porte*). In 2006 Bolivian Customs signed an agreement with Chilean Customs for the exchange of information by e-mail. It is working satisfactorily.

At Customs bonded warehouses it used to be mandatory to entrust the storage function to AADAA, a public body, which had a poor performance record. Now private partners have been brought into AADAA and it has been re-named Bolivia Port Services Administration (*Administracion de Servicios Portuarios de Bolivia*—ASPB), but it no longer has a monopoly. ANB is already operating joint inspections with Argentine customs at the Yacuiba border crossing, and is in negotiation with Peruvian customs to do likewise at Desaguadero.

Table 3.A.1. Leading Nontraditional Export Products, 2006–07

	2006			2007			
Exports (excl. minerals, oil and gas)	**Volume (000 tons)**	**Value (US$ mln.)**	**Share of value**	**Volume (000 tons)**	**Value (US$ mln.)**	**Share of value**	**Value Growth Rate**
Soya & derivatives	1,417	350	*32%*	1,274	378	*29%*	*8%*
Food products	165	74	*7%*	200	108	*8%*	*46%*
Wood & wood products	123	87	*8%*	137	99	*8%*	*14%*
Fruits/Brazil nuts	86	70	*6%*	82	77	*6%*	*10%*
Sugar	42	NA		81	NA		
Other products	504	528	*48%*	521	648	*49%*	*23%*
Total, nontraditional	2,337	1,109	*100%*	2,295	1,310	*100%*	*18%*
Total, all products	*18,390*	*4,080*		*19,179*	*4,780*		*17%*

Source: Instituto Nacional de Estadisticas, summarized in "Exportemos," IBCE.

Annex Note

1. At Tambo Quemado the Bank team saw a 500-ton consignment of soya being hauled by 20 trucks. In the past, the first truck would not be allowed to proceed until the last had arrived and been cleared, but the inefficiency of that procedure has been recognized and the first trucks are no longer required to wait.

CHAPTER 4

Export Competitiveness and Transport Logistics

An effective system of trade and transport logistics is of paramount importance for the export performance of a landlocked country like Bolivia. The first section of this chapter addresses issues related to export competitiveness in Bolivia. Comparative analysis suggests a persistent gap in Bolivia's capacity to take advantage of international market opportunities. To understand that gap, this section investigates: (i) the incentives that exporters face, (ii) the efficiency of service providers in the economy, and (iii) the effectiveness of trade support institutions. The second section analyzes inefficiencies in current practices and institutional weaknesses related to transport and logistics, to identify ways to reduce their impact on nontraditional export performance. In addition, the section puts forward recommendations for transport logistics to help nontraditional exports reach their exporting potential. The section focuses on the commodities and markets which today account for the largest export flows.

Export Competitiveness in Bolivia[1]

Strengthening export performance in Bolivia is a multifaceted challenge and requires attention to the (i) incentives that actual and potential exporters face, (ii) the efficiency of service providers in the economy, and (iii) the effectiveness of trade support institutions. These three elements of export competitiveness are discussed in turn.

The Incentive Regime: Macroeconomic and Trade Policy

Improving export performance will require movement of resources from less productive to more productive exporting firms, as the latter expand both the range of markets into which they sell, as well as exports per market. Resource mobility will also facilitate the export of higher quality products, which will tend to a have a different input mix than traditional or lower-quality products. Resources need to be flexible enough to allow the emergence of new export activities, including in nontraditional services. Hence, a key challenge for policy makers is to ensure that land, labor, capital, and technology are moving to: (i) sectors in which the country has a long-term capacity to compete and (ii) the most productive firms within sectors. This necessitates a clear understanding of how the business environment and trade and tax policies act as incentives to investment, output, and trade decisions.

Bolivia operates a duty drawback system, which makes it possible for exporters to claim back the duty paid on inputs of exported products. This arrangement is supposed to neutralize to some extent the effects of tariff policy for exporting firms. However, there are complaints from companies that the duty refunds are delayed, that pay-outs are partial, and that application procedures are cumbersome. In the absence of a smoothly operating duty relief mechanism, export manufacturers have to produce at higher cost than if they had full and easy access to production inputs at world prices. Therefore, their competitiveness in export markets is impaired.

The economic justification for relieving export producers of duties on imported inputs rests on the principle that no indirect taxes should be levied on goods that are not destined for domestic consumption. Following this principle, there is no ground for levying import duties, for instance, on goods in international transit, or on materials and components imported for incorporation into manufactured products that are subsequently exported. The failure to relieve export producers from import duties would effectively establish a tax on exports, increase their cost, and reduce the competitiveness of domestic manufacturers in export markets (Goorman, 2003). To help exporters survive in a highly competitive economic environment, it is important that policy makers and customs managers make available through an effective administration system the full (100 percent) relief from the duty burden on industrial inputs. The implementation of duty relief regimes clearly establishes a problem of customs control, and mechanisms need to be established to ensure that claims for duty relief are legitimate and correctly executed.

Another controversial trade policy measure on the agenda in Bolivia is the introduction of temporary export restrictions and bans for a number of staple food products, including rice, sugar, maize, vegetable oil, and meat. Exports of these products are prohibited if the domestic market situation is judged to be in deficit. The measure intends to ensure that even the less well off parts of the population can afford a healthy and varied diet, and are shielded from global increases in food prices. It is questionable, however, whether the regulation of product markets and seller-buyer transactions is an appropriate means to achieve the distributional policy objective. More direct policy interventions, such as targeted transfer programs, have in other countries proven to be more effective with less adverse effects on the economy.

These bans are detrimental to Bolivia's desire to promote inclusive exports. Staple food products are often produced by small and medium-sized firms, and depriving these producers of access to international markets for their products is adversely affecting their ability to achieve economies of scale and to learn about the quality requirements in international markets. Moreover, depressing the domestic price level through the imposition of export restrictions will reduce the value that farmers and agro-processors give to their produce and, hence, reduce their incentives to maintain the existing output and quality level. International experience shows that export restrictions introduce costly distortions into the domestic economy and most often fail to achieve their industrial development or distributional objectives (Piermartini, 2004). Also, it is unclear to what extent the restrictions will simply just encourage producers to trade informally and engage in smuggling.

The Efficiency of Service Providers

In today's global economy access to efficient backbone services inputs are critical to domestic exporting firms. Firms that have to pay more than their competitors for energy, telecommunications, transport and logistics, finance and security will find it hard to compete in both the domestic and overseas markets. Export diversification into products of higher quality tends to increase the importance of these backbone services more than traditional activities. Moreover, the rapidly expanding global export of services relies heavily on the use of other services as inputs. For example, telecommunications are a critical input into call centers and other business processing activities, and transport is vital to tourism.

The telecom infrastructure in Bolivia is not well-developed, adversely affecting the country's connectivity to international markets and its prospects of taking advantage of opportunities in dynamic services export sectors, such as call centers and outsourcing (Box 4.1). The penetration of fixed and mobile telephones is somewhat below the level in all neighboring countries and Andean Community partners (except Peru). A similar situation emerges with respect to the availability of Internet services, with only Ecuador having fewer Internet users per 1,000 people (Figure 4.1).

Box 4.1. The International Market for ICT and Other Service Exports

Services accounted for 19 percent of global exports in 2005, and more than doubled from 1995 to 2006. About 7 percent of all services trade is related to communication, computer, and information services (WTO, 2007). This expansion has been driven by considerable reductions in communications, transport, and transactions costs. Many service sector activities are becoming increasingly internationalized, especially since ICT enables the production of services to be increasingly location-independent. This development has led to the globalization of services activities, with associated changes in trade, cross-border investment, and employment patterns (OECD, 2006). Moreover, demand for services has high income elasticity—services tend to expand more than proportionally as countries grow richer. With the world economy projected to continue to grow at a strong pace, the prospects for service providers and services trade look bright.

More than 80 percent of global exports of ICT-enabled services continue to originate in OECD countries. Yet, a number of developing countries have experienced very dynamic trade patterns in recent years. One development that has fuelled the growth of ICT-enabled services is the growing trend in high income countries for firms to outsource back office and information technology functions to take advantage of advanced skills and lower labor costs of specialized service providers. Most of the contracting-out is still undertaken with companies in the country of origin ("on shoring"), but cross-border arrangements ("off shoring") have been becoming increasingly common.

The aggregate potential for outsourcing to low wage locations has been estimated to reach more than 18 million jobs in 2008. Due to the limited need for direct client contact, regional knowledge, and complex interactions, IT services and packaged software are activities that are particularly amenable to being moved abroad. About 3 million jobs, i.e. 44 percent of all ICT employment, could potentially be outsourced (McKinsey Global Institute, 2005). For some location-insensitive ICT-activities, such as call centers, the outsourcing rate could reach more than 90 percent.

Source: McKinsey Global Institute, 2005.

Figure 4.1. Telecommunications Connections (Ratio for Bolivia = 100)

Internet users per 1,000 people

Venezuela
Peru
Paraguay
Ecuador
Colombia
Chile
Brazil
Bolivia
Argentina

Telephones and mobiles per 1,000 people

Venezuela
Peru
Paraguay
Ecuador
Colombia
Chile
Bolivia
Argentina

0 50 100 150 200 250 300 350 400

Source: World Bank staff based on World Trade Indicators database.

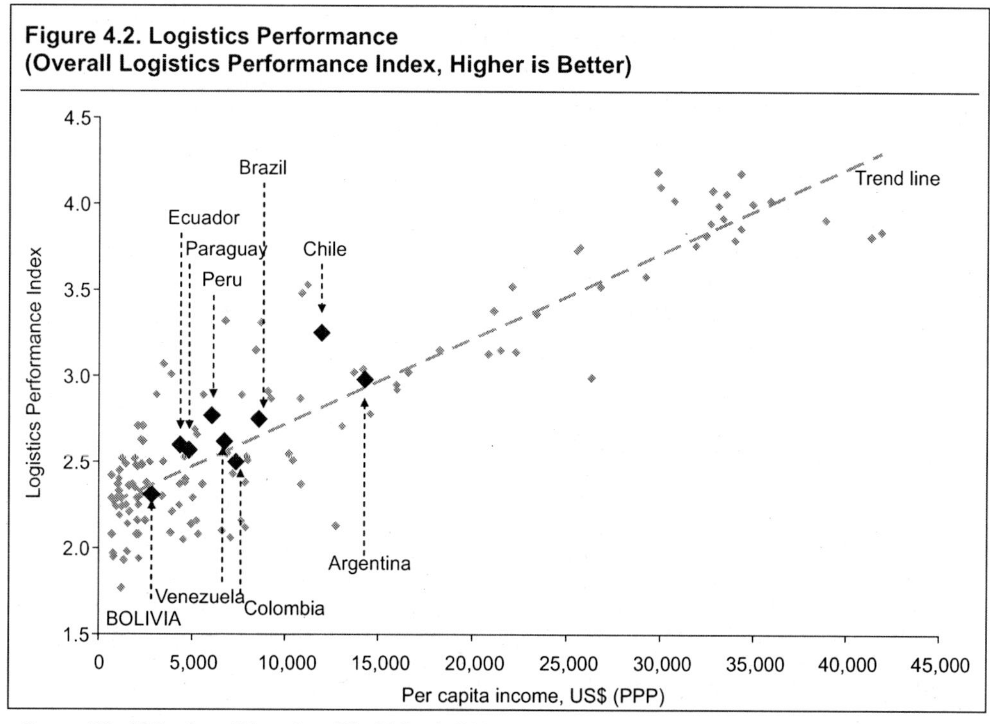

Source: World Bank staff based on World Bank (2007).

An effective system of trade and transport logistics is naturally of paramount importance for the export performance of a landlocked country like Bolivia. A newly developed Logistics Performance Index (World Bank, 2007), indicates that while most Latin American countries show results above the trend, Bolivia scores below the level of logistics performance that would be expected from its level of income (Figure 4.2). Areas of particular concern are Customs and coordination among border agencies, as well as facilitation infrastructure (see the next section of this chapter for a more detailed analysis of these issues). See Box 4.1 for a description of exports in services and Box 4.2 on the constraints to exports in services.

Box 4.2. Obstacles Limiting Exports of Services—New Survey Evidence

A survey* conducted by CEPROBOL and the International Trade Center (ITC) identified four key categories of services already being exported, in order of importance: (i) tourism; (ii) IT software; (iii) professional services such as consultancy, engineering; and (iv) call centers. Main destination markets are the United States (especially for IT), the EU, and neighboring countries like Peru and Brazil. Answers to survey questions regarding obstacles to service exporters indicate that limited knowledge of market opportunities (contacts abroad and market intelligence) is a critical factor that constrains expansion. Access to credit is also perceived to be as a major obstacle. The provision of telecom services, crucial for the activities of many services exporters, is not perceived to be an important obstacle.

Main obstacles to the exporting of services as perceived by Bolivian service exporters

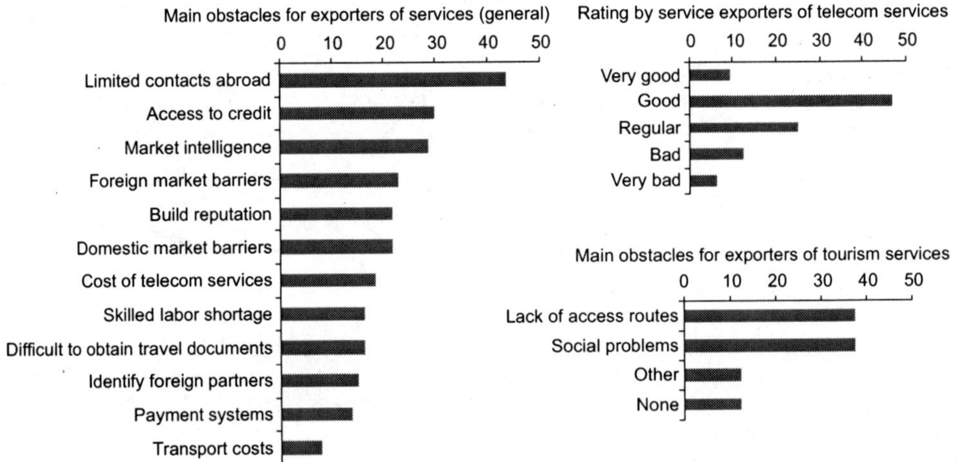

Source: CEPROBOL-ITC survey of 101 services exporters and 43 associations in La Paz, Cochabamba, and Santa Cruz.

There were, however, differences regarding perceptions about the main obstacles for services exporters across different sectors of activity. Access to credit was widely perceived to be a major obstacle among IT firms but not among those operating in the tourism sector. In the case of tourism, respondents consider that poor transport infrastructure (lack of access routes) is a key obstacle but, significantly, no more than the detrimental effect caused by social instability. Visa requirements to foreign visitors (in particular to U.S. citizens) were also noted as a limiting factor among respondents in the tourism sector. In the case of call centers, the lack of a specific regulatory framework specific that would allow for shift work was seen as a constraint for that type of activity.

(Box continues on next page)

Box 4.2 (continued)

The evidence uncovered by the CEPROBOL-ITC survey points to an already relatively diversified and dynamic base of services exports. Besides particular sector-specific issues that may need to be addressed, the key policy implications that can be drawn from the study is the need to further support Bolivian services firms to build up their capacity to identify market opportunities, and to achieve the standards of quality and reliability that will allow them to take advantage of those opportunities.

---

* M. Michel, "Estudio sobre el comercio de servicios en Bolivia," CEPROBOL-ITC, December 2007.

The Effectiveness of Trade Support Institutions

Both market and government failures tend to hamper developing countries as they seek to expand exports and growth. Laissez faire policies with low tariffs are rarely sufficient to prompt dynamic export drives or overcome obstacles in other areas. In many cases these constraints to competitiveness impinge more on higher quality and differentiated products, and require specific interventions and institutions to be overcome.

Overall, Bolivia's trade regime used to be rather liberal and subject to little government intervention. In the mid-1980s, as part of the stabilization program, multiple exchange rates were unified, tariffs were greatly simplified and reduced (capital goods pay a 0 or 5 percent tariff while consumption goods pay 10 percent) and nontariff barriers and discretionary licensing were mostly eliminated.[2] Until the recent introduction of export bans on food staples, Bolivia had no voluntary export restraints, export charges, or minimum export prices. Moreover, there are no export cartels or export quotas, aside from those negotiated within bilateral trade agreements. Policies to actively promote and boost exports have been generally focused on the following areas: (i) tax and tariffs reimbursement or suspension; and (ii) implementation of export promotion instruments and institutions. These are discussed in turn below.

Tax and tariff reimbursement authorities

Tax neutrality has been the main pillar of export policies since the mid-1980s. Bolivia applies a tax refund system and a temporary import regime with tax suspension to achieve neutrality. Several instruments were successively applied to fulfill these objectives since the mid 1980s (Candia and Antelo, 2005): *Certificado de Reintegro Arancelario* (CRA), *Certificado de Notas de Credito Negociables* (CENOCREN), *Bonos de Tesorería Redimibles* (BTR), and drawbacks and *Certificados de Devolución Impositiva* (CEDEIM). Currently, tax refund requirements are processed through CEDEIM while RITEX mechanism assures temporary import tariff suspension. CEDEIM are transferable securities negotiable on the Bolivian stock exchange that can be used to pay any tax to the customs or internal tax authorities. CEDEIM reimburses the value of tariffs, VAT and the special consumption tax (ICE) paid by traditional and nontraditional exports, but refunds require tax payments of up to 13 percent of the value of exports. Tariff refunds are automatic—for exports below $3 million the previous year with reimbursement amounting to 2 to 4 percent of the export value—or discretionary—for exports above $3 million, based on the government calculation of the industry's costs, although exporters can request a firm-specific calculation. RITEX temporarily suspends tariffs, VAT and ICE, to imported inputs used in the production process of export goods. The tax suspension applies only for 180 days and can not be requested for capital goods, fuel, hydrocarbons, or electric energy. However, RITEX is only used by a handful of exporters, which might be related to heavy administrative burdens that smaller, less frequent exporters are unwilling to shoulder.

Nevertheless, CEDEIM issuing has long delays and the RITEX use is limited. CEDEIM should be issued within no more than 35 days but, in the practice, delays run for more than eight months, affecting the exporter's competitiveness, particularly small and medium enterprises with low access to credit. These delays are caused by the high costs implied by customs exports verification, since most exports are very small—more than 90 percent of exports are below $1 million. Chronic treasury deficits were also a significant restriction until recently. In addition, there is a perception that the government considers CEDEIM as a subsidy to exporters instead of a reimbursement of taxes and tariffs that have already been paid. The government proposed to eliminate CEDEIM for extractive and forestry exports, although this proposal was not applied. Reimbursement requests are currently accumulating (Figure 4.4). Additionally, budgeted reimbursement through CEDEIMs is linked to past budgets instead of being linked to exports performance.

Figure 4.3. Gross CEDEIM Issuing and Nontraditional Exports

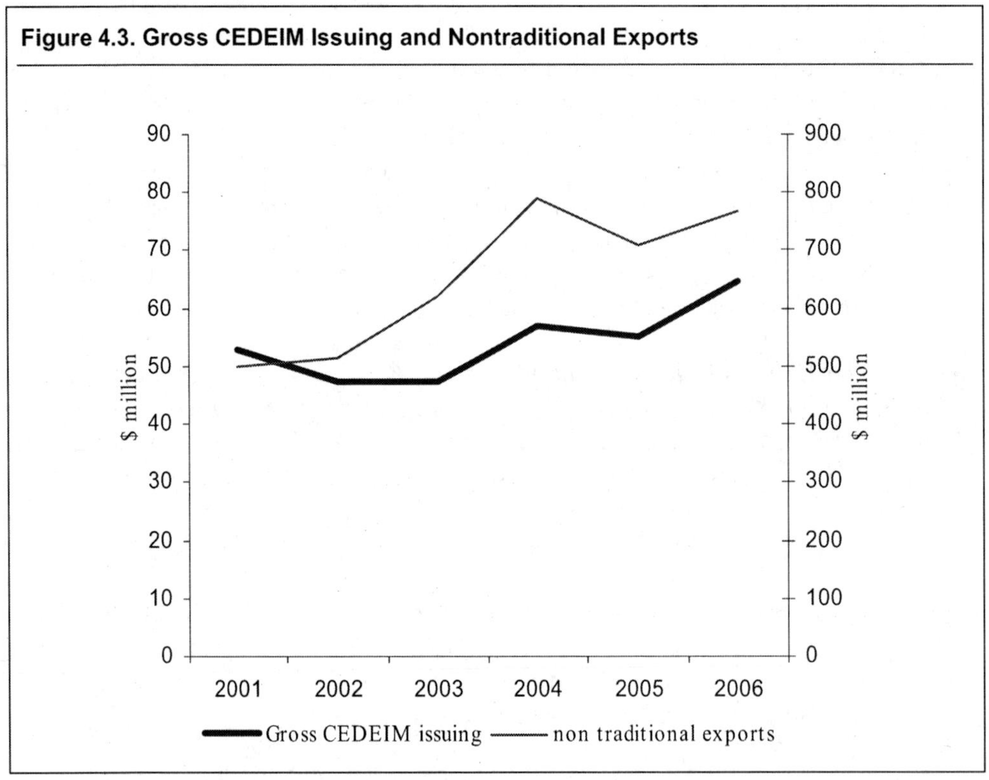

Source: UDAPE and BCB.

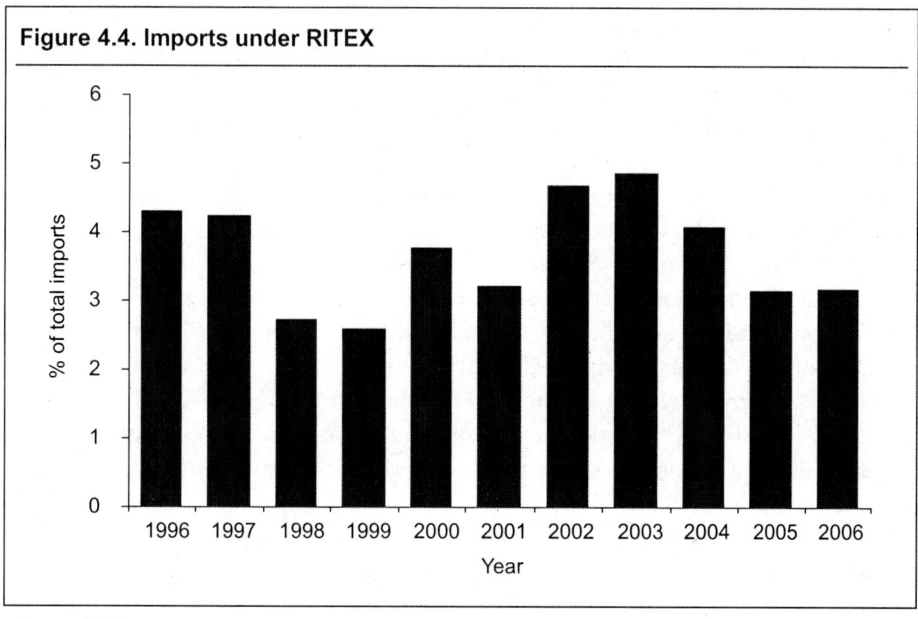

Figure 4.4. Imports under RITEX

Source: INE.

Export promotion instruments and institutions

The institutional framework supporting exports development began in the late 1980s, but it has faced difficulties consolidating. The Ministry of Exports and Economic Competitiveness (MECE), the export promotion agency (INPEX) and the one-stop shop for export procedures (SIVEX) were created in the second half of the 1980s. Those institutions were designed to, respectively, generate policies, provide technical assistance and information, and reduce red-tape. However, their dependency and competencies changed several times due to the modest outcomes attained. For instance, in late 1990, MECE was renamed Ministry of Exports, receiving more responsibilities including RITEX, SIVEX, and free trade zones management. Similarly, INPEX was renamed CEPROBOL, receiving the new responsibilities of promoting investment and tourism. The tax refund system management was transferred from the Ministry of Exports to the Finance Ministry. In this decade, the Ministry of Exports was eliminated and its competencies were transferred to the Ministry of Development and to the Ministry of Production and Micro-enterprises.

Some mechanisms to coordinate policy design and export promotion services have been launched, but they have been extremely weak. Although the line ministries formulate and execute trade policies, the National Export Council (CONEX) may suggest export promoting policies to the executive branch. This council is composed of ministries with competences in trade, and private sectors representatives. However, CONEX did not have a significant role, due to irregular meetings. Similarly, the National Council for Quality Control (CONACAL) has not been reactivated to provide information and coordinate to address issues of nontariff barriers binding exporters. The Productive Development and Export Promotion Network (REFO) was created in 2003 to support the production and competition by offering information and coordinating several related services: CEPROBOL, SIVEX, the Bolivian Institute of

Metrology (IBMETRO), the Bolivian Accreditation Body (OBA), the Bolivian Institute for Small Industries (INBOPIA), the Productivity and Competitiveness Unit (UPC), the National Intellectual Property Service (SENAPI), and the Technical Assistance Service (SAT). As REFO had only consultative attributions, proposals generated by their members were rarely implemented.

Due to CEPROBOL's institutional weakness and lack of resources, private sector institutions are providing export promotion services. CEPROBOL aims to provide technical assistance, information, and finance capacity building in the export sector. However, it has had very limited success due mainly to its very small budget, most of which is allocated to salaries, and also to inadequate institutional rearrangements. As a result, part of its role has been filled by private institutions, such as IBCE (*Instituto Boliviano de Comercio Exterior*). National Chamber of Commerce (CNC), National Chamber of Industry (CNI), and the Chamber of Exporters (CANEB) also provide technical assistance, information, and export promotion services to exporters at a regional level.

Additionally, a network of institutions supports quality and standards, but they are constrained by the legal framework and budget allocation. SENASAG controls quality and safety of imports, domestic production, and exports, while SNMAC has the objective of technically enhancing quality planning and control in production for internal and external markets, and is composed by IBNORCA, OBA, and IBMETRO. In both cases, there has been progress in developing norms for quality control and calibration services, and private firms and public institutions require accreditation to pre-established quality standards. However, the current Supreme Decree ruling the issue is insufficient to adequately define the relationship, roles, and responsibilities between SNMAC and other private quality-control institutions. Moreover, resources allocated to both SENASAG and SNMAC are insufficient to fulfill their obligations and growing demands.

The current administration is trying to re-launch the export promotion framework with emphasis on strengthening small producers. The government's main goal is to promote new markets, while strengthening existing ones, diversifying Bolivian exports and increasing added value, through fiscal incentives, financial instruments and revamped trade promotion institutions and instruments (Production and Micro-enterprises Ministry, 2007). The government is trying to re-launch REFO by including additional actors and increasing its decision-making capacity. Moreover, the government is replacing SIVEX with PAEX (*Plataforma de Atención al Exportador*), which is a comprehensive one-stop-shop for exporters opened in La Paz, following the model initiated in Cochabamba and Santa Cruz by the private sector. Complementing the PAEX initiative, the government is also designing the SIEX (*Sistema Integral de Inteligencia de Mercados para Exportadores Bolivianos*) to provide information and tendencies of export markets, including prices, procedures and external requirements. Finally, the diplomatic network is planning to implement the *Red Externa Boliviana* (REB) to attract foreign investments to export sectors and gather market information. An overarching new Exports Strategy document is in final preparation.

Other initiatives related to competitiveness and productivity are also being designed and implemented by the government, complementing export promotion activities. In an effort to build up productivity strengths among small producers and generate economies of scale, the I Buy Bolivian (*Compro Boliviano)* schema offers advantages to small producers in public procurement. It has recently been extended and revamped. An Information System for the National Market (SIM), parallel to the SIEX, is being designed. The Productive Development Bank is providing loans with lower interests and longer maturities than commercial banks to selected productive sectors which have export potential, such as textiles, manufacturing, leather, wood, food, and tourism. The government is also designing a comprehensive set of instruments to enhance small producers' productivity in the above mentioned sectors, including the *Servicio Nacional de Desarrollo Productivo* (SENADEPRO) that will provide managerial skills and technical assistance, and the Productive Clusters (*Complejos Productivos)* that intends to establish strong links among firms, both vertically and horizontally, in each prioritized sector. *Complejos Productivos* continue and extend the proposals generated in the *Sistema Boliviano de Productividad y Competitividad* (SBPC), which proposed a long-term strategy for productivity and competitiveness in early 2000. See Box 4.3 for international experiences with Export Promotion Agencies.

Box 4.3. International Experiences with Export Promotion Agencies

Most of the empirical literature that has assessed the effectiveness of export promotion agencies (EPAs) has concentrated on agencies in developed countries, although some studies with a developing country focus exist (Lederman, Olarreaga, and Payton, 2007). For example, in an influential study, Hogan, Keesing and Singer (1991) noted a number of weaknesses that impeded the performance of EPAs in developing countries. The major impediments to success concerned staffing with poorly trained civil servants who often had insufficient private sector experience, lack of incentives for staff to provide high-quality services to exporters, and excessive focus on marketing-related aspects while neglecting other supply constraints on exporters.

More recently, Alvarez (2004) provided evidence from a survey of almost 300 small-and-medium-sized exporters in Chile on the importance of an appropriate setup of export promotion efforts. He finds that the establishment of exporter committees composed of firms in similar industries to encourage cooperation in research, marketing and promotion was more likely to be successful than the organization of trade shows and trade missions.

Moreover, research by Macario (2000) in Brazil, Chile, Colombia, and Mexico suggests that cost-sharing should be used to help self-select dedicated exporters, and that any public agency support should not exceed 2-3 years in duration, that programs be subject to external review and evaluation, that EPAs should be run as public-private partnerships, and that export promotion efforts should be targeted at firms with new products or who are entering new markets. On the latter aspect, Boston Consulting Group (2004) suggest a nuance in recommending that EPAs should target firms that are "threshold" or "mature" exporters, as focusing on many small and inexperienced firms can be wasteful.

Issues for the Attention of Policy Makers

The earlier discussion highlighted a number of issues that need to be addressed in order to make better use of Bolivia's export potential. A corresponding set of policy reform priorities that warrants the attention of policy makers is listed below:

- Push within CAN for the establishment of a CET reduction schedule in order to attenuate the anti-export bias of high external tariff barriers and foster integration into international markets.
- Critically assess the effectiveness of existing export restrictions for staple food products with a view to phasing them out and thereby giving nontraditional exporters an opportunity to supply international markets.
- Expedite duty drawback refunds, pay them in full, and streamline the refund claim system in order to reduce the anti-export bias.
- Re-evaluate the institutional structure of export promotion efforts, including CEPROBOL, with a view to strengthen the involvement of the private sector, possibly through private-public-partnerships and matching grant programs.
- Undertake analytical work to assess the impact of high costs of key backbone services on the performance of small and medium-sized enterprises and benchmark the findings against the situation in comparator countries.

Transport and Logistics[3]

This section examines the issue of logistics, and in particular transportation logistics, in more detail. By all evidence, Bolivia's transport linkages from producers within the country to external markets—made all the more difficult because of the country's landlocked status and extremely dramatic terrain—are a critically binding factor inhibiting greater development of export products, especially nontraditional exports with greater value added. The first two subsections describe, in turn, main existing export routes and main modes of transportation. The next subsection presents trends and dynamics in the past decade and looking forward for the next 5–10 years, as well as a number of relevant issues and uncertainties facing the export sector. The final section concludes with policy recommendations.

Main Export Market and Export Routes

The principal markets for Bolivia's nontraditional exports are: (i) the United States and Europe, and (ii) South American neighbors, and especially Colombia, República Bolivariana de Venezuela, and Peru. The major nontraditional commodities exported today are: soya and soya derivatives, food products (including sugar, alcohol, beef, coffee and quinoa), wood and wood products, fruits (including Brazil nuts), and other products (including textiles, jewelry, and handicrafts). All categories grew in value from 2006 to 2007, by 18 percent overall. However, they account for little more than a quarter (27 percent) of total exports. Even though Bolivia is an associate member of MERCOSUR, the volumes of nontraditional exports from Bolivia to other MERCOSUR countries are small compared with those to the primary export markets.[4]

Table 4.1. Export Volumes and Values by Main Exit Points, 2005–06

	2005				2006			
	Volume (000 tons)	Value (US$ mil.)	$/ton	% of total value	Volume (000 tons)	Value (US$ mil.)	$/ton	% of total value
P Suarez, Brazil	12,162	$1,140	$94	40	13,174	$1,630	$124	50
T Quemado, Chile	461	$492	$1,067	17	528	$682	$1,292	21
Yacuiba, Argentina	2,539	$241	$95	8	2,637	$344	$130	11
Air freight	22	$219	$9,995	8	4	$249	$67,207	8
Desaguadero, Peru	622	$220	$353	8	576	$234	$406	7
Subtotal				81				97
Total	**17,181**	**$2,868**	**$167**		**17,381**	**$3,242**	**$187**	

Source: CEPROBOL.
Note: This table refers to all exports, including minerals and natural gas. At Puerto Suarez soya and soya products accounted for about 1 million tons, valued at about $500 million.

The main export routes for Bolivia's nontraditional exports are Chile's Pacific ports and inland waterways to the Atlantic (Table 4.1). Arica and Iquique (Chile) are the main ports for ocean shipment of containers to the United States, Europe, and the Far East, as well as to Colombia and República Bolivariana de Venezuela; and the Paraguay/Parana River ('Hidrovia') for soya oil, cake, and flour produced in Santa Cruz province and shipped via the Cuenca de la Plata ports: Rosario in Argentina and Nueva Palmira in Uruguay. Secondary export routes are: via Desaguadero for Peru by truck, and Yacuiba for northern Argentina by truck. In addition, Peru offers its southern ports of Ilo and Matarani, where handling facilities have recently been improved, but today's volumes of Bolivian traffic through these ports are insignificant, because of the additional distance compared to the Chilean ports. See the Map below.

Access routes to these main ports are of variable quality. The routes to Arica, Desaguadero and Yacuiba are all served by paved roads of recent construction that are in generally good condition. Former railway links to these destinations are now fully closed to Peru, temporarily closed to Arica (pending major repairs), or in bad condition to northern Argentina. In contrast, the railway to Brazil is still the only reliable year-round option for reaching the Hidrovia, as the parallel road is not yet paved throughout.

It is notable that Colombia and República Bolivariana de Venezuela are reached by containers going via the Pacific Coast ports, despite the geographic and cost obstacles of crossing the Altiplano (up to an altitude of 4,500 meters and down again) and the need to cross the Panama Canal. The explanation given is that Atlantic coast ports in Argentina are inefficient, unreliable and costly (charging as much $700 per TEU, against $85–90 at Arica, which is well equipped for loading containers and is well run), while Brazil's ports are congested and overland transport across Brazil is lengthy: Corumba to Santos (the port serving Sao Paulo) is nearly 1,800 km and to Paranagua (the main port for soya traffic) is about 2,200 km.

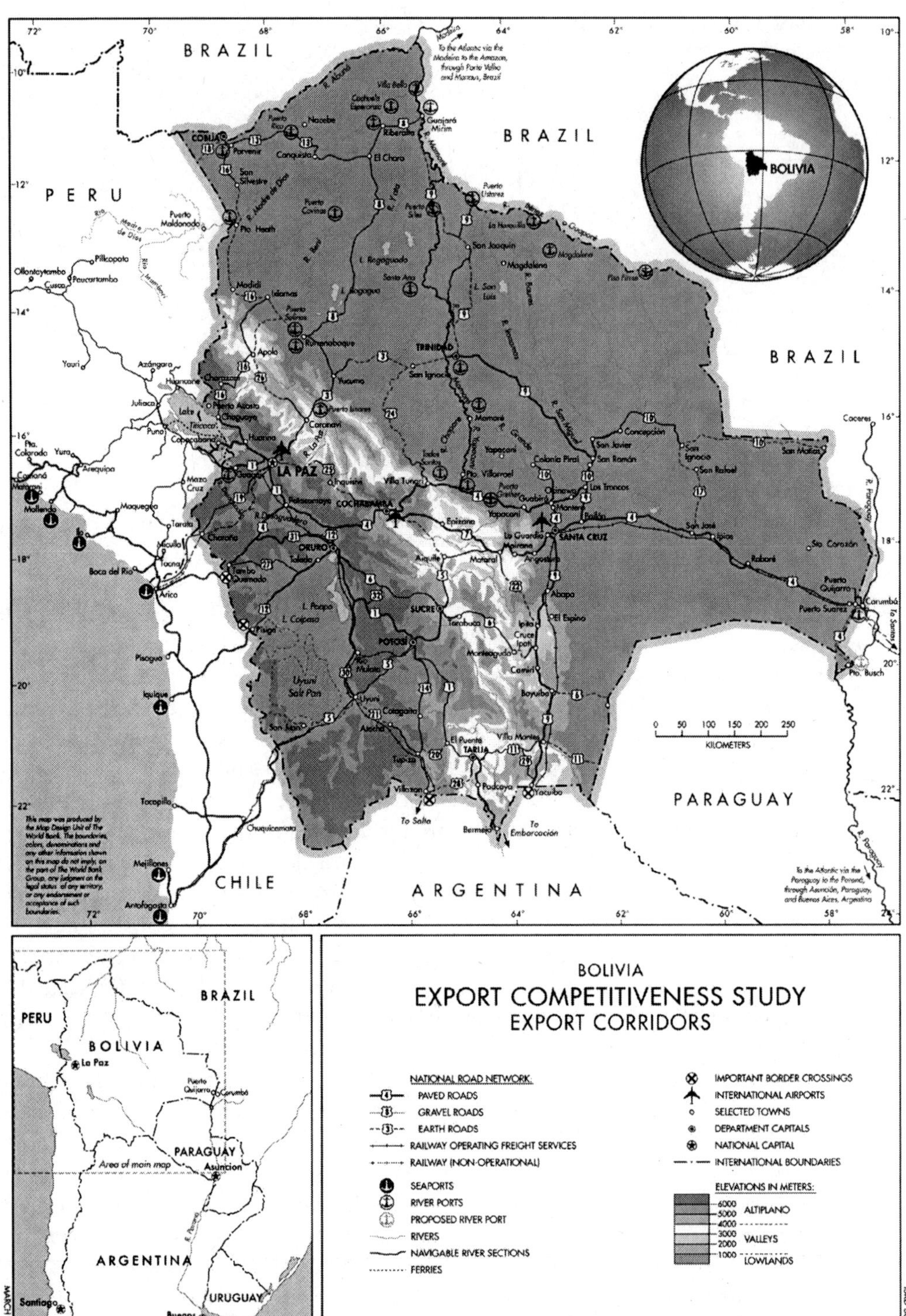
BOLIVIA
EXPORT COMPETITIVENESS STUDY
EXPORT CORRIDORS
NATIONAL ROAD NETWORK:
PAVED ROADS
GRAVEL ROADS
EARTH ROADS
RAILWAY OPERATING FREIGHT SERVICES
RAILWAY (NON-OPERATIONAL)
SEAPORTS
RIVER PORTS
PROPOSED RIVER PORT
RIVERS
NAVIGABLE RIVER SECTIONS
FERRIES
IMPORTANT BORDER CROSSINGS
INTERNATIONAL AIRPORTS
SELECTED TOWNS
DEPARTMENT CAPITALS
NATIONAL CAPITAL
INTERNATIONAL BOUNDARIES
ELEVATIONS IN METERS:
6000
5000
ALTIPLANO
4000
3000
2000
VALLEYS
1000
LOWLANDS
0 50 100 150 200 250
KILOMETERS
BRAZIL
PERU
CHILE
ARGENTINA
PARAGUAY
BOLIVIA
LA PAZ
COCHABAMBA
SANTA CRUZ
ORURO
SUCRE
POTOSÍ
TARIJA
TRINIDAD
COBIJA
To the Atlantic via the Madeira to the Amazon, through Porto Velho and Manaus, Brazil
To the Atlantic via the Paraguay to the Paraná, through Asunción, Paraguay, and Buenos Aires, Argentina
To Salta
To Embarcación
To Santos
This map was produced by the Map Design Unit of The World Bank. The boundaries, colors, denominations and any other information shown on this map do not imply, on the part of The World Bank Group, any judgment on the legal status of any territory, or any endorsement or acceptance of such boundaries.
Area of main map
La Paz
Puerto Quijarro
Corumbá
Asunción
URUGUAY
Buenos Aires
Montevideo
Santiago
MARCH 2006
IBRD 36000

Main Transport Modes

Different transport modes are considered in two groups: those commodities shipped in containers, and those shipped in bulk.

Containers

Use of containers for medium- and high-value exports has grown rapidly since the road to Arica was opened in the mid 1990s and, at about the same time, a reliable paved highway was completed between Santa Cruz and Cochabamba. These two new roads reduced the travel time between Santa Cruz and Arica from a week to three days (36 hours driving time), radically extending Arica's economic hinterland and boosting and redirecting export traffic generated in the Santa Cruz region. Further developments are expected to extend this trend: refrigerated containers are beginning to be used, which augurs well for opening new markets for meat, flowers, fruits, and vegetables sold to the northern countries of South America or even to the southern United States. Indicative tariffs for hauling containers from the four major cities to Arica are given in Table 4.2.

The above freight rates for containers may be compared with the rates for sawn wood hauled in open trucks, which are allowed to carry up to 20 tons (Table 4.3). The freight rate for bringing sawn wood from Pando to La Paz is about 20 percent of the delivered value of the wood (about $90 out of $500). By the time this wood is made into furniture and sold FOB at Arica, the product is worth $1,400-$1,600 per ton, of which transport that far will have cost about $120 per ton, or a little less than 10 percent of the FOB value. Forty-foot containers typically contain 20 tons of merchandise, worth (in this trade) $30-35,000, implying that the ocean rate to a European port is about 10 percent and the total transport cost about 15 percent of the CIF value, or a little less for containers bound for the United States (Table 4.3).

Table 4.2. Typical Truck Tariffs between Main Transport Nodes

Corridor	Distance (kms)	20' up to 23 tons	40' up to 27 tons	40' RF up to 27 tons
EXPORTS				
La Paz – Arica	501	$600	$660	$1,300
Oruro – Arica	580	$750	$900	$1,800
Cochabamba-Arica	668	$900	$1,100	$2,400
Santa Cruz – Arica	1,148	$1,400	$1,500	$3,500
IMPORTS				
La Paz – Arica	501	$1,140	$1,440	$2,300
Oruro – Arica	580	$1,200	$1,400	$2,800
Cochabamba-Arica	668	$1,380	$1,620	$3,000
Santa Cruz – Arica	1,148	$1,440	$2,040	$3,500

Source: Maersk Logistics, La Paz

Notes: RF = refrigerated containers.

All rates are in US$, quoted up to Customs or free zone warehouse. They do not include customs clearance and off-loading. All rates include empty return of container to port or Bolivian depot. Rates are all-in (including transport, MIC, Arica dispatch, border payment)

Table 4.3. Main Parameters for Exports of Wood from Northern Bolivia

Origin – destination	Distance (km)	Trucking cost per m^3 (US$)
Cobija- La Paz	1,250	$91
San Borja – La Paz	400	$50
Santa Cruz – La Paz	900	$50
Ocean freight		Per 40' container
El Alto – Arica	490	$680-750
Arica – U.S. port		$2,700-3,300
Arica – European port		$3,000-3,500

Source: Suma Pacha furniture manufacturer, El Alto.

Bulks

Shipping via the Hidrovia is inexpensive but it has limitations. The Hidrovia operates well with very large barge convoys (up to 45,000 tons capacity: 30 barges, each carrying 1,500 tons). These operations achieve very low costs for long-distance transport, typically $30 per ton for transport of 2,800 km from Corumba to Nueva Palmira, Uruguay. This is about 1 U.S. cent per ton-km,[5] as against 5–8 cents per ton-km for transport on paved main roads. However, volumes using the Hidrovia are subject to various constraints: the minimum water depth (2.8–3 meters in more favorable seasons of the year and less in other months), limited navigational aids especially for night navigation; and a limited supply of barges, the cost of steel having skyrocketed recently.

The Eastern Railway from Santa Cruz to Puerto Quijarro/Corumba has substantially improved its service since it was partially privatized in the 1990s, but it remains expensive. The railway has enlarged its freight car fleet, putting an end to complaints that cars were never made available when needed. However, its published tariff for soya products ($37 for 643 km) is no lower per ton-km than road tariffs between La Paz/El Alto and Arica ($29 for 495 km): 5.8 U.S. cents per ton-km. International good practice for bulks on low-density lines is closer to 2–3 cents. The road parallel to the Santa Cruz-Corumba railway is nearing completion; only the last 200 or so km remain to be paved, due in the second half of 2008. It is to be expected that completion of the road will put strong price pressure on the railway if it is to keep its customers.

Trends and Dynamics in Logistics

Past Decade

Road construction has improved Bolivia's links internally and to the Chilean port of Arica. The whole center of Bolivia, from La Paz to Santa Cruz, has benefited from the marked improvement in access ever since the paved road from Patacamaya (near Oruro) to Arica and that between Cochabamba and Santa Cruz were opened. Arica's economic catchment area now extends as far as Santa Cruz. Consistent with the 1904 treaty between Bolivia and Chile, Bolivian truckers enjoy full rights to deliver exports to the ports of Arica, Iquique, and Antofagasta and to pick up imports for their return leg (Box 4.4).

Box 4.4. Legal Framework for Bolivian Trucks Using Chilean Ports

Peace Treaty of 1904

Bolivia's right of transit through Chile is embodied in the peace treaty of 1904 between the two countries. In this treaty Chile recognized, in perpetuity, Bolivia's full right of commercial free transit through its territory and ports, without exception. The treaty also authorized both governments to maintain customs agents in the ports, and defined procedures for transit to and from Bolivia, and to store goods in secured facilities. This treaty remains in effect and has been honored with only small deviations over the past century.

Integrated Transit System at Arica

To ensure that the 1904 treaty is fully implemented, in 1975 the two countries agreed on an integrated transit system for the port of Arica, built around an Information and Coordination Center that brings together representatives of the Chilean port enterprise, the Arica-La Paz Railway, Chilean Customs, the Bolivian Autonomous Customs Warehouse Administration (which has subsequently been restructured under another name) and Bolivian users. Its purpose is to coordinate decisions about procedures and documentation, especially regarding the dispatching of cargoes. Documents have been simplified to conform to a standard layout. This system remains in effect today, and Bolivian exporters interviewed by the Bank team expressed general satisfaction with the port's performance.

The road from Oruro to Iquique, south of Arica, is now paved much of the way, opening up reliable access to a third Chilean port. Iquique has free zone facilities for Bolivia's use and offers economies of scale, in the form of direct weekly sailings to northern hemisphere markets. In 2007 Iquique handled 263,000 TEU, more than four times more than Arica's 58,000 TEU. Some Iquique traffic to La Paz may be entering via Tambo Quemado, since within Chile the road is paved throughout, and the extra distance compared to the direct route via Pisiga is not great (100–120 km). Using Iquique instead of Arica saves $300–400 per container by avoiding the transshipment in Callao. Furthermore, the import/export balance of containers at Iquique is far worse than at Arica (two out of three outbound are empty). This suggests that rates on outbound containers through Iquique should be heavily discounted. It is to be expected that the Tambo Quemado border post, today prone to congestion, will lose traffic when paving of the Pisiga route is completed.

The last 15 years have seen substantial growth in soya production east of Santa Cruz, from virtually nothing to approaching a million tons per year (Table 4.4). This sea-change in the land use of eastern Santa Cruz province owes much to private investment in modern storage and loading facilities on a waterway entering the Paraguay River. This was tied into the Eastern Railway and the privately-funded building of grain silos for short-term storage and efficient loading into rail freight cars at stations along that line. Once the regular movement of substantial volumes of bulk soya was established, it became financially attractive to process at least part of the soya into oil and cake at plants near the Río Paraguay terminals, creating the relatively new export flow of soya derivatives down the Hidrovia. The soya traffic now represents three-quarters of total tonnage of nontraditional exports, and about half in value.

Table 4.4. Bolivian Exports via the Paraguay-Parana Waterway, 1997–2006

Year	Total export volume (000 tons)	Growth rate per year
1997	361	
1999	270	−14%
2000	754	180%
2002	901	9%
2004	1,016	6%
2005	1,302	28%
2006	1,500	15%

Source: CADEX.

The use of air freight remains limited for lack of air transport capacity. Bolivia is served by few international air routes, none using specialized freight aircraft. Air freight is carried in the bellies of passenger aircraft. The bankruptcy of Lloyd Aereo Boliviano, which ceased operations in late March 2007, has set back the supply of air freight services. Santa Cruz airport has the greatest potential to develop air freight, because the Santa Cruz market is the largest and its airport facilities are the best. Air freight rates from Santa Cruz to Miami penalize small shipments, varying from about $2,900 per ton for a one-ton shipment to about $460 for a 100-kg load. Consolidation of ten such small loads into one would save about 37 percent of the tariff.

Cochabamba has potential to develop exports utilizing air freight, but service is currently very limited. Cochabamba sits in a benign geographic zone at middle altitude, above the tropical lowlands of Santa Cruz but below the dry and infertile high plateau of the La Paz region. As a result the region enjoys favorable temperatures, rainfall and soils for a wide variety of fruits, vegetables, and flowers, as well as other specialized exports derived from agriculture (textiles and leather). Such products are good candidates for air freight, either because of their perishable nature or because of their high value per ton (Box 4.5). However, Cochabamba has only limited passenger air services, with no direct flights to relevant international destinations. Secondary handling at Santa Cruz, the preferred hub for most international flights, adds to costs and delivery times.

Box 4.5. Cochabamba's Many Small-Scale Nontraditional Exporters

The Cochabamba region has more than 500 exporters, who export more than 2,000 different products. Almost all these firms (85–90 percent) are small and medium enterprises. The three biggest exporters have annual sales of only $9 million, $5 million, and $2 million (whereas the largest exporter in Santa Cruz has sales of $120 million).

Exporters of wood products sell hardwood furniture in the United States through mass retailers like WalMart and Home Depot. Bananas grown in Chapare, as a replacement crop for coca, are sold to Chile, Argentina, France, and Germany. Papaya, pineapples (fresh), palm hearts in cans, sweet onions, dry eucalyptus, quinua paste (a substitute for gluten), and camucamu (a fruit whose Vitamin C content is said to be 120 times stronger than citrus) are exported to the United States and Europe, often marketed through deli groceries and organic food stores. Chicha (fermented maize beer) is exported to Spain in tetra packs for Bolivian guest workers. Other products include frozen pichon (meat), rabbit meat, honey, bee-based medicines, flavored teas, toilet paper, and flavored salt, as well as alpaca textiles, blue jeans, T-shirts and blue marble.

Most of these products are exported by container via Arica. The tropical fruits and meats are transported in refrigerated containers. Leather goods, handbags and the like, as well as hardwood doors with glass, have a high enough value per ton to warrant transport by air freight.

A Cochabamba exporter interviewed exports high-end leather goods to Italy worth (on average) about $35 per kg ex factory. Short lead times and reliable delivery are important attributes demanded by his customers. Thanks to the regularity of his business he has been able to negotiate a substantial discount on the air freight rate, so that the air transport from Santa Cruz constitutes about 10 percent of the CIF price at destination. This allows him to remain competitive with Chinese producers.

Prospects for the Next 5-10 Years

The Santa Cruz department and other lowland areas will continue to grow in population and production faster than the Altiplano cities of La Paz, Oruro, Potosí, and Sucre. This differential has been shifting Bolivia's economic center of gravity eastward over the past two decades. In 1986 Santa Cruz contributed only 6 percent of Bolivia's total exports (in value), whereas by 2006 it accounted for 50 percent. This trend is likely to continue.

The driving force of Santa Cruz's growth, soya, faces a price risk, but diversification is starting to offset that risk. Soya and its derivatives, being commodities, remain vulnerable to international price movements and tariffs, Bolivia producers face competition with Brazil and Argentina as major world producers, whereas Bolivia accounts for only 1 percent of world supply. At the same time, one of Bolivia's main customers for soya, Peru, can now import soya from the United States duty-free. Off-setting this threat, lowland agriculture and the harvesting of forest wood have been growing more diverse and extensive, and this diversification reduces the risks of price shocks to individual commodities. Extension of all-weather roads in the eastern lowlands between Santa Cruz and the Brazilian border, now well underway can be expected to consolidate this trend. It remains to be seen whether the produce of this region will prefer the Chilean ports to reach international markets, or the ports of Brazil and Argentina. Trip costs to the ports are about equal in today's circumstances: $55–60 per ton, while travel times favor the Pacific ports: three days by road to the Pacific against 15 days by rail and river to the Atlantic. There exists potential to lower costs and transit times in both directions.

Recent developments suggest that traffic demand in Bolivia's 'Far East' (around Corumba) will grow strongly and sustain the eastward shift. The Paraná-Paraguay River system is comparable in configuration and scale to the Mississippi-Missouri River, and Corumba's location vis-à-vis the Hidrovia is similar to one of the large cities of the U.S. Midwest such as Omaha or Minneapolis. From the northernmost navigable waters near Caceres in Brazil's Mato Grosso state to Nueva Palmira, at the mouth of the Paraná, is 3,450 km (2,130 miles). This is very similar to the navigable length of the Mississippi, and also of the Rhine-Danube waterway. Corumba is about 2,770 km upriver, yet the water level there is only 100m above sea level. The river's slope is extremely gradual: 1 meter in 30 km. The minimal current is favorable for vessels navigating upriver, but the many meanders greatly lengthen the distance to be traveled. Between Cáceres and the Paraguayan section, with Corumba roughly in the middle, the River Paraguay flows through a vast seasonal wetland, known by its Portuguese term *Pantanal*. This is the largest and biologically most diverse wetland in the world.

Brazil would benefit from an increased use of the Hidrovia and of adjoining roads in Bolivia to evacuate its own soya and beef from Mato Grosso. Upstream from Corumba the Brazilian bank of the River Paraguay is wetlands, whereas the Bolivian bank is high and dry. Co-financing options between the two countries of some transport infrastructure within Bolivia may be of interest to Brazil. This could lead to Bolivia playing a transit role for Brazilian exports.

The current patterns in the use of the Hidrovia would be changed once the vast iron ore reserves of Mutún are exploited. While this issue falls outside the scope of this study, the exploitation of the iron ore reserves of Mutún, very close to the Brazilian border outside Corumba, would have significant implications for the use of the Hidrovia. The proposed project to mine iron ore in large quantities (estimated at 7–11 million tons per year) near the source will transform the character of the Puerto Suarez/ Puerto Quijarro/Corumba area, attracting employment and secondary investment to serve what is likely to become a large industrial complex.

Santa Cruz is seeking to build a new river port at Puerto Busch. The Santa Cruz business community is talking of 'realizing a dream' that it has harbored for decades of building a new high-capacity river port within Bolivian territory but directly on the Paraguay River at Puerto Busch, some 140 km south of Corumba at Bolivia's southeastern-most point. Environmental objections are likely to be strong, but probably not strong enough to prevent the complex becoming a reality. This in turn would create new access opportunities for the soya and other agri-based exports of the eastern lowlands. Project defenders argue that it will be Bolivia's first and only port on the River Paraguay proper (Puerto Quijarro being on the Tamengo Channel, a tributary that has limited draft) and it will avoid bridges near Corumba that force barge convoys to break up and re-form. Bolivia would no longer depend on the benevolence of its neighbor countries, but would have its own sovereign port on an international waterway. (This is true in principle, but downriver countries can still disrupt shipping if they so choose.)

The technical arguments for the proposed port are debatable. The lower reaches of the River Paraguay have the same limiting depth as the Tamengo Channel, so even if Puerto Busch will have deeper draft, shipping will draw no benefit from the extra draft. And barge convoys coming up-river routinely break up at the southeastern end of Corumba anyway, since each convoy contains barges for various wharves in and around the city. For traffic going down river regrouping large convoys downstream from the last bridge is a minor inconvenience, probably not enough to justify the investment in wholly new facilities for the current traffic of 1-2 million tons per year. The cost of building a road or railway line to Puerto Busch would be at least $65-70 million (130 km at $0.5 million per km). The railway investment, including locomotives and freight cars, has been estimated at $84 million.[6] Furthermore, careless construction of a road or railway extension to Puerto Busch could do serious and irreversible damage to the Pantanal and wildlife of that area.

On the other hand, the 7-11 million tons of sponge iron proposed to be shipped out within eight years is a different order of magnitude. Fortunately for soya, its season for exports coincides with the months when the water level of the Tamengo Channel and the Paraguay is high. In contrast, the proposed export of iron ore and its derivatives will have to take place year-round. The ore could be stockpiled during the months of low water, but economic and political pressures will undoubtedly build for dredging the Paraguay to maintain adequate draft in the dry months.

Box 4.6. Institutional Arrangements for Managing the Paraguay-Paraná River Waterway ("Hidrovia")

In 1996 Argentina, Bolivia, Brazil, Paraguay, and Uruguay signed the Accord for River Navigation on the Paraguay and Paraná Rivers. It provides for "free navigation, equal treatment, free transit and reciprocity, multi-lateral treatment of cargo reservations, transport and trade facilitation, and port navigational services." In 1989 the Intergovernmental Committee for the Waterway (*Comite Intergubernamental de la Hidrovia*—CIH) was set up by the governments of the five riparian countries to coordinate use of the Paraguay, Paraná, and Uruguay Rivers as an integrated system. A permanent secretariat is based in Rosario, Argentina.

In the interest of safety, CIH regulates barge operators, their crews, and pilots for all countries, sets standards for navigation, and provides information to users of the waterway, especially about depth available for navigation, which varies throughout the year. The CIH also coordinates proposals for navigational improvements. Some dredging to deepen the shipping channel has been carried out in the Paraná's lower reaches, between Santa Fe (Argentina) and the Atlantic, and also in Paraguay. Proposals to remove rock shelves by blasting in the Pantanal section have drawn strong opposition from environmental groups, because of the likely negative impacts of changes in the river's flow on the Pantanal and its vegetation and wildlife. These objections have led Brazil to ban dredging in its section. But in 1998 Bolivia dredged the Tamengo Channel to guarantee a minimum depth of 2.8 meters. Fortunately for Bolivia, the Paraguay River is today navigable during at least half of the year. Soybean harvesting and shipping in eastern Bolivia occur in April, May and June, when the river is full and presents little problems for navigation.

The River Plate Basin Permanent Transport Commission (*Comision Permanente de Transporte de la Cuenca del Plata*—CPTCP) is a forum for barge operators to lobby with CIH and each country's bodies responsible for the waterway. It was set up at the same time as the CIH. At a recent meeting, for example, the agenda included a proposal by the Mato Grosso government that barge operators should contribute to the construction cost of structures to protect the piers of the road bridge at Corumba and serve as moorings (conditionally accepted), and the cost of installing a navigation simulator for crew training in Buenos Aires (rejected).

Two international institutions manage the Hidrovia (Box 4.6). An intergovernmental permanent commission representing the five riparian countries is responsible for co-coordinating safety on the waterway and licensing and regulating barge companies, as well as any dredging or other major proposed infrastructure investment. The environmental objections to major dredging are not to be underestimated. The second body is a consultative private-sector body bringing together the main barge companies using the waterway. In both bodies the temptation for 'free riders' is always present.

The governments of Brazil, Bolivia and Chile are considering developing the whole east-west corridor between Central Brazil and northern Chile, called the *Corredor Bi-oceánico*. The presidents of the three countries signed this agreement in La Paz on December 17, 2007. Despite this political initiative, it does not seem to be economically attractive for Brazil to make much use of the ports of northern Chile. Much depends on whether the ports of Argentina, Uruguay, and southern Brazil can raise their efficiency to levels more competitive with Chile's. There is also talk of Chile exploiting a natural deepwater harbor (Mejillones) north of Antofagasta for very large ships, which could prove attractive. But at the same time Buenos Aires is said to be on the way to creating a hub for fourth-generation (post-Panamax) containerships operating to China, Japan and Korea via the Indian Ocean, that could throw development in its favor. These potential developments, clearly, are beyond Bolivia's control.

Issues and Uncertainties

Trucking industry tariffs and regulation

Despite the difficult terrain and the thinness of its markets, the Bolivian long-distance trucking industry offers relatively low tariffs per ton-km: 5-8 U.S. cents. This corresponds to $1.001.20 per truck-km, an average load in the full direction of about 20 tons (maximum permitted load of 24 tons), and relatively low rates of back-haul—that is, most return trips are less than fully loaded or even empty (Table 4.2 in previous section). Containerized imports to Bolivia via the Chilean ports substantially exceed containerized exports. This explains the substantially lower tariffs for exports from La Paz, Oruro and Cochabamba (a discount of 35–45 percent), because they are mostly back-hauls. Santa Cruz's containerized exports are more balanced in volumes with its imports, explaining the smaller discount on exports from there to Arica.

Several factors tend to keep truck operating costs per ton-km low:

- Wage costs are low because drivers receive no social benefits.
- Profits are kept low as the trucking industry can be characterized as non-monopolistic.
- Diesel fuel is heavily subsidized at a set price throughout Bolivia (in December 2007 it was about $0.50 per liter—cheaper by one-third than in the United States).
- The capital cost of most trucks is low, because they are bought second hand from richer countries, particularly Sweden.
- Maintenance costs are low because spare parts are imported second hand (or not from the original vehicle manufacturer), and labor is cheap.
- Overloading is widespread (and minimally controlled—Box 4.7).

Box 4.7. Design Road Pavements to Withstand Overloaded Trucks

Overloading of trucks is likely to continue; enforcement is difficult in the best of countries. Chile is one of the very few countries in the world that has consistently enforced axle-load limits. This suggests that Bolivia should take advantage of its proximity to seek best practice. But in the absence of consistent enforcement—pavements should be built thicker, designed for expected actual loading rather than loading assuming compliance with the axle-load limits. It will increase the construction cost but substantial savings in vehicle operating costs and road maintenance expenditure will soon pay off the extra investment.

However, the distances are great—the nearest seaport is 500 km from the capital and 1,200 km from the biggest commercial city—so Bolivia remains at a disadvantage vis-à-vis competitor countries. Driving from the eastern lowlands up to the Altiplano is bound to be costly, by reason of generally poor road geometry and steep slopes, deteriorated pavements, and low fuel efficiency at high altitude.[7] From Santa Cruz trucks typically make only two to three round trips a month. This is due to long idle times between one trip and the next, waiting for unloading and loading, and to a lesser degree waiting times at border checkpoints. Efforts should be focused on measures that would reduce these idle times and raise the number of trips per month.

One obvious way to trim road transport costs would be to give truck semi-trailers separate license plates from tractors (the engine cab). Current laws and decrees make no provision for tractor units to operate separately from their trailers—for example, leaving a trailer in Arica or Iquique for unloading and immediately picking up another loaded trailer to take back to Santa Cruz. If allowed, this could cut days off the round-trip journey time and allow several roundtrips per month instead of just two or three. This would reduce the cost per truck-km by about 10 percent—at least $150 off the cost of hauling a 40-foott container from Santa Cruz to Arica.

Time on the road could be reduced if the government were to abolish the toll stations and replaced this cost recovery mechanism by an equivalent surcharge on fuels or annual vehicle registration fees. Between Santa Cruz and the border with Chile a truck passes through 8–10 such toll stations, paying a total of about $100 per trip. This is a reasonable approximation to the road wear and tear cost caused by heavy trucks. However, studies have shown that traffic volumes on Bolivia's inter-urban roads (rarely more than a few hundred vehicles per day) fall far short of the minimum volumes deemed efficient internationally, in terms of the revenue collected compared to the administrative cost of collecting it, the delay to commercial vehicles, and the high risk of revenue leakage.

The above two recommendations may not be practicable in today's circumstances, since they imply a significant shift in the collection and allocation of fiscal revenues between the central government and the provinces. On the other hand, they balance each other to the extent that the shifting of revenue collection to the Center is offset by the obligation on the Center to redistribute budget to the provinces, to increase funds available for maintenance of key national highways. But this option should be held in mind until political circumstances are more favorable.

The predictability of truck trip times is an important consideration, since most container ships operate out of Arica to a timetable only once a week. Roads in the Valleys region are vulnerable to seasonal damage when it rains because of landslides and damage to bridges. A measure the Ministry of Transport could take to reduce the variability in trip times is to provide budget support to the regional highway departments to strengthen their emergency maintenance capacity.

Border Control Management—Customs and Other Border Control Reforms[8]

Although border controls tend to impinge more on imports, they are also relevant for considering export efficiency. Border control issues are considered for three reasons. First, delays imposed on trucks bringing in imports lower the efficiency of their use and drive up the costs of trucking generally, as well as making delivery times unpredictable. Second, among the controls imposed by border control agencies on exports, the provision of certificates of origin has been cited by many exporters as onerous and often causing lengthy delays. A related common complaint is that unpredictable processing times often cause trucks hauling exports to fail to reach the seaport in time for loading of the container onto the ships. And third, the widespread smuggling of imported consumer goods tends to perpetuate mistrust between the border control agencies and the trading community. This discourages the effective introduction of 'good faith' clearance techniques not only for imports but also for exports.

The computerized processing of Customs declarations using ASYCUDA++ is working well and has greatly enhanced the efficiency of most processes. UN standard documentary formats are being used, and this also appears to be working well. Once the planned system of risk-based selection for inspections is put in place, it will be far easier to determine from a computer check in real time whether a particular truck has a good performance record.

The ANB aims to extend and consolidate the reforms launched in 2000–04 as its medium-term priorities (Box 4.8). These priorities primarily address the needs of imports and importers, but some initiatives will benefit exporters directly, while others will benefit them indirectly insofar as they allow long-distance trucks to be used more efficiently, and truck tariffs can then be lowered and delivery times made more predictable.

Customs practices require trucking firms to put up financial transit guarantees to cover duty owed on imports when the importer processes the Customs declaration at an inland site rather than at the point of entry into the country. The same principle applies to trucks crossing a third country without unloading in that country. Bolivia's current system requires each trucking firm to put up a bank guarantee or equivalent for values up to $15–20,000, using a smart card with an embedded chip. This system has the virtue of simplicity and has been adequate for deterring truck operators from failing to declare their inbound cargo at a Customs depot. ANB has proposed to simplify the system further by doing away with the smart cards, since all the relevant information is now available on-line at any Customs control point.

Box 4.8. Priorities of the Aduana Nacional de Bolivia

- Set up a risk-based selectivity process for inspections, relying on computerized data bases and algorithms with which to analyze traders' patterns, and the training of specialized staff to operate the system.
- Upgrade core software from ASYCUDA++ to the next level, or transition to other software, off-the-shelf or customized, that ANB may judge more cost-effective.
- Acquire IT hardware and other equipment for border stations, including X-ray scanners (with associated training in their use).
- Improve the transit regime, allowing trucks to be cleared at or near their intended destination within Bolivia rather than at the border entry point.
- Develop and pilot testing a single window system for coordinated processing of import transactions with the other border agencies (including enhanced integration of strategic planning, functional Websites, and training).
- Put in place integrated border facilities jointly with the Customs of neighbor countries at two or three pilot sites.
- Tackle smuggling through introduction of a satellite-based tracking system and other surveillance and control systems.
- Strengthen capacity for valuation.
- Setting up an outreach (liaison) service to communicate better with merchants.

Box 4.9. Transport International Routier System

This system offers several advantages over the present domestic system. First, it guarantees the duty and tax revenue at risk rather than a fixed amount per truck, and the maximum coverage is several times larger (advantage for Customs). Second, the cost per trip is small: less than $100, or 0.2 percent of the maximum coverage (advantage for the trucker). This is achieved through the pooling of risk over the large number of reputable operators covered by the TIR system in 55 member countries. Third, it is an internationally recognized system that imposes on its participants minimum standards of professional conduct (an advantage for all parties).

It also has several disadvantages. First, it is designed for international transit and therefore is accepted only in countries that have adopted the TIR convention. So far the only South American country to do so is Uruguay. It will only make sense for Bolivia to adopt TIR if the neighbor countries through which its imports and exports pass also become members. Second, the TIR system requires, as part of the international guarantee chain, the setting up and approval by the IRU of a national collective guarantee association adhered to and financially backed by all Bolivian truckers engaged in international haulage. This may be difficult to put in place and sustain, considering the small size of most Bolivian trucking operations, and the thinness of the Bolivian market. Third, the TIR carnet is a paper document; it has not yet been updated to take advantage of IT technology. However, the IRU is examining options for automating the system with a smart card or bar-code reading technology.

Consideration is also being given to moving to a broader system that will facilitate transit of Bolivian trucks through neighboring countries and vice versa. The obvious candidate is the international Transport International Routier (TIR) system, overseen by the International Road Transport Union (IRU), a United Nations agency (Box 4.9). This system protects Customs against loss of duty and tax revenue up to $50,000 per truckload, and $100,000 in the case of alcohol and tobacco.

Some of the anomalies in the way transit is managed derive from efforts to frustrate specific contraband tricks, mostly driven by a desire to claim duty drawback refunds on phantom exports. As discussed in the previous section, reportedly long delays to obtain duty drawback affect exporters' finances. The disruption to their cash flow is often passed on to the trucking firms. Issues related to smuggling make it hard for Customs and other border control agencies to take seriously the official policy of 'good faith' vis-à-vis traders and the vehicles they use.

The plant and animal health control agency SENASAG is unable to fulfill its mandate due to a lack of capacity and a lack of resources. Would-be exporters in remote locations are reportedly affected by delays in obtaining certification—as the agency is not decentralized—to the point where their ability to export was jeopardized. Lack of technical capacity and leadership, lack of resources, and a lack of decentralization have gutted the agency's capacity.

Logistic centers

Cochabamba has implemented a simple logistics center bringing together into one place all services required for exporting: brokers, Customs, banks, cold storage, and air freight. It uses existing buildings abandoned by the airport in the 1990s when it built a new runway and terminal. These buildings have been subject to minor upgrading. The scale, however, is very small, constrained in part by lack of airfreight capacity (as noted above, Cochabamba has very few international flights). The scale of operations is at present so small that the various service providers are likely to lose money and the center will not be financially sustainable. The question then arises as to who should carry the financial cost of creating the real estate, who should operate it and under what incentives. It seems that the desired economies of scale are unlikely to be achieved unless major exporters are attracted or bigger air freight operators—a classic chicken and egg problem. There are no easy solutions, but some approaches are offered below.

The Bolivian government should make a concerted effort to facilitate air freight, within the constraints of the market. Air freight offers any landlocked country the opportunity to escape the penalties of having no seaport within its territory. As has been noted, Cochabamba has the best resource endowment for developing export industries in goods that are of high value per ton, and perishable fruits, vegetables and flowers that could sell at high margins if they could reliably reach affluent markets within (say) 24 hours. But on the supply side, Santa Cruz has daily passenger flights to Miami and to European capital cities, mostly via Buenos Aires. It follows that a close working relationship will be needed between manufacturers, growers and sellers based in Cochabamba and one or more airlines operating daily out of Santa Cruz to the United States or Europe. The local airline operating flights between Cochabamba and Santa Cruz will also need to be a partner in this collaborative effort. The Chamber of Exporters of Cochabamba would be in the best position to launch such an initiative, perhaps contracting with a freight forwarder specialized in air freight to define a business model for consolidating loads and using whatever economies of scale this generates in negotiating tariffs and terms with the airlines.

Policy Implications

Pursue reforms in coordinated border control management (Customs and other border control agencies). Continue Customs reform to make life easier for legitimate traders while pursuing the struggle against corruption and smuggling. Ensure continuous attention to the public throughout the opening hours at border control. Pursue the experiment currently under way at Yacuiba for combined operations with Argentine border controls in joint facilities and repeat the experiment at Desaguadero with Peruvian border controls. Set up a system of border crossing performance indicators, especially to include total waiting times from the arrival of a truck at the outgoing checkpoint to its departure from the checkpoint in the neighboring country.

Improve coordination between Customs and other border control agencies, especially SENASAG. This probably requires radical strengthening of SENASAG, including authorization of an adequate budget, appointment and training of qualified personnel, simplification of procedures and documentation, and further decentralization to get closer to the clients.

Build trust between public and private sectors. Consider the merits of setting up a public/private committee responsible for facilitating trade, bringing together representatives of the business community (who would be expected to provide most of the operating budget) and of the government control agencies: Customs, plant and animal health inspections, immigration and border police, and the transport ministry. Today Bolivia has bodies with this objective in the private sector (notably the chambers of exporters) and separately in the public sector (PAEX under the Ministry of

Production and CEPROBOL under the Ministry of Foreign Affairs). The merit of a joint body would be to build bridges of mutual trust and cooperation between the two sides, and assure greater continuity of funding for the public sector functions.

Encourage the Cochabamba chamber of exporters to develop a viable business model for consolidating air freight consignments to be channeled via Santa Cruz to North American and European markets.

Give truck trailers their own license plate. Allow tractor units to have separate registration from trailers, so that tractor units can keep moving—and earning revenue—while trailers wait to unload and reload. The present law considers the tractor and trailer as a single unit for purposes of registration. This change would greatly enhance the efficient utilization of the truck fleet, allowing tariffs to be lowered by 10 percent or more. An alternative solution would be to allow a single plate to be retained for both units, but the trailer plate could be switched from one trailer to the next.

Abolish road tolls in favor of a distribution to each province of part of the fuel tax revenue. Many studies have shown that because of the low traffic volumes found almost everywhere in Bolivia, tolls yield little revenue to the treasury, encourage corruption, and often impose costly waiting times and harassment on truckers.

Ensure adequate funding for emergency maintenance of existing roads. Allocate more funds to emergency services that can unblock roads after landslides and flooding, which are common. These would be most appropriately supplied by prefectures, but legally the main roads are controlled at the national level. Some resolution needs to be found for this.

Curtail diesel fuel subsidies and smuggling. Subsidies of diesel have heightened contraband of fuel to neighbor countries (the price in neighboring Peru is more than double the Bolivian pump price and in Brazil closer to three times higher). Smuggling has fiscal costs in terms of foregone duties to be paid to the government but also a distortion effect of unfair competition to formal productive firms.

Give more concerted attention to options for making greater use of the Paraná-Paraguay waterway. In principle, the Hidrovia offers a low-cost export corridor for the products of eastern Bolivia, one that requires relatively little investment in public infrastructure and which has considerable potential for carrying increased volumes without congestion. However, such development has to face openly the two big challenges: how to coordinate the waterway's use with the governments of the four other riparian countries; and how to reconcile its increased use with valid concerns about damage to the environment, especially the fragile eco-systems of the Pantanal.

Notes

[1] This section is based on contributions from Peter Walkenhorst.

[2] This is except for a few related to health or sanitary issues.

[3] The section on transport logistics is based on contributions from Graham Smith and Hector Revuelta.

[4] Bolivia is bound to remain a price-taker on almost all of these commodities. This means that the key calculation for producers is the residual income ('net-back') after deducting from the international price the cost of transport and logistics to reach the international markets.

[5] Apart from some diesel fuel imported, most upstream operations are empty, for lack of appropriate cargo. Standard barges are not adapted for carrying containers, though recently there has been some experimentation in this regard.
[6] Source: "Foro Puerto Busch," CADEX.
[7] Fuel consumption could be improved by engine adjustment to suit the altitude, but trips to and from the seaports take trucks from sea level to 4,500m in the same day.
[8] For a brief description of the results of a Bank field mission to investigate the functioning of Bolivia's border management systems, see Annex 3.1.

CHAPTER 5

A Firm-Level Analysis of the Factors Affecting Export Performance

This chapter uses firm level data to explore the characteristics of exporting firms and the constraints affecting them. The first section investigates whether Bolivian exporters are more productive than non exporters. The second section analyzes the constraints exporting firms face based on enterprises surveys. The final section provides an empirical analysis of the propensity to export in Bolivia as compared to other countries in the Latin America Region.

Is There a 'Productivity Premium' for Bolivian Exporters?[1]

In most countries exporting firms are on average more productive, larger, older, and have more skilled workers than nonexporters. Much empirical research over the last decades has been devoted to study the characteristics of exporters.[2] In particular, a number of studies have focused on the estimation of the differences in productivity between exporting and nonexporting firms using firm-level data. Even though the estimates from these studies are not directly comparable (given the heterogeneity in datasets and techniques used), one robust finding is that, exporters are on average more productive, larger, older and employ more skilled workers than nonexporters. This 'productivity premium' of exporters is typically explained by two different hypotheses: (i) self-selection of more productive firms into exporting, and (ii) 'learning by exporting,' which suggests that firms that start exporting become more productive by virtue of doing so (see Box 5.1 for a review of the theoretical arguments).

The first objective of this chapter is to estimate the productivity differential between exporters and nonexporters in the manufacturing sector in Bolivia. In order to estimate the exporters' productivity premium, we start by analyzing the differences in the cost structure between exporters and nonexporters in Bolivia using information from the Enterprise Survey on Investment Climate (2006), and the Exporters' Survey from the National Institute of Statistics (2005) of Bolivia. The basic features of these two surveys are laid out in Table 5.1 below.

**Box 5.1. Why Are Exporting Firms More Productive?
A Review of the Theoretical Arguments**

Two arguments are commonly given as to why exporting firms may display a 'productivity premium' vis-à-vis nonexporting firms.

A first hypothesis suggests that the most productive firms self-select into exporting. The reasoning is that only the most productive firms can afford the additional costs associated with entering into new markets. A number of empirical studies support this hypothesis. For example, Baldwin and Gu (2003) find that labor productivity and its growth in Canada is higher for new exporters than for nonexporters even before they start exporting. Alvarez and Lopez (2004) find the same in Chilean firms, and in addition, firms made conscious efforts to increase their productivity before staring to export (Wagner, 2005). Clerides, Lach, and Tybout (1998) find support for the self-selection hypothesis in Colombia, Mexico, and Morocco. Bernard and Jensen (1999) and Liu et al. (1999) find the same in the cases of United States and Taiwan, China.

A second hypothesis argues that firms increase their productivity as a result of exporting. The reasoning is that exporting firms are more exposed to competition and to the knowledge acquired from buyers and competitors. In support of this hypothesis, exporters' productivity has been found to increase with export intensity in China (Kray 1999), Brazil (Fajnzylber 2004) and in Colombia (Fernandes and Isgut 2005)—especially for young Colombian manufacturers.

Although more evidence tends to favor the self-selection hypothesis, there is no clear consensus. Both hypotheses may be at work depending on the particular case analyzed and, in fact, they should not be seen as being mutually exclusive. There are in fact studies that provide evidence of both hypotheses being at play (for example, Girma, Greenaway, and Kneller, 2002). Likewise, Van Biesebroeck (2003) finds in Africa that most productive firms engage in exporting, however, also that exporters increase their productivity after entry into the export market.

Recent theoretical models of trade have shed light on what type of costs may contribute to the self-selection of more productive firms into exporting. For example, Melitz (2003) presents a model in which the existence of fixed (overhead) and variable costs implies that only the more productive firms are able to export. Similarly, Bernard, Eaton, Jensen, and Kortum (2003) develop a model in which heterogeneous firms compete a la Bertrand and the existence of variable costs explains why the firms that are more productive are exporters. Helpman, Melitz and Rubinstein (2007) develop a model that predicts trade flows across pairs of countries, allowing the number of exporting firms to vary across destinations, depending on the interaction of different fixed costs. As a result, they decompose the impact of trade frictions on trade flows into the intensive and extensive margins (the volumes traded vs. how many firms export).

One important point about these models is that they emphasize the importance of evaluating the fixed costs to exporting. In this context, extensive empirical work has been devoted to that purpose. In particular, the fixed costs studied have been associated to the operation in the domestic and overseas markets. For instance, restrictive trade and customs regulations have been found to discourage exporting in African countries (Clarke 2005). The author argues that policies aiming at facilitating exports have a role in increasing productivity at the firm level in eight African countries. Likewise, having a good investment climate has been found to be positively associated with exporting, even after controlling for geographic and national level policies (Dollar, Hallward-Driemeier and Mengistae 2005). Infrastructure, and institutional quality have also been found to be significant determinants of export levels and also of the likelihood that exports will take place at all (Francois and Manchin, 2007).

Table 5.1. Characteristics of Firm-Level Data Sources on Bolivian Exporters

Year		Enterprise survey 2005		INE survey 2004
Sample size	Exporters	72 (18% of sample)		330
	Nonexporters	333		0
	Total	405		330
Sample firms by industry		Exporters	Non-exporters	Exporters
	Food manuf.	14	106	67
	Garments manuf.	35	86	39
	Chemicals manuf.	9	50	14
	Non-metal manuf.	2	17	16
	Other manuf.	12	74	194
Sample firms by size		Exporters	Non-exporters	Exporters
	5 to 19 workers)	11	146	159
	20 to 99 workers	37	147	103
	100 or more workers	24	40	3

Source: World Bank and INE.

Preliminary inspection of the data confirms that Bolivian exporters pay higher wages and use more capital than nonexporting firms. Data from the Enterprise Survey suggests that the average wage and compensations paid to all workers in the exporting sectors is larger than in nonexporting firms, especially for medium exporters (see Figure 5.1, left panel). These higher wages are paid mostly in the chemicals and food

Figure 5.1. Labor Costs, Capital Stocks, and Revenue of Exporting and Nonexporting Firms in Enterprise Survey for Bolivia

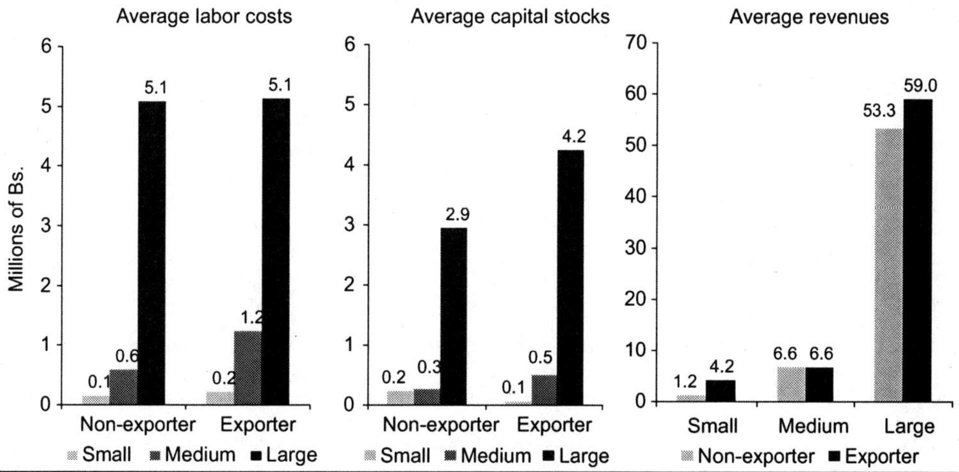

Source: Staff calculations based on Enterprise Survey for Bolivia (2005).
Note: Data refers to 2005.

industries. In terms of capital, the average capital stock per firm (machinery and buildings) is clearly higher for large-sized exporters, and slightly larger for medium-sized exporters. In the segment of small firms, nonexporters seem to have higher capital stocks (see Figure 5.1, middle panel). Exporters also appear to have higher revenues than nonexporters. We observe that the difference is larger for the group of small firms, while the difference does not appear to be that large for bigger firms (see Figure 5.1, right panel). In any case, this suggests that a closer look at the difference between exporters and nonexporters should take account of firm size in a more rigorous way – as it is done below.

Bolivian exporters pay higher wages and use more capital than nonexporting firms even when controlling for firm size, industry, and region where the firms are located. In order to evaluate whether the above-mentioned differences between exporters and nonexporters are statistically significant once controlling for variables such as the size of the firm, the industry, and the location of the firm, we estimated a number of simple cross-section regressions using the Enterprise Survey dataset for Bolivia (see Table 5.2 below). The results suggest that, once controlling for firm size, the average wage paid by exporters is 41 percent higher than the average wage paid by a non-exporter, and the result is statistically significant. Similarly, exporters have on average 91 percent more capital stock than nonexporters, and they also employ more workers and are on average older firms. Overall, the evidence so far indicates that Bolivian exporters have on average many of the same characteristics of exporters studied elsewhere: they pay higher wages, have more capital stocks, are larger, and are older. This is particularly true for medium and larger exporters. However, the regression analysis for Bolivian exporters does not show significant higher sales on average for exporters once controlling for size, industry, and location.

Table 5.2. Bolivian Exporters' Premium on Wages, Capital, and Sales after Controlling for Size, Industry, and Location

Dependent variable	Exporters' premium[a]	t statistic[b]	N[c]	Interpretation[d]
Wages	0.34	1.88*	317	Exporters pay on average wages that are 41% higher than nonexporters
Capital stock	0.65	2.42**	201	Exporters have on average capital stock that is 91% higher than nonexporters
Sales	0.26	1.39	338	Higher sales of exporters are not statistically significant
Age	0.16	1.54*	498	Exporters are on average 18% older than nonexporters
Labor[e]	0.93	6.10***	399	Exporters employ on average 152% more workers than nonexporters

Source: Bank staff based on Enterprise Survey data.

Notes: Data refers to 2005. All regressions are of the form $log(y) = \alpha + \beta_1\ exporter + \beta_2\ size + \mu$ where y is the variable of interest (wages, capital, etc), exporter is a dummy variable that takes the value of one if the firm is an exporter and zero otherwise, and *size* refers to the number of workers in the firm $ln(L)$. All regressions include industry and region fixed effects.

a. Exporters' premium refers to the coefficient on the dummy *exporter*; b. Robust t statistics, * Statistically significant at 10% ** Statistically significant at 5%, *** statistically significant at 1%; c. Number of observations in the regression; d. As per formula $(exp(\beta1)-1)*100$; e. Regression as follows: $log(y) = \alpha + \beta1\ exporter + \mu$.

We now turn our attention to the analysis of productivity differentials between exporters and nonexporters. In the analysis that follows we will use three measures of productivity. Firstly, as suggested by the recent study by the International Study Group on Exports and Productivity (World Bank, 2007), we will take revenue per worker as a general measure of labor productivity. Secondly, we will also use the value added per worker as an alternative measure and for robustness check purposes. The caveat with this latter measure is that due to missing information on intermediate inputs, it is only available for a smaller group of observations in the sample. As a third measure of productivity, and following Escribano and Guasch (2005), we estimate the Total Factor Productivity (TFP) correcting for the simultaneity bias in the selection of inputs by using the investment climate variables as instruments. We then proceed, following Wagner (2005), to run the cross-industry regressions using our measures of productivity as the dependent variable and, as explanatory variables, whether a firm exports or not, its size, and controls for industry and region.

The available evidence, however, does not provide robust evidence that Bolivian exporters are more productive than nonexporters. As shown in Table 5.3, the analysis suggests that the 'productivity premium' of exporters is statistically significant only when using sales per employee as a measure of productivity. Once controlling for size the result is no longer statistically significant regardless of the productivity measure used. While these results may suggest that the size of the domestic market is a general constraint for the productivity of all Bolivian producers—whether exporters or not—they should not be interpreted as evidence that export markets are unimportant for Bolivian firms. One has to bear in mind that productivity is not a measure that can be directly observed but that is constructed on the basis of other data, potentially compounding measurement errors. This may be a source of concern in particular given the relatively short sample of data available.

Table 5.3. Productivity Premium of Bolivian Exporters

Productivity measure	(1) Ln(sales/L)	(2) Ln(VA/L)	(3) Ln(TFP)	(4) Ln(sales/L)	(5) Ln(VA/L)	(6) Ln(TFP)
Exporter	0.43	0.19	0.24	0.26	0.00	−0.14
	(2.56)**	(0.98)	(1.54)	(1.39)	(0.01)	(1.00)
Ln(L)				0.18	0.20	0.37
				(2.49)**	(2.39)**	(6.63)***
Constant	11.07	10.52	5.47	10.48	9.88	4.13
	(70.60)***	(63.08)***	(38.21)***	(41.04)***	(33.09)***	(18.40)***
Observations	338	247	146	338	247	146
R-squared	0.19	0.16	0.22	0.20	0.18	0.41

Source: Bank staff based on Enterprise Survey data.

Notes: Data refers to 2005. Regressions (1) to (3) are of the form $log(y) = \alpha + \beta_1\ exporter + \mu$ where y is the productivity measure of interest, and *exporter* is a dummy variable that takes the value of one if the firm is an exporter and zero otherwise. Regressions (4) to (6) control also for firm size, *Ln(L)*. All regressions include industry and region fixed effects.

Overall, the mixed results on the existence of a 'productivity premium' among exporters call for a cautious interpretation. As noted above, Bolivian exporters pay higher wages on average than nonexporters. How can exporters pay higher wages but not display higher productivity? Three reasons may help to explain away this puzzle. First, measures of productivity like value added and TFP may be estimated imperfectly. It is worth noting that there is evidence of a productivity premium for exporters under the simpler measure of productivity used in the analysis (sales per worker). It is under more data-intensive measures of productivity that the relationship breaks down. Second, when controlling for firm size in the regressions we must bear in mind that the variable is highly correlated with our simpler measure of productivity (sales per worker). There may simply be not enough variation in the sample – other than can be explained by firm size – to establish a statistically significant relationship between exporting and productivity. Third, we must bear in mind that any survey data will inevitably suffer from measurement errors, which may be inadvertently be compounded when constructing variables based on that data.

What Factors Affect Exporters?

The second objective of this chapter is to examine the factors affecting the firms' export performance. In this section we do so by exploring the reasons that firms themselves cite as crucial factors. The first source of data on firms' perceptions about constraints for their operation comes from the Investment Climate Assessment surveys conducted in Bolivia and in many other countries. The second source of data is a survey of exporters conducted by the INE (as discussed in Table 5.1 above). Evidence from surveys can provide a useful backdrop for the later econometric analysis.

Enterprise Survey data suggests that the perceptions of Bolivian exporters of what are the key problems for firms do not differ greatly from the perceptions of nonexporters. As shown in the left panel of Figure 5.2, political and macroeconomic instability are among the top four issues perceived to be as major or severe problems for both exporters and nonexporters. The proportion of exporters that consider a specific issue to be a major or severe problem tends to be lower than for nonexporters but the rankings of the top ten problems are the same for both groups. Customs regulations are seen as a major or severe problem for only 8 percent of Bolivian exporters, not unlike the situation in other countries (see right panel in Figure 5.2). More broadly, compared to the perceptions of exporters in other countries Bolivian exporters are more concerned about political instability, corruption, and competition from informal firms than the average of exporters in a sample of 33 Enterprise Surveys.

Figure 5.2. Factors Perceived to be Major or Severe Problems for Firm Performance

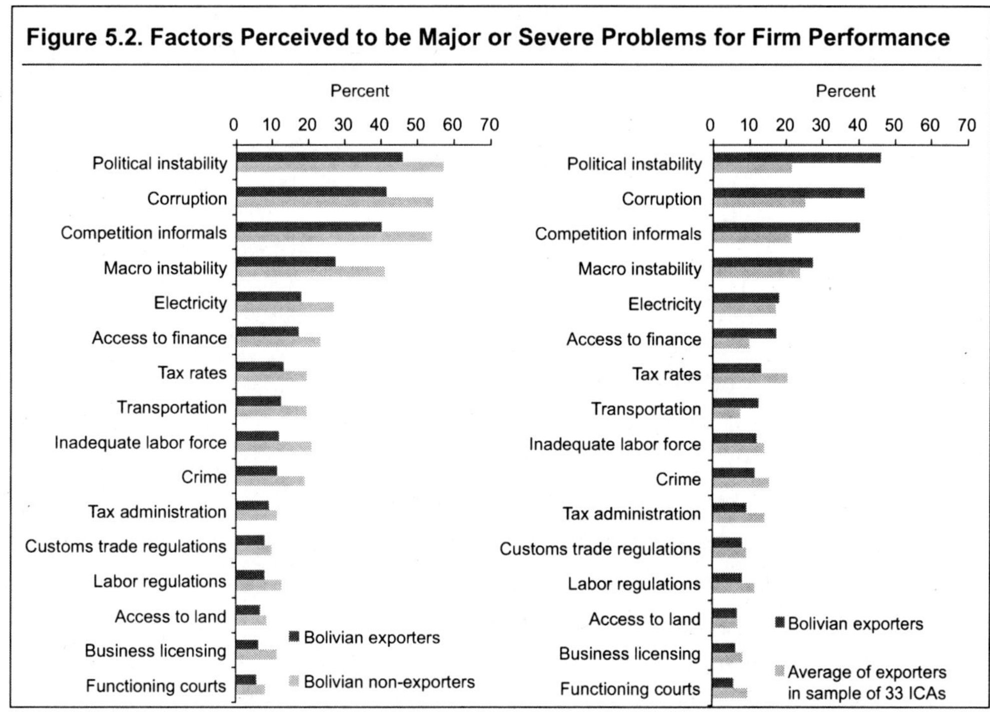

Source: World Bank Enterprise Surveys and Latin America and the Caribbean Regional Study on Economic Growth (2007).
Note: Table shows percent of firms that state that a certain issue is a major or severe problem.

Based on the INE survey, exporters consider a large set of factors as key for their performance. While the INE survey of exporters asks questions about perceptions in a different way than the Enterprise Survey, it provides a ranking of what factors are perceived to be most important for exporters. The results suggest that exporters find a large number of factors, ranging from inputs availability to legal protection as important or very important for their business. Given the large number of factors with high percentages it is worth noting those factors that have the lowest responses: exchange rate policy, financial costs, and regional integration policies (left panel in Figure 5.3).

The INE survey also shows that the road network elicits the most complaints among a range of infrastructure surveys. The INE survey includes additional questions that shed light on other issues that might pose problems to exporters. In terms of the quality of transport networks, the survey finds that a third of the exporters considered the quality of the roads to be either bad or very bad. In the case of the other transport network types, the percentage of exporters that perceive these other networks as bad or very bad is much lower. Electricity, telecommunications, and water services seem to be perceived as being of largely acceptable quality, but appear to represent major restraints to producers in some cases (see Figure 5.2).

Figure 5.3. Perceptions of Bolivian Exporters on Key Factors for Firm Growth and on Infrastructure and Network Services

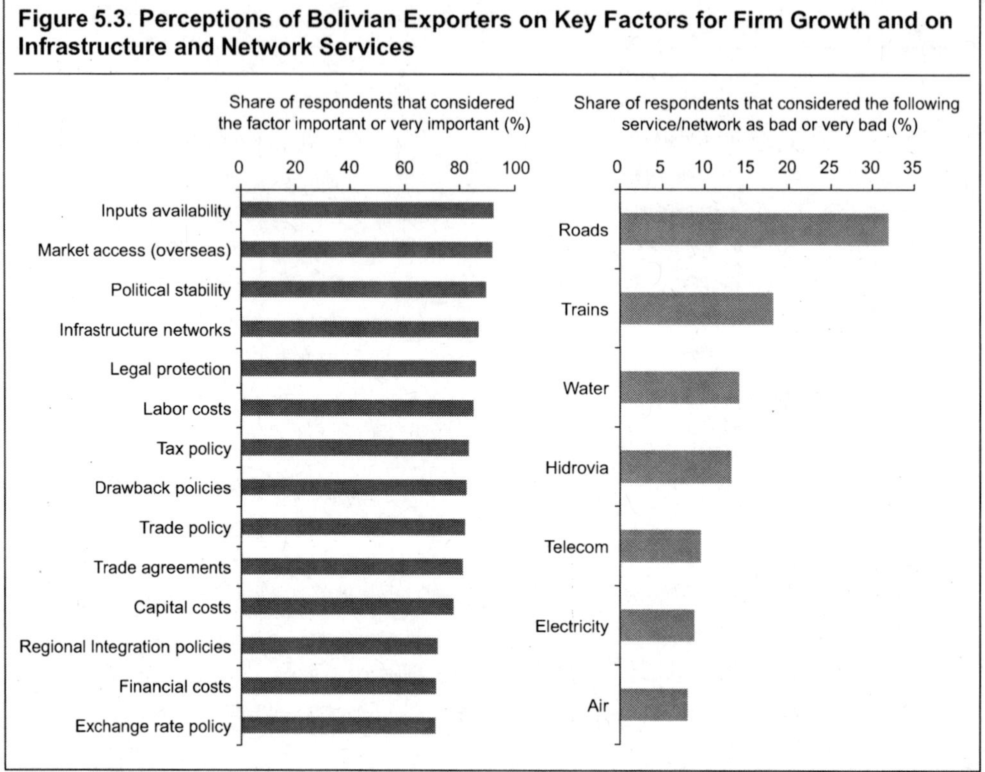

Source: INE.

The INE survey also points to 'social problems' as a key concern of exporters (reminiscent of the concern with political and macro instability in the Enterprise Survey). As noted above, while the INE survey asks questions in a somewhat different form than in the Enterprise Survey, the results from the questions on governance issues appear to be consistent with the evidence from the Enterprise Survey that political and macro instability, as well as corruption and competition from informal firms are key concerns of exporters. As shown in Figure 5.4 below, there is an almost unanimous agreement with the statement that 'social problems' (the wording used in the INE survey) generate large costs, while corruption is perceived to be as a problem for a majority of exporters and less than half agrees or somewhat agrees that assets are duly protected by laws. In addition, bureaucracy (and the number of procedures related to it) is perceived to be as a factor slowing down export shipments.

Figure 5.4. Perceptions of Bolivian Exporters on Governance Issues

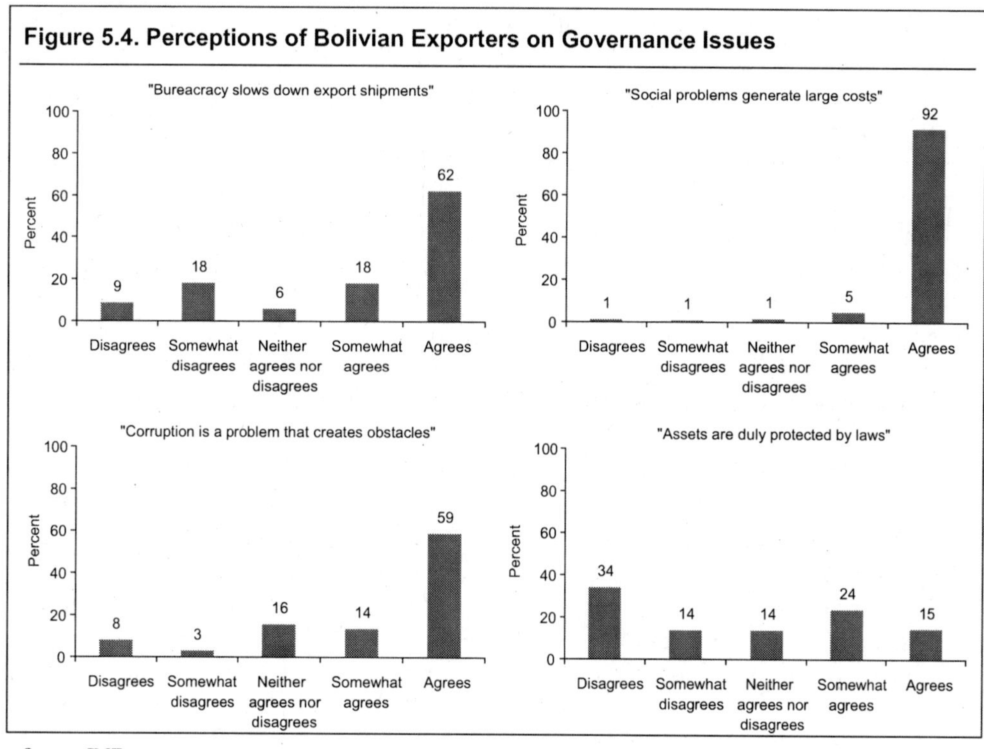

Source: INE.

What Factors Affect the Decision to Export? Estimating the Propensity to Export

In this section we continue to explore the factors that affect the firms' decision to export based on a simple model of international trade. The methodology used to study the determinants of the propensity to export is based on a well-known trade model (Melitz, 2003). The intuition behind the model is that whether a firm exports or not can be explained by two sets of factors: (i) heterogeneity among firms in terms of how productive they are, and (ii) different variable and fixed costs involved in the production of goods for the domestic and the foreign markets. The basic idea is that for each export market that the firm enters there are additional variable costs to serve that market (transport, tariffs, etc.) as well as a fixed cost that is specific to that market and to that product, such as advertising or compliance with particular technical standards and regulations. These costs to exporting are product-specific and in addition to the costs that the firm faces when serving the domestic market.

Empirically, we estimate the propensity to export among firms in different industries using a sample of Enterprise Surveys for a broader set of countries. From an empirical perspective we are interested in estimating the conditional probability that a firm exports, given a set of variables that will capture the fixed and variable costs involved in the production and export of goods. The estimation techniques appropriate for answering this question are probabilistic regression analyses. In principle we could estimate the propensity to export using Enterprise Survey data for Bolivian firms only. However, using firm-level information regarding the fixed and variable costs reported to the Enterprise Survey would create reverse causality issues in the sense that the export status (our dependent variable) can be related to some of the explanatory variables. For example, the fact that a firm exports might be the reason why a firm has more access to finance or is more exposed to bureaucracy. A common solution to this problem is to replace the firm-level data on costs with industry/region averages. However, given the fact that there are only 12 such industry/region clusters for Bolivia this avenue is not feasible in our case. Therefore, to correct for endogeneity problems, we follow the approach suggested by the World Bank's 2007 LAC regional study "Economic Growth in Latin America and the Caribbean: A Microeconomic Perspective" and include more countries that have Enterprise Surveys to expand the number of observations and use the averages by cluster used in the regional study.[3]

This method allows us to identify the causality running from the explanatory variables (fixed costs, etc) to the probability of exporting. The econometric approach followed here overcomes the endogeneity concerns discussed above because the industry/region average is not substantially affected by each individual firm's responses. In addition, the impact of the explanatory variables on the probability to export is assessed while holding basic firm characteristics such as size and age constant. However, the estimated coefficients will reflect the factors affecting the probability to export based on the entire sample and not only on Bolivia-specific data. While we cannot draw different policy conclusions for the different countries in the sample, one additional advantage of the approach followed is that it increases the robustness of the results found. In our case, the use of region/industry averages is justified not only from an empirical perspective but also from a theoretical one since, as we mentioned previously, our theoretical model suggests that the fixed costs are product-specific.

The explanatory variables were selected based on whether they had a significant and robust effect on the exporter status. Following the World Bank's 2007 LAC regional study on Economic Growth, we proceed to select the explanatory variables as follows. First, we use Enterprise Survey variables that can be thought to reflect key categories of factors identified in our theoretical model and in previous empirical work: (i) innovation costs; (ii) domestic costs—including access to finance, infrastructure, and governance; and, (iii) export costs—including both fixed and variable. Second, within each category we estimate a probit regression using only firm characteristics and one variable at a time. We discard the variables that are not significant in this partial analysis. Whenever we had more than one significant variable within each category, we employed principal components analysis to construct a synthetic index. This ensures that we incorporate the information content while avoiding potential problems of collinearity. Details of the variables used and selection process can be found in Box 5.2.

Box 5.2. Econometric Methodology to Estimate the Export Propensity among Bolivian Firms

The equation that we estimate is:

$$pr_{ijk}(X > 0 / observed\ \mathrm{var}) = \Phi(F_{Ijk}, F_{Djk}, \varphi_{jk}, F_{Xjk}, age_i, ownership_i, size_i, \zeta, \gamma)$$

where, pr_{ijk} the conditional probability to export of firm i in industry j in country k, conditional on the observed variables; F_{Ijk} is the innovation cost of introducing a new product in industry j in country k, F_{Djk} the domestic fixed cost of entering the domestic market in industry j in country k such as cost of compliance with technical regulations, Φ_{jk} is the variable cost of exporting product j to country k, and F_{Xjk} is the fixed cost of exporting in industry j in country k; ζ and γ are the industry and country fixed effects respectively.

The variables regarding innovation and domestic fixed costs come all from the Enterprise Surveys, whereas trade costs are taken from TRAINS, and Doing Business. The final list of the variables selected is:

Innovation costs: Dummy variables indicating (a) whether the firm uses technology from a foreign country, (b) whether it invests in R&.D and (c) whether it offers formal training for its employees. We also considered other variables for such as the use of a website to communicate with suppliers/clients and the introduction of new products or new production processes in the last years. However, we did not include these variables in the final analysis because none of them had a significant effect on the exporter status.

Domestic costs: As mentioned in the main text, based on the findings from the World Bank's LAC regional study on economic growth, we controlled for variables that reflect domestic constraints in the following areas: (a) Infrastructure quality (the number of days to get an electrical connection and the losses due to power outages as a percent of sales), (b) Governance (the time spent on dealing with regulations, the cost of security and the losses due to crime, as a percent of sales), and (c) Access to finance (whether the firm is constrained or not in their access to bank credit and how much of their working capital and fixed assets has been financed from private banks). Other variables initially considered were losses due to problems in water supply and delays to get a phone connection (on infrastructure), number of tax inspections per year, bribes and tax evasion (on governance), availability of overdraft facilities and lines of credit (on access to finance). However, Most of these variables did not turn out to be significant to explain the exporter status.

Export costs: As far as fixed export costs, we use as a proxy the information from Doing Business on how to start a new business (number of procedures, costs and time it takes to start a business) and on the number of procedures it takes to clear imports/exports from customs (which is almost the same regardless the size of the shipment). For variable trade costs, we use the information on tariffs by product from TRAINS (we also used data on nontariff barriers from the overall trade restrictiveness index database, however, they were insignificant). Finally, we also include the number of days it takes to clear imports and exports from customs at home (from the Enterprise Surveys) and at the destination markets (from Doing Business) which are considered in our analysis as variable costs since there is substantial variation in these variables depending on shipment size.

One point worth noting with respect to the building of indexes for trade costs at the destination markets is that we face a limitation of our dataset from the Enterprise Surveys due to the lack of information on the destination markets where exporters in our sample sell (there is a question about the main country of destination for the main product exported but the response rate for that question is very low.) To overcome this shortcoming as much as possible we built a trade weighted average of the top ten destinations by product—at the 3-digit ISIC Rev.3 classification—for each country in the sample and assumed that the destination markets of the exporters in our samples were the same as the destination markets for the exports of that product from that country as a whole.

As predicted by the model, results suggest that trade costs (fixed and variable) negatively affect the probability to export. The coefficient on the indices for trade costs, both fixed and variable, can be interpreted in a straightforward way as higher costs can be expected to decrease the probability of exporting. When interpreting the results (see Table 5.4) for the other variables (the indices for infrastructure, governance, access to finance and innovation) one has to bear in mind the way the principal components were defined. For example, in the case of both infrastructure and governance the underlying variables reflect factors that can be expected to negatively impact the probability of exporting. In contrast, in the case of innovation and access to finance the underlying variables reflect factors that can be expected to positively impact the probability of exporting. As expected, the marginal effect of each index (calculated at the means) on the probability of exporting reflects the appropriate signs. Overall, the results are robust across different estimation techniques and under different definitions of what an exporter is (when firms declare they export at least 1 percent or 10 percent of their annual sales). The idea behind this sensitivity analysis was to check that the presence of marginal exporters (those exporting 1–10 percent of their sales) did not affect the results.

Table 5.4. Estimated Factors Affecting the Probability to Export

	Probit		Logit	
Dependent variable: export status	**(1) Export (>1%)**	**(2) Export (>10%)**	**(3) Export (>1%)**	**(4) Export (>10%)**
Cost indices				
Export fixed costs	-0.038	-0.038	-0.036	-0.035
	(0.018)**	(0.017)**	(0.018)**	(0.017)**
Variable trade costs	-0.033	-0.026	-0.034	-0.026
	(0.013)**	(0.012)**	(0.014)**	(0.013)**
Infrastructure (energy)[a]	-0.025	-0.021	-0.026	-0.021
	(0.013)**	(0.012)*	(0.013)**	(0.012)*
Governance	-0.017	-0.008	-0.016	-0.007
	(0.007)**	(0.007)	(0.007)**	(0.007)
Innovation	0.024	0.015	0.024	0.014
	(0.009)***	(0.007)**	(0.009)***	(0.007)**
Access to finance	0.023	0.024	0.023	0.024
	(0.008)***	(0.008)***	(0.009)***	(0.008)***
Control variables				
Log of firm's age	0.024	-0.003	0.025	-0.002
	(0.010)**	(0.008)	(0.010)**	(0.008)
Ownership (=1 if foreign)	0.231	0.198	0.215	0.161
	(0.023)***	(0.021)***	(0.021)***	(0.016)***
Size (medium)	0.222	0.172	0.224	0.168
	(0.016)***	(0.015)***	(0.015)***	(0.014)***
Size (large	0.508	0.410	0.486	0.338
	(0.022)***	(0.029)***	(0.026)***	(0.024)***
Observations	11,604	11,596	11,604	11,596

Source: Bank staff based on Enterprise Survey data.

Notes: Table shows marginal effects from the maximum likelihood estimations (clustered) All regressions include country and industry fixed effects. Robust standard errors in parentheses. * statistically significant at 10%, ** Statistically significant at 5%, *** statistically significant at 1%.

a. As noted in Box 5.2 the components of the infrastructure index are the number of days to get an electrical connection and the losses due to power outages as a percent of sales, therefore we label the variable as *infrastructure (energy)* to make clear to the reader that transport and telecommunications variables are not reflected in this variable.

We can investigate further the relative importance of the factors under consideration by undertaking some simulations. To help identify the areas that constrain the probability of exporting the most we undertake some simple simulations as follows. First, for each policy variable in our regressions, we take the mean value within the Bolivian sample to obtain the average predicted probability of exporting in Bolivia. Second, we simulate what the predicted probability of exporting would be under alternative values for the policy variable in question. In particular, we use the mean values of that policy variable in different country groupings. We can then compare these two predicted probabilities, giving us an idea of the impact of improvements in each policy variable on the probability of exporting. We can answer the question of what would be the probability of exporting among Bolivian firms if the underlying policy variables were similar to those found in other countries of the region.

The results of these simulations suggest that potential reductions in trade costs (such as further reducing delays at customs) may have a substantial effect on exporters, suggesting that the positive efforts of customs reform should be continued particularly in cross-border management. The bars in Figure 5.5 represent the percentage point change in the predicted probability to export in the event that – with regard to the variable in question – Bolivia was able to achieve: the mean value that based on the Enterprise Surveys is characteristic in the Andean countries, in MERCOSUR countries, in all of Latin America and the Caribbean, and, finally if Bolivia were to achieve the value of the top 75th percentile in the region for each policy variable. The results suggest that the largest potential lies in achieving reductions in customs delays (the measure of variable trade costs used in these simulations). In contrast, the simulations show a limited impact in other categories. In those cases, the limited (and sometimes negative) impact does not mean that Bolivian exporters' probability would not increase with improvements in these areas; it only implies that the indicators for infrastructure, innovation and access to finance are not the ones mainly constraining Bolivian exporters probability to export from achieving the levels observed in the median across the sample.

Policy Implications

The analysis of firm-level data confirms that Bolivian exporters pay higher wages than nonexporters of similar size. This result provides a rationale for policies that promote export growth as a way to improve the lot of workers. While there is mixed evidence on the existence of a 'productivity premium' among exporters, the confirmation that exporters pay higher wages—controlling for other firm characteristics such as size—calls for policy interventions aimed at increasing exports as a way to positively affect the welfare of workers.

Figure 5.5. Differences in the Predicted Probability to Export among Bolivian Firms under Different Scenarios

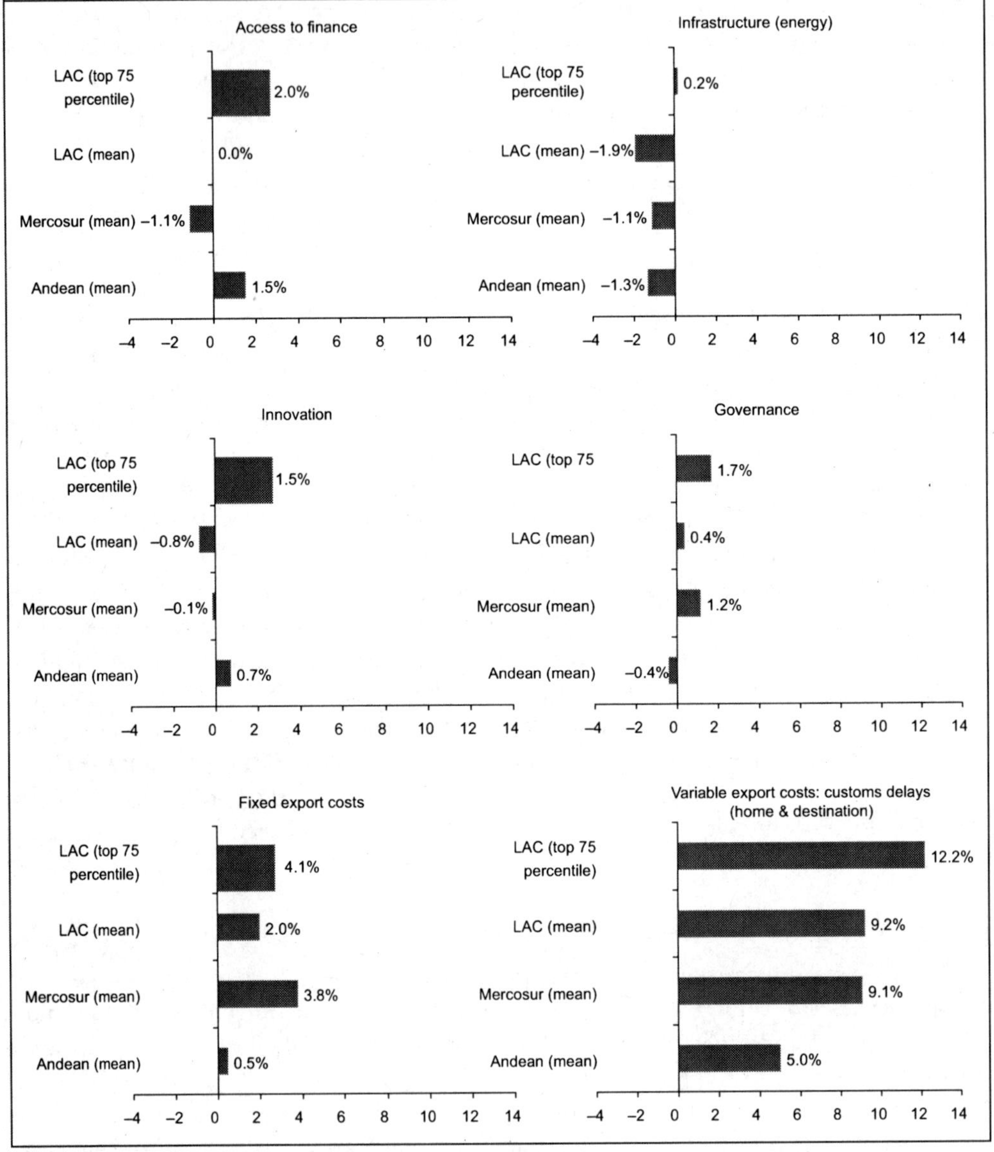

Source: Staff calculation based on Enterprise Survey data.
Note: The bars represent how more (or less) likely to export a Bolivian firm would be if the country were to enjoy the same infrastructure, access to finance, etc, as in other countries.

The econometric estimations on the factors affecting the exporter status of firms suggest that Bolivian exporters would benefit from policy actions towards reductions in costs related to the time shipments are delayed at customs. The operation of customs (either in terms of the paperwork required or the delay to clear imports/exports) was identified as the area where achieving the underlying levels of service common in comparator countries would have the greatest impact in terms of increasing the likelihood to export among Bolivian firms. In this regard it is worth stressing that the 'delays at customs' has to be interpreted in a broad sense, referring to issues such as complying with certifications, phytosanitary regulations, and so forth, since all of these tend to be lumped together by respondents of surveys such as the Enterprise Survey. It is in this broad sense that the econometric results produced in this chapter lend support to the more detailed analysis conducted in Chapter 3 laying out areas where there is room for improvement in the customs-related areas.

Finally, the analysis makes it clear that a key concern among exporters refers to political and economic stability, raising a broad policy agenda about the business environment. One finding that comes out from the different surveys on exporters is that they perceive political and economic instability as a key concern and limitation to a better firm performance. Most significant is that this perception among Bolivian exporters is much more pronounced than among exporters from other countries where Enterprise Surveys have been conducted (see Figure 5.2, right panel). While the policy agenda to address those concerns lies outside the scope of this study, it is nevertheless important to highlight that improvements in those areas can be expected to go a long way in supporting export growth. This conclusion is supported by the simulations conducted in this chapter regarding the predicted probability to export among Bolivian firms in the event that Bolivia were to improve in indicators of the business environment to the levels seen in comparator countries.

Notes

[1] This chapter is based on a background paper by D. Pierola Castro (2008).

[2] For a comprehensive survey on this literature, see Tybout (2001) or Wagner (2005).

[3] The countries included are, besides Bolivia, Argentina, Brazil, Chile, Colombia, Costa Rica, Ecuador, El Salvador, Guatemala, Guyana, Honduras, Mexico, Nicaragua, Panama, Paraguay, Peru, Uruguay, Mauritius, República Bolivariana de Venezuela, South Africa, Turkey and Mauritius.

References

Aguilar, M. 2003. "Estimación del Tipo de Cambio Real de Equilibrio para Bolivia". Central Bank of Bolivia. *Revista de Analisis*, Vol. 6, No 1. Junio 2003.

Alvarez, Roberto. 2004. "Sources of Export Success in Small and Medium-Sized Enterprises: The Impact of Public Programs." *International Business Review* 13, 383–400.

Alvarez and Lopez 2004. "Exporting and Firm performance: Evidence from Chilean plants." University of Chile, mimeo.

Andriamananjara, S. and Valenzuela, E. 2008. "Economic Impacts of Different Trade Policy Scenarios on the Bolivian Economy." Background paper, World Bank.

Awokuse, Titus O. 2003. "Is the export-led growth hypothesis valid for Canada?" *Canadian Journal of Economics* 36(1): 126–36.

Awokuse, Titus O. 2006. "Export-led growth and the Japanese economy: evidence from VAR and directed acyclic graphs." *Applied Economics* 38: 593–602.

Bahmani-Oskooee, M., and O. Maharouf. 2007. "Export growth and output growth: an application of bounds testing approach." *Journal of Economics and Finance* 31(1): 593–602.

Baldwin and Gu. 2003. "Participation on Export Markets and Productivity Performance in Canadian Manufacturing." *Canadian Journal of Economics* 36(3): 634–657.

Bernard, Eaton, Jensen, and Kortum. 2003. "Plants and Productivity in International Trade." *American Economic Review* 93(4): 1268–1290.

Biesebroeck. 2003. "Exporting Raises Productivity in Sub-Saharan African Manufacturing Plants." NBER Working Papers 10020. NBER, Cambridge, MA.

Boston Consulting Group. 2004. "Export Development and Promotion: Lessons from Four Benchmark Countries." Mimeo.

Bouët, A., Decreux, Y., Fontagné L., Jean, S., Laborde, D. 2008. "Assessing applied protection across the world." *Review of International Economics* 16(5): 850–863.

Brenton, P. and R. Newfarmer. 2007, "Watching More Than the Discovery Channel: Export Cycles and Diversification in Development." Policy Research Working Paper 4302. World Bank, Washington, DC.

Cadot, O., and L. Dutoit. 2008. "Does Bolivia Undertrade?" Background paper, World Bank.

Cadot, O., and E. Fonseca. 2008. "ATPDEA: Effects on Bolivian Real Income." Background paper, World Bank.

Cadot, O., and A. Molina. 2008. "Sunset over the ATPDEA: Implications for Bolivian Employment" Background paper, World Bank.

Candia F., and E. Antelo. 2005. "Políticas Sectoriales para Promover la Competitividad en Bolivia". In: *Políticas Sectoriales en la Región Andina.* Corporación Andina de Fomento.

Carrère, C. 2006. "Revisiting the Effects of Free Trade Agreements on Trade Flows with the Proper Specification of the Gravity Trade Model." *European Economic Review* 50(2): 223–47.

Carrère, C., J. de Melo, and B. Tumurchudur. 2007. "Market Access for ASEAN Members in an ASEAN-EU FTA." Mimeo, World Bank, December

Central Bank of Bolivia. 2008. *Informe de Politica Monetaria.* January 2008.

Clarke. 2005. "Beyond Tariffs and Quotas: Why Don't African Manufacturers Export More?" Policy Research Working Paper No. 3617. World Bank, Washington, DC.

Clerides, Lach, and Tybout. 1998. "Is Learning by Exporting Important? Micro-Dynamic Evidence from Colombia, Mexico, and Morocco." *Quarterly Journal of Economics* 113(3): 903–947.

Dawson, P. J. 2006. "The Export-income Relationship and Trade Liberalization in Bangladesh." *Journal of Policy Modeling* 28: 889–96.

Development Planning Ministry. 2006. "Plan Nacional de Desarrollo: Bolivia Digna, Soberana, Productiva y Democrática para Vivir Bien." Bolivia.

Dollar, D., M. Hallward-Driemeier, and T. Mengistae. 2005. "Investment Climate and Firm Performance in Developing Economies." In *Economic Development and Cultural Change*. University of Chicago Press.

Escobar, F., and P. Mendieta. 2004. "Inflación y Depreciación en una Economía Dolarizada: el Caso de Bolivia." Central Bank of Bolivia. *Revista de Análisis* Vol. 7 No.1 . June 2004.

Escribano and Guasch. 2005. "Assessing the Impact of the Investment Climate on Productivity using Firm-Level Data: Methodology and the Cases of Guatemala, Honduras and Nicaragua". Policy Research Working Paper No. 3621. World Bank, Washington, DC.

Fajnzylber. 2004. "Learning Before or From Exporting? Evidence from Brazilian Manufacturing Firms." World Bank: Washington DC.

Fernandes, A. M., and A. E. Isgut. 2005. "Learning-by-Doing, Learning-by-Exporting, and Productivity: Evidence from Colombia." Policy Research Working Paper 3544. World Bank, Washington, DC.

Francois, J., and M. Manchin. 2006. "Institutional Quality, Infrastructure, and the Propensity to Export." Policy Research Working Papers No 4152. World Bank, Washington, DC.

Fretes-Cibils, V., M. Giugale, and C. Luff, eds. 2006. *Bolivia: Public Policy for the Well-being of All.* World Bank, Washington, DC.

Ghatak, S., C. Milner, and U. Utkulu. 1997. "Exports, Export Composition and Growth: Cointegration and Causality Evidence for Malaysia." *Applied Economics* 29: 213–23.

Girma, Greenaway, and Kneller. 2002. "Does Exporting Lead to Better Performance? A Microeconometric Analysis of Matched Firms." *GEP Research Paper* 02/09.

Giussani, Bruno, and Marcelo Olarreaga. 2006. "Trade and Integration Policies." In *Bolivia: Public Policy Options for the Well-Being of All.* Washington, DC: World Bank.

Goorman, A. 2003. "Duty Relief and Exemption Control." In De Wulf, L., and J. Sokol, eds., *Customs Modernization Handbook.* Washington, DC: World Bank.

Guterman, L. 2008. "Distortions to Agricultural Incentives in Colombia." Ch. 5 in *Distortions to Agricultural Incentives in Latin America,* edited by K. Anderson and A. Valdes. Washington, DC: World Bank.

Hausman, J. A., and W. E. Taylor. 1981. "Panel Data and Unobservable Individual Effects." *Journal of Econometrics* 16(1): 155–155.

Heitz, Benoît, and Gilbert Rini 2006. "Reinterpreting the contribution of foreign trade to growth." *Trésor-Economics letter* No. 6, December.

Helpman, Elhanan, Marc J. Melitz, and Yona Rubinstein. 2007. "Estimating trade flows: Trading partners and trading volumes." NBER Working Paper 12927. NBER, Cambridge, MA.

Hertel, T. 1997. *Global Trade Analysis: Modeling and Applications.* Cambridge: Cambridge University Press.

Hertel, T., R. Keeney, M. Ivanic, and A. Winters. 2007. "Distributional Effects of WTO Agricultural Reforms in Rich and Poor Countries." *Economic Policy* (April): 289–337.

Hoekman, B., and C. Özden, eds. 2007. *Trade Preferences and Differential Treatment of Developing Countries.* Cheltenham: Edward Elgar.

Hogan, Paul, Donald Keesing, and Andrew Singer. 2001. "The Role of Support Services in Expanding Manufactured Exports in Developing Countries." Economic Development Institute, World Bank.

Humerez, J. 2005. "Reexaminando el Desalineamiento del Tipo de Cambio Real." UDAPE. Analisis Economico. Junio 2005.

International Monetary Fund. 2007a. Country Report No. 07/248, Staff Report for the 2007 Article IV Consultation. July, Washington DC.

———. 2007b. *World Economic Outlook.* October 2007.

Jones, B. F., and B. A. Olken. 2007. "The Anatomy of Start-Stop-Growth." *Review of Economics and. Statistics,* forthcoming.

Kee, H.L., A. Nicita, and M. Olarreaga. 2006. "Estimating Trade Restrictiveness Indices." World Bank Working Paper No. 3840. World Bank, Washington, DC.

Kray, A. 1999. "Exports and Economic Performance: Evidence from a Panel of Chinese Enterprises. *Revue d'Economie du Developpement* 0(1-2): 183–207.

Lara, G., and I. Soloaga. 2007. "Bolivia." In *Global Trade and Poor Nations,* edited by B. Hoekman and M. Olarreaga. Center for the Study of Globalization. Yale University and Groupe d'Economie Mondiale. Sciences Po.

Lederman, D., M. Olearraga, and L. Payton. 2007. "Export Promotion Agencies: What Works and What Doesn't." Workshop on "Export Growth and Diversification: Incentive Regimes and Pro-active Policies in the Export Cycle." World Bank, Washington DC.

Lederman, D., and W. Maloney. 2006. *Natural Resources: Neither Destiny nor Curse.* Stanford University Press and World Bank.

Lin, Justin Yifu, and Yongjun Li. 2002. "Export and Economic Growth in China: A Demand-Oriented Analysis." China Center for Economic Research, Peking University.

Liu, Jin-Tan, M.-W. Tsou, and J. K. Hammitt 1999. "Export activity and productivity: Evidence from the Taiwan electronics industry." *Review of World Economics* 127(4): 675–691.

Love, Jim and Ramesh Chandra 2005. "Testing export-led growth in Bangladesh in a multivariate VAR framework." *Journal of Asian Economics* 15: 1155–68.

Loza, G. 2000. "Tipo de Cambio, Exportaciones e Importaciones: El Caso de la Economía Boliviana." Central Bank of Bolivia. *Revista de Análisis* 3(1), June.

Ludeña, C., and R. Telleria. 2006. V6.2 Documentation I-O Tables: Bolivia. GTAP Resource #2151. Available at https://www.gtap.agecon.purdue.edu/resources/res_display.asp?RecordID=2151.

Macario, Carla. 2000. *Export Growth in Latin America: Policies and Performance*. Lynne Rienner Publishers.

Maddala, G. S. 1986. "Limited-Dependent and Qualitative Variables in Econometrics." Econometric Society Monographs, Cambridge University Press.

McCulloch, N. 2005. "The Impact of Structural Reforms on Poverty: A Simple Methodology with Extensions." In M. Bussolo and J. I. Round, eds., *Globalisation and Poverty: Channels and Policy Responses*. London: Routledge.

McKinsey Global Institute. 2005. "The Emerging Global Labor Market: How Supply and Demand for Offshore Talent Meet." San Francisco.

Melitz. 2003. "The Impact of Trade on Intra-industry Reallocations and Aggregate Industry Productivity". *Econometrica* 71 (6), November, 1695-1725.

Orellana, W., and J. Requena. 1999. "Determinantes de la Inflación en Bolivia." Central Bank of Bolivia. *Revista de Análisis* 3(1), June.

Organization for Economic Co-operation and Development (OECD). 2006. " Potential Impact of International Sourcing on Different Occupations." Document DSTI/ICCP/IE(2006)1/FINAL. Paris.

Piermartini, R. 2004. "The Role of Export Taxes in the Field of Primary Commodities." *WTO Discussion Papers* No. 4. World Trade Organization, Geneva.

Pierola M. D. 2008. "A Firm-level Analysis of the Factors Affecting Export Performance in Bolivia." Background paper, World Bank.

Production and Micro-enterprise Ministry. 2007. "Plan de Desarrollo Productivo con Soberanía para Vivir Bien." Bolivia.

Rauch, J. E. 1999. "Networks versus Markets in International Trade." *Journal of International Economics* 48: 7–35.

Richards, Donald G. 2001. "Exports as a Determinant of Long-Run Growth in Paraguay, 1966–96." *Journal of Development Studies* 38(1): 128–46.

Rodríguez Álvarez, G. 2004. "Apertura Económica y Exportadores en Bolivia: El Papel del Estado (1980–2003)." Instituto Boliviano de Comercio Exterior.

Quintana, H. 2002. "Promoción de Exportaciones. In: Estado de la Situación de la Competitividad en Bolivia." Unidad de Productividad y Competitividad. Sistema Boliviano de Productividad y Competitividad.

Tybout, James. 2001. "Plant and Firm-Level Evidence on "New" Trade Theories." NBER Working Paper No. 8418. NBER, Cambridge, MA.

Unidad de Políticas Sociales y Económicas. 2006. "El ATPDEA. Un análisis de situación y perspectivas." *Notas de Coyuntura* No 3, November.

Valenzuela, E., T. Hertel, R. Keeney, and J. Reimer. 2007. "Assessing Global Computable General Equilibrium Model Validity Using Agricultural Price Volatility." *American Journal of Agricultural Economics* 89(2): 383–397.

Valenzuela, E., S. Wong, and D. Sandri. 2008. "Distortions to Agricultural Incentives in Ecuador." Ch. 7 in *Distortions to Agricultural Incentives in Latin America,* edited by K. Anderson and A. Valdes. Washington DC: World Bank.

Wagner, Joachim. 2005. "Exports and Productivity: A Survey of the Evidence from Firm-level Data." *The World Economy* 30(1): 60–82.

World Bank. 2005. "Bolivia Country Economic Memorandum—Policies to Improve Growth and Employment." October 2005. World Bank, Washington, DC.

———. 2006. Investment Climate Assessment Surveys—Bolivia. World Bank, Washington, DC.

———. 2007a. "Exports and Productivity—Comparable Evidence for 14 Countries." The International Study Group on Exports and Productivity. Policy Research Working Paper No. 4418. World Bank, Washington, DC.

———. 2007b. "Economic Growth in Latin America and the Caribbean: A Microeconomic Perspective." World Bank, Washington, DC.

World Bank 2007c. "Connecting to Compete: Trade Logistics in the Global Economy." World Bank, Washington, DC.

World Bank and International Financial Corporation 2007. *Doing Business 2007.* Washington, DC.

World Economic Forum Reports 2007–2008.

World Trade Organization. 2005. "Trade Policy Review: Bolivia." Report by the Secretariat, WTO Trade WT/TPRS/S/154/Rev.1, Geneva Switzerland, September.

———. 2007. *International Trade Statistics 2006.* Geneva.

Zambrana, Calvimonte Humberto Sergio. 2002. "La Apertura Externa en Bolivia." *Análisis Económico,* Unidad de Análisis de Políticas Sociales y Económicas (UDAPE).

Eco-Audit

Environmental Benefits Statement

The World Bank is committed to preserving Endangered Forests and natural resources. We print World Bank Working Papers and Country Studies on postconsumer recycled paper, processed chlorine free. The World Bank has formally agreed to follow the recommended standards for paper usage set by Green Press Initiative—a nonprofit program supporting publishers in using fiber that is not sourced from Endangered Forests. For more information, visit www.greenpressinitiative.org.

In 2008, the printing of these books on recycled paper saved the following:

Trees*	Solid Waste	Water	Net Greenhouse Gases	Total Energy
355	16,663	129,550	31,256	247 mil.
*40 feet in height and 6–8 inches in diameter	Pounds	Gallons	Pounds CO_2 Equivalent	BTUs